HUMANISTIC PRAGMATISM

HUMANISTIC PRAGMATISM

The Philosophy of F. C. S. Schiller

Edited,
with an Introduction by
REUBEN ABEL

Fp

THE FREE PRESS, *New York*
COLLIER-MACMILLAN LIMITED, *London*

Copyright © 1966 by The Free Fress

A DIVISION OF THE MACMILLAN COMPANY

Printed in the United States of America

Collier-Macmillan Canada, Ltd., Toronto, Ontario

FIRST FREE PRESS PAPERBACK EDITION 1966

Contents

General Introduction

IN HIS *Sceptical Essays* (1928), Bertrand Russell remarked, "The three founders of pragmatism differ greatly *inter se;* we may distinguish James, Schiller, and Dewey as respectively its religious, literary, and scientific protagonists." This division of philosophical labor is not quite accurate, but it serves to remind us of Schiller's stature. The "literary" leg of the tripod —the only Britisher of the three—deserves to be better known in the United States.

Ferdinand Canning Scott Schiller's dates are 1864-1937. He was born in the Danish part of Schleswig-Holstein. His schooling was at Rugby, and then at Oxford, where he was to spend the major portion of his life. There was an American interlude, however, from 1893 to 1897, when he was an instructor at Cornell, and made his first contact with William James. At Oxford, he continued as tutor, senior tutor, and fellow, until 1935. Then he moved to the University of Southern California, where he married (at the age of 71).

Dewey came to philosophical maturity by reacting to Hegelianism; Schiller's Goliath was the Absolute Idealism of Anglo-Hegelianism. This movement—including chiefly F. H. Bradley, J. M. E. McTaggart, Bernard Bosanquet, and T. H. Green— dominated British philosophy at the turn of the century. Schiller opposed their absolutism, authoritarianism, monism, rationalism, and intellectualism. His own views were anathema to them: that reality was incomplete, that truth was pragmatic, that thought was personal, that God was not omnipotent. Furthermore, Schiller was interested in such academically dubious subjects as eugenics and psychical research. Thus his Oxford career was stormy. Russell wrote,[1] however, "I always thought that he rather enjoyed being hated by the other Oxford philosophers."

Schiller was a prolific writer and vigorous polemicist. His bibliography includes hundreds of items. For decades, his essays and book reviews filled the pages of the scholarly and popular publications. His major works are the two from which

1 Personal communication.

7

the present volume is selected: *Humanism: Philosophical Essays* (1903) and *Studies in Humanism* (1907). There are two other collections of essays: *Must Philosophers Disagree?* (1934) and *Our Human Truths* (posthumously, 1939). In the special field of logic, his contributions are *Formal Logic* (1912), which is an attack on the traditional interpretation, and *Logic for Use* (1929), a constructive new approach. He wrote a long essay on "Axioms as Postulates" for an Oxford anthology called *Personal Idealism* (1902), edited by Henry Sturt. An early metaphysics, *Riddles of the Sphinx* (1891), represents his pre-pragmatic phase.

The core of Schiller's vision is his conviction that all acts and all thoughts are irreducibly the products of individual human beings, and are therefore inescapably associated with the needs, desires, and purposes of men. Thus such terms as "truth" and "reality" denote nothing absolute; rather, they are intertwined with human intentions and deeds. Man makes his "truth," just as he makes his other values, "beauty" and "goodness." Even "axioms" are never God-given, but man-made. They are not a priori verities, but postulates, or working hypotheses, whose truth grows or diminishes within our experience. The logic we employ in gathering knowledge is dynamic and functional, rather than, as was taught in the universities, eternally fixed. Our "data" are not "what is given" but "what is taken." Thus man's active role is made focal both to theory of knowledge and to metaphysics. There is therefore genuine novelty in our growing universe, and no theoretical limit to man's freedom. That is why Schiller chose the name "Humanism,"[2] although at various times he referred to his system as Pragmatism, Voluntarism, and Personalism.

Schiller's relations with his American contemporaries varied. He admired James enormously, both as a philosopher and as a man. Schiller claimed to have arrived at his own position independently. He wrote Leroux[3] that he had not read a word of James before 1891. However, his debt to James, who was twenty-two years his senior, is patent, and was acknowledged often and freely. There was always a certain amount of disagreement between the two. Sometimes this was merely termi-

---

[2] The term "humanism" has had a wide usage, in literature, education, theology, and elsewhere in philosophy. These are all irrelevant to Schiller's use.

[3] Emanuel Leroux, *Le Pragmatisme Américain et Anglais* (Paris, 1932), p. 119.

nological: Schiller regarded Pragmatism as a subdivision of Humanism, whereas James would have reversed this relation. James wrote,[4] "As I myself understand Dewey and Schiller, our views absolutely agree, in spite of our different modes of statement." Thus Schiller said that Pragmatism is "in reality only the application of Humanism to the theory of knowledge"; but James referred to Schiller's "butt-end foremost statement of the humanist position." James reviewed Schiller's *Humanism* for *The Nation*[5] favorably:

> [*Humanism*] expresses the essence of the new way of thought, which is, that it is impossible to strip the human element out from even our most abstract theorizing. All our mental categories without exception have been evolved because of their fruitfulness for life, and owe their being to historic circumstances just as much as do the nouns and verbs and adjectives in which our languages clothe them.

With Dewey, Schiller had less contact, and perhaps less sympathy. Dewey believed that "the antecedents of humanism, via personal idealism, were distinctly an idealistic metaphysics,"[6] whereas Schiller was not attracted by Dewey's naturalism. In his otherwise approving review of *Humanism*,[7] Dewey took care to express his "almost total dissent from the position taken in the essays entitled 'Activity and Substance' and 'Philosophy and the Scientific Investigation of a Future Life.'" Elsewhere Dewey wrote[8] of Schiller:

> ... while I have a great regard for his writings, it seems to me that he gave Humanism an unduly subjectivistic turn. He was so interested in bringing out the elements of human desire and purpose neglected in traditional philosophy that he tends ... to a virtual isolation of man from the rest of nature.

4 *The Meaning of Truth* (New York, 1909), p. 169.
5 LXXVIII (1904), p. 175; reprinted in *Collected Essays and Reviews*, ed. R. B. Perry (New York, 1920), p. 450.
6 Quoted in Perry, *Thought and Character of William James*, II, p. 528.
7 *Psychological Bulletin*, I (1904), p. 335.
8 In a letter to Corliss Lamont, quoted in *Journal of Philosophy*, LVIII (1961), p. 26.

Peirce and Schiller respected each other's views, but their contacts seem to have been tangential. Peirce once wrote,[9] "Schiller . . . is a pragmatist, although he does not very well understand the nature of pragmatism." And, at another time:[10]

> The brilliant and marvelous human thinker, Mr. F. C. S. Schiller, who extends to the philosophic world a cup of nectar stimulant in his beautiful *Humanism,* seems to occupy ground of his own, intermediate . . . between those of James and mine.

For his part, Schiller credited Pragmatism to James and Peirce jointly, and regarded it as one of the nine great philosophical discoveries of all time.[11]

All these thinkers are in a sense the intellectual progeny of Kant. For it was his great insight (loosely formulated) that if man's mind had been different, so would the world have been. Schiller's unique contribution to philosophy may be stated as his emphasis on the effective creativity of the mind of man. He clarifies the function of human intelligence in organizing the universe of human experience, and in remaking "reality" more nearly in accordance with human values and aspirations.

We are today in a position to see certain unexpected relations between Humanism and two other broad movements in philosophy, later in time and quite different in theme.

The first of these is Existentialism. Sartre also has used the term "humanism"; he has said,[12] "Man is the being as a result of whose appearance a world exists." And the Existentialists share with Schiller their stress on the significance of the act of free choice or decision, although with them that act is more crucial.

The second is modern linguistic philosophy and Logical Empiricism. We have no evidence that Wittgenstein was influ-

9 *Collected Papers,* ed. Hartshorne and Weiss (Cambridge, Mass., 1931-35), V, par. 13.
10 *Ibid.,* par. 466.
11 The other eight were: the Absolute or One of Monism (the Hindus and Parmenides); Pure Spirit (Plato); Universals (Plato); Formal Logic (Aristotle); the Self (Descartes); Epistemology, or the Critical Problem (Locke, Kant); the Problem of Value (post-Kantians); and Darwinian evolution.
12 *Literary and Philosophical Essays,* quoted in *Partisan Review,* XXIII (1956), p. 113.

enced by Schiller, yet there is a substantial similarity between some of their views. Wittgenstein denied that there were any abstract Platonic entities called "meanings." He frequently asserted that "the meaning is the use"; Schiller often said, "no form of words has any actual meaning until it is used." Thus Humanism may have foreshadowed the verifiability theory of meaning.

Schiller's style was sprightly and spirited. In the great English tradition of Locke, Berkeley, Hume, and Mill, he wrote so that he could be understood by the layman. His role as philosophic *enfant terrible* is amply supported in the present volume. We have here selected four of the nineteen essays in *Humanism: Philosophical Essays,* and eight of the twenty in *Studies in Humanism* (in each case from the Second Edition, 1912). We have also reprinted the important Preface to each volume. Many of the essays had been originally written for publication in periodicals, and they therefore retain a certain sturdy independence which neither Schiller nor the present editor could quite overcome. This selection is intended to show the range of Schiller's constructive thought, rather than his polemical sallies. We have rearranged the selections, for more systematic presentation, in three sections, each with introductory comments,[13] as follows:

    I. Humanism, Pragmatism, and Metaphysics
    II. Truth and Meaning in Logic and Psychology
    III. Faith, Ethics, and Immortality.

We have also selected, as an Appendix, some samples of Schiller's wit and scorn, as they appeared in a celebrated burlesque of the eminent British philosophical periodical, *Mind.* Like much good humor, it has a serious intention behind it. Thus the frontispiece is a blank page, which is designated a portrait of the Absolute.

REUBEN ABEL

[13] A critical study of his entire philosophy is Reuben Abel, *The Pragmatic Humanism of F. C. S. Schiller* (New York, 1955).

Preface to the First Edition
of *Humanism*

I

THE APPEARANCE of this volume demands more than the usual amount of apology. For the philosophic public, which makes up for the scantiness of its numbers by the severity of its criticism, might justly have expected me to follow up the apparently novel and disputable position I had taken up in my contribution to *Personal Idealism* with a systematic treatise on the logic of "Pragmatism." And no doubt if it had rested with me to transform wishes into thoughts and thoughts into deeds without restrictions of time and space, I should willingly have expanded my sketch in *Axioms as Postulates* into a full account of the beneficent simplification of the whole theory of knowledge which must needs result from the adoption of the principles I had ventured to enunciate. But the work of a college tutor lends itself more easily to the conception than to the composition of a systematic treatise, and so for the present the philosophic public will have to wait.

The general public, on the other hand, it seemed more feasible to please by an altogether smaller and more practicable undertaking, viz., by republishing from various technical journals, where conceivably the philosophic public had already read them, the essays which compose the bulk of this volume. I have, however, taken the opportunity to add several new essays, partly because they happened to be available, partly because they seemed to be needed to complete the doctrine of the rest. And the old material also has been thoroughly revised and considerably augmented. So that I am not without hopes that the collection, though discontinuous in form, will be found to be coherent in substance, and to present successive aspects of a fairly systematic body of doctrine. To me at least it has seemed that, when thus taken collectively, these essays not only reinforced my previous contentions, but even supplied the ground for a further advance of the greatest importance.

It is clear to all who have kept in touch with the pulse of

thought that we are on the brink of great events in those intellectual altitudes which a time-honoured satire has described as the "intelligible" world. The ancient shibboleths encounter open yawns and unconcealed derision. The rattling of dry bones can no longer fascinate respect nor plunge a self-suggested horde of fakirs in hypnotic stupor. The agnostic maunderings of impotent despair are flung aside with a contemptuous smile by the young, the strong, the virile. And there is growing up a reasonable faith that even the highest peaks of speculation may prove accessible to properly equipped explorers, while what seemed so unapproachable was nothing but a cloud land of confused imaginings. Among the more marked symptoms that the times are growing more propitious to new philosophic enterprise, I would instance the conspicuous success of Mr. Balfour's *Foundations of Belief;* the magnificent series of William James's popular works, *The Will to Believe, Human Immortality,* and *The Varieties of Religious Experience;* James Ward's important Gifford Lectures on *Naturalism and Agnosticism;* the emergence from Oxford, where the idealist enthusiasm of thirty years ago long seemed to have fossilized into sterile logic-chopping or to have dissolved into Bradleian scepticism, of so audacious a manifesto as *Personal Idealism;* and most recently, but not least full of future promise, the work of the energetic Chicago School headed by Professor Dewey.[1] It seemed therefore not impolitic, and even imperative, to keep up the agitation for a more hopeful and *humaner* view of metaphysics, and at the same time to herald the coming of what will doubtless be an epoch-making work, viz., William James's promised *Metaphysics.*

II

The origin of great truths, as of great men, is usually obscure, and by the time that the world has become cognizant of

[1] They have published a number of articles in the *Decennial Publications* of the University; their *Studies in Logical Theory* are announced, but have not yet reached me. Though proceeding from a different camp, the works of Dr. J. E. McTaggart and Prof. G. H. Howison should also be alluded to as adding to the salutary ferment. For while ostensibly (and indeed ostentatiously) employing the methods of the old a priori dogmatism, they have managed to reverse its chief conclusions, in a charming but somewhat perplexing way. I have on purpose confined this enumeration to the English-speaking world; but in France and even in Germany somewhat similar movements are becoming visible.

them and interested in their pedigree, they have usually grown old. It is not surprising, therefore, that the central thought of our present Pragmatism, to wit, the purposiveness of our thought and the teleological character of its methods, should have been clearly stated by Professor James so long ago as 1879.[2] Similarly I was surprised to find that I had all along been a pragmatist myself without knowing it, and that little but the name was lacking to my own advocacy of an essentially cognate position in 1892.

But Pragmatism is no longer unobserved; it has by this time reached the "Strike, but hear me!" stage, and as the misconceptions due to sheer unfamiliarity are refuted or abandoned, it will rapidly enter on the era of profitable employment. It was this latter probability which formed one of my chief motives for publishing these essays. The practical advantages of the pragmatist method are so signal, the field to be covered is so immense, and the reforms to be effected are so sweeping, that I would fain hasten the acceptance of so salutary a philosophy, even at the risk of prematurely flinging these informal essays, as forlorn hopes, against the strongholds of inveterate prejudice. It is in the hope, therefore, that I may encourage others to cooperate and to cultivate a soil which promises such rich returns of novel truth that I will indicate a number of important problems which seem to me urgently to demand treatment by pragmatic methods.

I will put first *a reform of logic*. Logic hitherto has attempted to be a pseudoscience of a nonexistent and impossible process called "pure thought." Or at least we have been ordered in its name to expunge from our thinking every trace of feeling, interest, desire, and emotion, as the most pernicious sources of error.

It has not been thought worthy of consideration that these influences are the sources equally of all truth and all-pervasive in our thinking. The result has been that logic has been rendered nothing but a systematic misrepresentation of our actual thinking. It has been made abstract and wantonly difficult, an inexhaustible source of mental bewilderment, but impotent to train the mind and to trace its actual workings, by being assiduously kept apart from the psychology of concrete thinking.

2 In his "Sentiment of Rationality" in *Mind*, O.S. No. 15.

Yet a reverent study of our minds' actual procedures might have been a most precious aid to the self-knowledge of the intellect. To justify in full these strictures (from which a few only of modern logicians, notably Professors Sigwart and Wundt, and Mr. Alfred Sidgwick,[3] can be more or less exempted) would be a long and arduous undertaking. Fortunately, however, a single illustration may suffice to indicate the sort of difference Pragmatism would introduce into the traditional maltreatment.

Let us consider a couple of actual, and probably familiar, modes of reasoning. (1) *The world is so bad that there must be a better;* (2) *the world is so bad that there cannot be a better.* It will probably be admitted that both of these are common forms of argumentation, and that neither is devoid of logical force, even though in neither case does it reach "demonstration." And yet the two reasonings flatly contradict each other. Now my suggestion is that this contradiction is not verbal, but deep-rooted in the conflicting versions of the nature of thought which they severally exemplify. The second argument alone, it would seem, could claim to be strictly "logical." For it alone seems to conform to the canons of the logical tradition which conceives reasoning as the product of a "pure" thought untainted by volition. And as in our theoretical reflections we can all disregard the psychological conditions of actual thinking to the extent of selecting examples in which we are interested merely as examples, we can all appreciate its abstract cogency. In arguing from a known to an unknown part of the universe, it is "logical" to be guided by the indications given by the former. If the known is a "fair sample" of the whole, how can the conclusion be otherwise than sound? At all events, how can the given nature of the known form a logical ground for inferring in the unknown a complete reversal of its characteristics?

Yet this is precisely what the first argument called for. Must not this be called the illogical caprice of an irrational desire? By no means. It is the intervention of an emotional postulate which takes the first step in the acquisition of new knowledge. But for its beneficent activity we should have acquiesced in our

---

[3] Whose writings, by reason perhaps of the ease of their style, have not received from the experts the attention they deserve.

ignorance. But once an unknown transfiguration of the actual is *desired,* it can be *sought,* and so, in many cases, *found.* The passionless concatenations of a "pure" thought never could have reached, and still less have justified, our conclusion; to attain it our thought needs to be impelled and guided by the promptings of volition and desire.

Now, that such ways of reasoning are not infrequent and not unsuccessful will, I fancy, hardly be denied. Indeed, if matters were looked into, it would turn out that reasonings of the second type *never* really occur in actual knowing, and that when they seem to do so, we have only failed to detect the hidden interest which incites the reason to pretend to be "dispassionate." In the example chosen, e.g., it may have been a pessimist's despair that clothed itself in the habiliments of logic, or it may have been merely stupidity and apathy, a want of imagination and enterprise in questioning nature. But, it may be said, the question of the justification *de jure* of what is done *de facto* still remains. The votary of an abstract logic may indignantly exclaim: "Shall I lower my ideal of pure thought because there is little or no pure thinking? Shall I abandon *Truth,* immutable, eternal, sacred Truth, as unattainable, and sanction as her substitute a spurious concretion of practical experience, on the degrading plea that it is what we need to live by, and all we need to live by? Shall I, in other words, abase myself? No! Perish the thought! Perish the phenomenal embodiment of Pure Reason out of Time and Place (which I popularly term 'myself') rather than that the least abatement should be made from the rigorous requirements of my theory of Thought!"

Strong emotional prejudices are always hard to reason with, especially when, as here, their nature is so far misconceived that they are regarded as the revelations of Pure Reason. Still, in some cases, the desire for knowledge may prove stronger than the attachment to habitual modes of thought, and so it may not be wholly fruitless to point out (1) that our objections are in no wise disposed of by vague charges of a "confusion of psychology and logic"; (2) that the canons of right thought must, even from the most narrowly logical of standpoints, be brought into some relation to the procedures of actual thinking; (3) that in point of fact the former are derived from the latter; (4) that if so, our first mode of reasoning must receive logical recognition, because (5) it is not only usual, but useful in the "discovery" of "Truth"; (6) that a process which yields valuable results must in some sense be valid, and (7) that, conversely, an ideal of validity which is not realizable is not valid, even as an ideal. In short, how can a logic which professes to be the theory of thought set aside as irrelevant a normal feature of our thinking? And if it cannot, is it not evident that, when reformed by Pragmatism, it must assume a very different complexion, more natural and clearer, than while its movements were shackled by the conventions of a strait-laced Intellectualism?

Secondly, Pragmatism would find an almost inexhaustible field of exploration in the sciences, by examining the multifarious ways in which their "truths" have come to be established, and showing how the practical value of scientific conceptions has accelerated and decided their acceptance. Nor is it oversanguine to suppose that a clearer consciousness of the actual procedure of the sciences will also lead to the critical rejection of notions which are not needed, and are not useful, and facilitate the formation of new conceptions which are needed.[4]

In the field of ethics, Pragmatism naturally demands to know what is the actual use of the ethical "principles" which are handed on from one textbook to another. But it speedily discovers that no answer is forthcoming. Next to nothing is known about the actual efficacy of ethical principles: ethics is a dead tradition which has very little relation to the actual facts of moral sentiment. And the reason obviously is that there has not been a sufficient desire to know to lead to the proper researches into the actual psychological nature and distribution of the moral sentiments. Hence there is implicit in Pragmatism a demand for an inquiry to ascertain the actual facts, and pending this inquiry, for a truce to the sterile polemic about ethical principles. In the end this seems not unlikely to result in a real revival of ethics.

If finally we turn to a region which the vested interests of

4 Most opportunely for my argument, the kind of transformation of our scientific ideas which Pragmatism will involve has received the most copious and admirable illustration in Professor Ostwald's great *Naturphilosophie*. Professor Ostwald is not a professional philosopher at all, but a chemist, and has very likely never heard of Pragmatism; but he sets forth the pragmatist procedure of the sciences in a perfectly masterly way.

time-honoured organizations, the turbid complications of emotion, and a formalism that too often merges in hypocrisy, must always render hard of access to a sincere philosophy, and consider the attitude of Pragmatism towards the religious side of life, we shall find once more that it has a most important bearing. For *in principle* Pragmatism overcomes the old antithesis of faith and reason. It shows on the one hand that "faith" must underlie all "reason" and pervade it, nay, that at bottom rationality itself is the supremest postulate of faith. Without faith, therefore, there can be no reason, and initially the demands of "faith" must be as legitimate and essentially as reasonable as those of the "reason" they pervade. On the other hand, it enables us to draw the line between a genuine and a spurious "faith." The spurious "faith," which too often is all theologians take courage to aspire to, is merely the smoothing over of an unfaced scepticism, or at best a pallid fungus that, lurking in the dark recesses of the mind, must shun the light of truth and warmth of action. In contrast with it, a genuine faith is an ingredient in the growth of knowledge. It is ever realizing itself in the knowledge that it needs and seeks—to help it on to further conquests. It aims at its natural completion in what we significantly call the "making true" or "verification," and in default of this must be suspected as mere make-believe. And so the identity of method in science and religion is far more fundamental than their difference. Both rest on experience and aim at its interpretation; both proceed by postulation; and both require their anticipations to be verified. The difference lies only in the mode and extent of their verifications: the former must doubtless differ according to the nature of the subject; the latter has gone much further in the case of science, perhaps merely because there has been so much less persistence in attempts at the systematic verification of religious postulates.

III

It is clear, therefore, that Pragmatism is able to propound an extensive programme of reforms to be worked out by its methods. But even Pragmatism is not the final term of philosophic innovation; there is yet a greater and more sovereign principle now entering the lists of which it can only claim to have been the forerunner and vicegerent. This principle also has long been working in the minds of men, dumb, unnamed, and unavowed. But the time seems ripe now formally to name it, and to let it loose in order that it may receive its baptism of fire.

I propose, accordingly, to convert to the use of philosophic terminology a word which has long been famed in history and literature, and to denominate Humanism the attitude of thought which I *know* to be habitual in William James and in myself, which seems to be sporadic and inchoate in many others, and which is destined, I believe, to win the widest popularity. There would indeed be no flavour of extravagance and paradox about this last suggestion, were it not that the professional study of philosophy has so largely fallen into the hands of recluses who have lost all interest in the practical concerns of humanity, and have rendered philosophy like unto themselves, abstruse, arid, abstract, and abhorrent. But in itself there is no reason why this should be the character of philosophy. The final theory of life ought to be every man's concern, and if we can dispel the notion that the tiresome technicalities of philosophy lead to nothing of the least practical interest, it yet may be. There is ground, then, for the hope that the study of a *humaner* philosophy may prove at least as profitable and enjoyable as that of the "humaner" letters.

In all but name, Humanism has long been in existence. Years ago I described one of its most precious texts, William James's *Will to Believe*,[5] as a "declaration of the independence of the concrete whole of man with all his passions and emotions unexpurgated, directed against the cramping rules and regulations by which the Brahmins of the academic caste are tempted to impede the free expansion of human life," and as "a most salutary doctrine to preach to a biped oppressed by many ' -ologies,' like modern man, and calculated to allay his growing doubts whether he has a responsible personality and a soul and conscience of his own, and is not a mere phantasmagoria of abstractions, a transient complex of shadowy formulas that Science calls 'the laws of nature.' " Its great lesson was, I held, that "there are not really any eternal and nonhuman truths to prohibit us from adopting the beliefs we need to live

[5] In reviewing it for *Mind* in October, 1897 (N.S. No. 24, p. 548).

by, nor any infallible a priori tests of truth to screen us from the consequences of our choice." Similarly Professor James, in reviewing *Personal Idealism*,[6] pointed out that "a re-anthropomorphized universe is the general outcome of its philosophy." Only for "re-anthropomorphized" we should henceforth read "rehumanized." "Anthropomorphism" is a term of disparagement whose dyslogistic usage it may prove difficult to alter.[7] Moreover, it is clumsy, and can hardly be extended so as to cover what I mean by Humanism. There is no need to disclaim the truth of which it is the adumbration, and a nonanthropomorphic thought is sheer absurdity; but still what we need is something wider and more vivid.

Similarly I would hint at affinities with the great saying of Protagoras, that "Man is the measure of all things." Fairly interpreted, this is the truest and most important thing that any thinker ever has propounded. It is only in travesties such as it suited Plato's dialectic purpose to circulate that it can be said to tend to scepticism; in reality it urges science to discover how Man may measure, and by what devices make concordant his measures with those of his fellowmen. Now measurement is that in which ancient science failed. Protagoras alone demanded it, and Humanism need not cast about for any sounder or more convenient starting point.

For in every philosophy we must take some things for granted. Humanism, like common sense, of which it may fairly claim to be the philosophic working out, takes Man for granted as he stands, and the world of man's experience as it has come to seem to him. This is the only natural starting point, from which we can proceed in every direction, and to which we must return, enriched and with enhanced powers over our experience, from all the journeyings of science. Of course, this frank, though *not* therefore "uncritical," acceptance of our immediate experience and experienced self will seem a great deal to be granted by those addicted to abstruser methods. They have dreamt for ages of a priori philosophies "without presuppositions or assumptions," whereby Being might be conjured out of Nothing and the sage might penetrate the secret

---

6 *Mind* for January, 1903 (N.S. No. 45, p. 94).
7 I tried to do this in *Riddles of the Sphinx*, ch. V, §§ 9-12. But I now think the term needs radical rewording.

of creative power. But no obscurity of verbiage has in the end succeeded in concealing the utter failure of such preposterous attempts. The a priori philosophies have all been found out.

And what is worse, have they not all been detected in doing what they pretended to disclaim? Do they not all take surreptitiously for granted the human nature they pride themselves on disavowing? Are they not trying to solve human problems with human faculties? It is true that in form they claim to transcend our nature, or to raise it to the superhuman. But while they profess to exalt human nature, they are really mutilating it—all for the kingdom of Abstraction's sake! For what are their professed starting points—Pure Being, the Idea, the Absolute, the Universal I—but pitiable abstractions from experience, mutilated shreds of human nature, whose real value for the understanding of life is easily outweighed by the living experience of an honest man?

All these theories then, de facto, start from the immediate facts of our experience. Only they are ashamed of it, and assume without inquiry that it is worthless as a principle of explanation, and that no thinker worthy of the name can tolerate the thought of expressly setting out from anything so vulgar. Thus, so far from assuming less than the humanist, these speculations really must assume a great deal more. They must assume, in addition to ordinary human nature, their own metempirical starting points and the correctness (always more than dubious) of the deductions whereby they have de facto reached them.

"Do you propose then to accept as sacrosanct the gross unanalysed conceptions of crude common sense, and to exempt them from all criticism?" No, I only propose to start with them, and to try and see whether we could not get as far with them as with any other, nay, as far as we may want to get. I have faith that the process of experience that has brought us to our present standpoint has not been wholly error and delusion, and may on the whole be trusted. And I am quite sure that, right or wrong, we have no other, and that it is, e.g., grotesque extravagance to imagine that we can put ourselves at the standpoint of the Absolute. I would protest, therefore, against every form of "a priori metaphysical criticism" that condemns the results of our experience up to date as an illusory "appearance" *without trial*. For I hold that the only valid criticism they can receive must come in, and through, their actual *use*. It is just where and in so far as common-sense assumptions fail to work that we are theoretically justified, and practically compelled, to modify them. But in each such case, sufficient reasons must be shown; it is not enough merely to show that other assumptions can be made, and couched in technical language, and that our data are abstractly capable of different arrangements. There are, I am aware, infinite possibilities of conceptual rearrangement, but their discovery or construction is but a sort of intellectual game, and has no real importance.

In point of method, therefore, Humanism is fully able to vindicate itself, and so we can now define it as the philosophic attitude which, without wasting thought upon attempts to construct experience a priori, is content to take human experience as the clue to the world of human experience, content to take man on his own merits, just as he is to start with, without insisting that he must first be disembowelled of his interests and have his individuality evaporated and translated into technical jargon, before he can be deemed deserving of scientific notice. To remember that man is the measure of all things, i.e., of his whole experience-world, and that if our standard measure be proved false, all our measurements are vitiated; to remember that man is the maker of the sciences which subserve his human purposes; to remember that an ultimate philosophy which analyses us away is thereby merely exhibiting its failure to achieve its purpose—that, and more that might be stated to the same effect, is the real root of Humanism, whence all its auxiliary doctrines spring.

It is a natural consequence, for instance, that, if the facts require it, "real possibilities, real indeterminations, real beginnings, real ends, real evil, real crises, catastrophes and escapes, a real God and a real moral life, just as common sense conceives these things, may remain in Humanism as conceptions which philosophy gives up the attempt either to 'overcome' or to reinterpret."[8] And whether or not Humanism will have to

8 James, *The Will to Believe* (p. ix). I have substituted *"Humanism"* for *"empiricism."*

recognize the ultimate reality of all the gloomier possibilities of James's enumeration, it may safely be predicted that its "radical empiricism" will grant to the possibilities of "pluralism" a more careful and unbiassed inquiry than monistic preconceptions have as yet deigned to bestow upon them. For seeing that man is a social being, it is natural that Humanism should be hospitable to the view that the universe is ultimately "a joint-stock affair." And again, it will receive with appropriate suspicion all attempts to explain away the human personality, which is the formal and efficient and final cause of all explanation, and will rather *welcome* it in its unmutilated, undistorted immediacy as (though in an uncongenial tongue) the "a priori condition of all knowledge." And so it will approve of that "personal idealism" which strives to redeem the spiritual values an idealistic absolutism has so treacherously sold into the bondage of naturalism.

With "common sense" it will ever keep in touch by dint of refusing to value or validate the products of merely speculative analyses, void of purpose and of use, which betoken merely a power to play with verbal phrases. Thus Humanism will derive, combine, and include all the doctrines which may be treated as anticipations of its attitude.

For Pragmatism itself is in the same case with Personal Idealism, Radical Empiricism, and Pluralism. It is in reality only the application of Humanism to the theory of knowledge. If the entire man, if human nature as a whole, be the clue to the theory of all experience, then human purposiveness must irrigate the arid soil of logic. The facts of our thinking, freed from intellectualistic perversions, will clearly show that we are not dealing with abstract concatenations of purely intellectual processes, but with the rational aims of personal thinkers. Great, therefore, as will be the value we must claim for Pragmatism as a method, we must yet concede that man is greater than any method he has made, and that our Humanism must interpret it.

IV

It is a well-known fact that things are not only known by their affinities but also by their opposites. And the fitness of the term Humanism for our philosophic purpose could hardly better be displayed than by the ready transfer of its old associations to a novel context.

A *humanist* philosopher is sure to be keenly interested in the rich variety of human thought and sentiment, and unwilling to ignore the actual facts for the sake of bolstering up the narrow abstractions of some a priori theory of what "all men must" think and feel under penalty of scientific reprobation. The humanist, accordingly, will tend to grow *humane,* and tolerant of the divergences of attitude which must inevitably spring from the divergent idiosyncrasies of men. *Humanism,* therefore, will still remain opposed to *Barbarism.* But Barbarism may show itself in philosophy in a double guise, as barbarism of temper and as barbarism of style. Both are human defects which to this day remain too common among philosophers. The former displays itself in the inveterate tendency to sectarianism and intolerance, in spite of the discredit which the history of philosophy heaps upon it. For what could be more ludicrous than to keep up the pretence that all must own the sway of some absolute and unquestionable creed? Does not every page of every philosophic history teem with illustrations that a philosophic system is a unique and personal achievement of which not even the servilest discipleship can transfuse the full flavour into another's soul? Why should we therefore blind ourselves to the invincible individuality of philosophy, and deny each other the precious right to behold reality each at the peculiar angle whence he sees it? Why, when others cannot and will not see as we do, should we lose our temper and the faith that the heavenly harmony can only be achieved by a multitudinous symphony in which each of the myriad centres of experience sounds its own concordant note?

As for barbarism of style, that too is ever rampant, even though it no longer reaches the colossal heights attained by Kant and Hegel. If Humanism can restore against such forces the lucid writing of the older English style, it will make philosophy once more a subject gentlemen can read with pleasure. And it can at least contend that most of the technicalities which disfigure philosophic writings are totally unneeded, and that the stringing together of abstractions is both barbarous and dangerous. Pedagogically it is barbarous, because it nauseates the student, and because abstract ideas need to be illumined by concrete illustrations to fix them in mind; logically it is dangerous, because abstractions mostly take the form of worn-out metaphors which are like sunken rocks in navigation, so that there is no more fatal cause of error and deception than the trust in abstract dicta which by themselves mean nothing, and whose real meaning lies in the applications, which are not supplied.

In history, however, the great antithesis has been between Humanism and Scholasticism. This also we may easily adopt, without detracting from its force. For Scholasticism is still one of the great facts in human nature, and a fundamental foible of the learned world. Now, as ever, it is a spirit of sterilizing pedantry that avoids beauty, dreads clearness, and detests life and grace, a spirit that grovels in muddy technicality, buries itself in the futile burrowings of valueless researches, and conceals itself from human insight by the dust clouds of desiccated rubbish which it raises. Unfortunately the scholastic temper is one which their mode of life induces in professors as easily as indigestion, and frequently it renders them the worst enemies of their subjects. This is deplorable but might be counteracted, were it not thought essential to a reputation for scientific profundity at least to *seem* scholastic. Humanism therefore has before it an arduous fight with the dragon of Scholasticism, which, as it were, deters men from approaching the golden apples that cluster on the tree of knowledge in the garden of the Hesperides.

And lastly, may we not emphasize that the old associations of the word would still connect with Humanism a Renascence of philosophy? And shall we not accept this reminiscence as an omen for the future? For it is clear, assuredly, that Philosophy has still to be born again to enter on her kingdom, and that her votaries must still be born again to purge their systems of the taint of an inveterate barbarism. But some of these suggestions verge, perhaps, upon the fanciful; it suffices to have shown that Humanism makes a good name for the views I seek to label thus, and that in such extension of its meaning its old associations lose no force but rather gain a subtler flavour.

To claim that in its philosophic use Humanism may retain

its old associations is not, however, to deny that it must enter also into new relations. It would be vain, for instance, to attempt concealment of the fact that to Naturalism and Absolutism its antagonism is intrinsic. Naturalism is valid enough and useful as a method of tracing the connexions that permeate reality from the lowest to the highest level; but when taken as the last word of philosophy, it subjects the human to the arbitrament of its inferior. Absolutism, on the other hand, cherishes ambitions to attain the superhuman; but rather than admit its failure, it deliberately prefers to delude itself with shadows, and to reduce concrete reality to the illusory adumbration of a phantom Whole. The difference thus is this, that whereas Naturalism is worthy of respect for the honest work it does, and has a real use as a partial method in subordination to the whole, Absolutism has no use, and its explanatory value is nothing but illusion. As compared with these, Humanism will pursue the middle path; it will neither reject ideals because they are not realized, nor yet despise the actual because it can conceive ideas. It will not think the worst of nature, but neither will it trust an Absolute beyond its ken.

I am well aware that the ideas of which the preceding pages may have suggested the barest outline are capable of endless working out and illustration. And though I believe myself to have made no assertion that could not be fully vindicated if assailed, I realize most keenly that a complete statement of the humanist position far transcends not only my own powers, but those of any single man. But I hoped that those who were disposed to sympathy and open-mindedness would pardon the defects and overlook the gaps in this informal survey of a glorious prospect, while to those who are too imperviously encased in habit or in sloth, or too deeply severed from me by an alien idiosyncrasy, I knew that I could never hope to bring conviction, however *much,* nor to avoid offence, however *little,* I might try to say. And so I thought the good ship *Humanism* might sail on its adventurous quest for the Islands of the Blest with the lighter freight of these essays as safely and hopefully as with the heaviest cargo.

F. C. S. SCHILLER

Oxford, August, 1903

Preface to the First Edition
of Studies in Humanism

OF THE essays which compose this volume, about half have appeared in various periodicals—*Mind*, the *Hibbert Journal*, the *Quarterly Review*, the *Fortnightly Review*, and the *Journal of Philosophy*—during the past three years. Additions have, however, grown so extensive that of the matter of the book, not more than one-third, and that the less constructive part, can be said, to have been in print before. That the form should still be discontinuous is due to the fact that the conditions under which I have had to work greatly hamper and delay the composition of a continuous treatise, and that it seemed imperative to deal more expeditiously with the chief strategic points of the philosophic situation. I hope, however, that the discontinuity of the form will not be found incompatible with an essential continuity of aim, argument, and interest. In all these respects the present *Studies* may most naturally be regarded as continuous with *Humanism* and *Axioms as Postulates*, without, however, ceasing to be independently intelligible. They have had to reflect the developments of philosophy and the progress of discussion, and this has rendered them, I fear, slightly more technical on the whole than *Humanism*. Nor can their main topic, the meaning of Truth, be made an altogether popular subject. On the other hand, they touch more fully than *Humanism* on subjects which are less exclusively technical, such as the nature of our freedom and the religious aspects of philosophy.

That in the contents construction should be somewhat largely mixed with controversy is in some respects regrettable. But whether one can avoid controversy depends largely on whether one's doctrines are allowed an opportunity of peaceful development. Also on what one has undertaken to do. And in this case the most harmless experiments in fog-dispelling have been treated as profanations of the most sacred mysteries. It is, however, quite true that the undertaking of the new philosophy may be regarded as in some ways the most stupendous in the history

29

of thought. Heine, in a well-known passage, once declared the feats of the German Transcendentalists to have been more terrific than those of the French Revolutionaries, in that they decapitated a deity and not a mere mortal king. But what was the Transcendental boldness of Kant, as described by Heine, when, armed only with the *Pure Reason*, and attended only by his "faithful Lampe" and an umbrella, he "stormed Heaven and put the whole garrison to the sword," to the transatlantic audacity of a Jacobin philosophy which is seriously suspected of penetrating into the "supercelestial" heavens of the Pure Reason, and of there upsetting the centre of gravity of the Intelligible Universe, of dethroning the "Higher Synthesis of the Devil and the Deity," the Absolute, and of instituting a general *Götzendämmerung* of the Eternal Ideas? Even its avowed aim of *humanizing* Truth, and bringing it back to earth from such altitudes, seems comparable with the Promethean sacrilege of the theft of fire. What wonder, then, that such transcelestial conflagrations should kindle burning questions on the earth, and be reflected in the heating of terrestrial tempers?

But after all, the chief warrant for a polemical handling of these matters is its strict relevance. The new truths are most easily understood by contrast with the old perplexities, and the necessity of advancing in their direction is rendered most evident by the impossibility of advancing in any other.[1]

That the development of the new views, then, should have been so largely controversial was probably inevitable. It has been all the more rapid for that. For the intensity of intellectualistic prejudice and the intolerance of Absolutism have compelled us to attack in sheer self-defence, to press on our counterstatements in order to engage the enemy along his whole front, and to hurry every new argument into the line of battle as soon as it became available.

The result has been an unprecedented development of converging novelties. Within the past three or four years (i.e., since the preface to *Humanism* was written) there have appeared in the first place the important *Studies in Logical Theory* by Professor Dewey and his coadjutors. These, it is becoming more and more evident, have dealt a death blow, not only to the "correspondence-with-reality" view of truth, but also to all the

[1] Cp. pp. 194–95.

realisms and idealisms which involve it. And so far no absolutism has succeeded in dispensing with it. Professor Dewey and
his pupils have also contributed a number of weighty and valuable papers and discussions to the philosophic periodicals
(*Mind*, the *Journal of Philosophy*, and the *Philosophical Review*). Mr. C. S. Peirce's articles in the *Monist* (1905) have
shown that he has not disavowed the great pragmatic principle
which he launched into the world so unobtrusively nearly thirty
years ago, and seemed to leave so long without a father's care.
William James's final metaphysics, on the other hand, is still in
the making. But he has expounded and defended the new views
in a series of brilliant articles in the *Journal of Philosophy* and
in *Mind*. In England the literature of the question has been
critical rather than constructive. In the forefront may be mentioned Mr. Henry Sturt's *Idola Theatri*, a singularly lucid
and readable study of the genesis, development, and ailments of
English Absolutism. But the masterly (and unanswered) criticisms by Captain H. V. Knox and Mr. Alfred Sidgwick of the
most essential foundations of absolutist metaphysics should not
be forgotten.[2] And lastly, Professor Santayana's exquisite *Life of
Reason* should be cited as a triumph, not only of literary form,
but also of the pragmatic method in a mind which has espoused
a metaphysic very different from that which in general Pragmatism favours. For Professor Santayana, though a pragmatist
in epistemology, is a materialist in metaphysics.[3]

The new movement is also in evidence beyond the borders
of the English-speaking world, either in its properly pragmatic forms or in their equivalents and analogues. It is most
marked perhaps in France, where it has the weighty support in
philosophy of Professor Bergson of the Collège de France, who
has followed up the anti-intellectualism of his *Données im-
médiates de la Conscience* by his *Matière et Mémoire*, and in
science of Professor Henri Poincaré of the Institute, whose *La
Science et l'Hypothèse* and *La Valeur de la Science* expound the
pragmatic nature of the scientific procedures and assumptions
with unsurpassable lucidity and grace. He seems, indeed, as
yet unwilling to go as far as some of the ultrapragmatic fol-

[2] *Mind*, N.S. Nos. 54 and 53.
[3] I have discussed the relations of his work to the Pragmatic movement in
reviewing it for the *Hibbert Journal* (January and July, 1906).

lowers of Professor Bergson, e.g., MM. Leroy and Wilbois, and imposes some slight limitations on the pragmatic treatment of knowledge, on the ground that knowledge may be conceived as an end to which action is a means. But this perhaps only indicates that this pre-eminent man of science has not yet taken note of the work which has been done by philosophers in the English-writing world on the nature of the conception of truth and the relation of the scientific endeavour to our total activity. At any rate he goes quite far enough to make it clear that whoever henceforth wishes to uphold the traditional views of the nature of science, and particularly of mathematics, will have in the first place to confute Professor Poincaré.

In Italy, Florence boasts of a youthful, but extremely active and brilliant, band of avowed Pragmatists, whose militant organ, the *Leonardo*, edited by Signor Giovanni Papini, is distinguished by a freedom and vigour of language which must frequently horrify the susceptibilities of academic coteries. In Denmark, Professor Höffding is more than sympathetic, and the Royal Academy of Science has recently made the relations of Pragmatism and Criticism the subject for the international prize essay for which Schopenhauer once wrote his *Grundlage der Moral*.

In Germany alone the movement seems slow to take root *eo nomine*. Nevertheless, there are a goodly number of analogous tendencies. Professors Ostwald and Mach and their schools are the champions of a pragmatic view of science. Various forms of "Psychologism," proceeding from the same considerations as those which have inspired the Anglo-American pragmatisms, disturb the old conceptions of logic. Among them Professor Jerusalem's *Der kritische Idealismus und die reine Logik* is particularly noteworthy. The "school of Fries," and conspicuously Dr. Julius Schultz, the author of the brilliant *Psychologie der Axiome*, excellently emphasize the postulation of axioms, though as their polemic against empiricism still presupposes the Humian conception of a passive experience, they prefer to call them a priori.[4] The *humanistic* aspects of the movement find a close parallel in the writings of Professor Eucken. But on the whole Germany lags behind, largely because these various tendencies have not yet been connected or

4 Cp. *Mind*, XV, 115.

brought to a common focus. I have, however, reason to believe that this deficiency may soon be remedied.

What, meanwhile, is the situation in the camp of Intellectualism, which is still thronged with most of the philosophic notables? Although the technical journals have been full of controversial articles, and the interest excited has actually sent up the circulation of *Mind*, singularly little has been produced that rises above the merest misconception or misrepresentation; and nothing to invalidate the new ideas. Mr. F. H. Bradley has exercised his great talents of philosophic caricature, but a positive alternative to Pragmatism, in the shape of an intelligible, coherent doctrine of the nature of truth, is still the great desideratum of Intellectualism.

The most noteworthy attempt, beyond doubt, to work out an intellectualistic ideal of truth, which has proceeded from the Anglo-Hegelian school, is Mr. H. H. Joachim's recent *Nature of Truth*. But it may be doubted whether its merits will commend it to the school. For it ends in flat failure, and avowed scepticism, which is scientifically redeemed only by the fact that its outspokenness greatly facilitates the critic's task in laying his finger on the fundamental flaw of all Intellectualism. With the exception of Plato's *Theaetetus*, no book has, consequently, been of greater service to me in showing how fatal the *depersonalizing* of thought and the *dehumanizing* of truth are to the possibility and intelligibility of knowledge, and how arbitrary and indefensible these abstractions really are.

It would seem, therefore, that the situation is rapidly clearing itself. On the one hand we have a new method with inexhaustible possibilities of application to life and science, which, though it is not primarily metaphysical, contains also the promise of an infinity of valuable, and more or less valid, metaphysics; on the other, opposed to it on every point, an old metaphysic of tried and tested sterility, which is condemned to eternal failure by the fundamental perversity of its logical method. And now at last is light beginning to penetrate into its obscurities. It is becoming clear that Rationalism is not rational, and that "reason" does not sanction its pretensions. Absolutism is ending as those who saw its essentially inhuman character foresaw that it must. In its "Hegelian" as in its Bradleian form, it has yielded itself wholly up to scepticism, and Mr. Bradley was evidently not a day too soon in comparing it to Jericho. For its defences have crumbled into dust, without a regular siege, merely under the strain of attempts to man them. Its opponents really are not needed for their demolition; they need merely record and applaud the work of self-destruction.

But that this process should provoke dissatisfaction and disintegration in the ranks of the absolutists is no wonder, nor that the signs of their confusion should be multiplying. No one seems to know, e.g., what is to be done about the central point, the conception of truth; whether the "correspondence view" is to be reaffirmed or abandoned, and in the former case, *how* it can be defended, or in the latter, *how* it can be discarded.[5] Nay, the voice of mutiny is beginning to be heard. The advice is openly given to the "idealist" host to shut up their Bradley and their Berkeley, and to open their Plato and their Hegel.[6] As regards Hegel, this recommendation is not likely to be fruitful, because nothing will be found in him that bears on the situation; Plato, on the other hand, is likely to provide most salutary, but almost wholly penitential, reading. For, I believe, these *Studies* will be found to fulfil a pledge given in *Humanism,* and to show that Intellectualism may be confuted out of the mouth of its own founder and greatest exponent. For Plato had in fact perceived the final consequence of Intellectualism, viz., that to complete itself *it must dehumanize the Ideal and derealize the Real,* with superior clearness. His unwillingness either to avoid or to conceal this consequence is what has engendered the hopeless crux of the "Platonic problem" from his day to this, and from this difficulty no intellectualism can ever extricate itself. It may rail at humanity and try to dissolve human knowledge; but the only real remedy lies in renouncing the abstractions on which it rests. Our only hope of understanding knowledge, our only chance of keeping philosophy alive by nourishing it with the realities of life, lies in going back from Plato to Protagoras, and ceasing to misunderstand the great teacher who discovered the measure of man's universe.

I cannot conclude this Preface without recording my indebtedness to my friend Captain H. V. Knox, who has read a

5 Cp. Chapter 9.
6 *Mind,* N.S. No. 59, XV, 327.

large part of these *Studies* in proof and in manuscript, and with whom I have had the pleasure of discussing some of the knottiest points in the theory of knowledge. I have profited thereby to such an extent that I should find it hard to say how far some of the doctrines here enunciated were his or mine.

Sils Maria, September, 1906

PART ONE

Humanism, Pragmatism, and Metaphysics

Editor's Introduction

THE DISTINCTIVE aspect of Schiller's world view is his statement that "reality" is plastic, incomplete, and piecemeal. This must be understood in opposition to Absolute Idealism, which was described by H. J. Paton as "Hegelianism modified by Anglo-Saxon caution." Briefly (and inaccurately) it maintained that only the spiritual is real; that Reality is a seamless logical unity, not a mere disjointed plurality of items; that in the Absolute all separateness vanishes; that nothing finite, nothing which changes, not even human personality, is ever quite real; and that there is something makeshift, transitory, and unsatisfactory about individual thoughts and acts. But this last, says Schiller, is precisely all we ever have or know about. An independent or Absolute Reality which does not somehow enter into our experience, or explain our knowledge, is irrelevant to us. He further declares Absolute Idealism to entail solipsism; it is, in short, obsolete idealism. (He could never resist a pun.)

We must ask, then, says Schiller, not What is Reality? but What can I know as real? Ontology must be conditioned by epistemology. It is our actual knowings which are decisive. What these reveal is a reality which is not rigid, but is evolving, and is necessarily related to our needs and purposes. Our freedom, accordingly, is genuine. We can't know just how malleable the universe will be; that will be determined in the course of our efforts. You will see that Schiller wriggles a bit in developing this theory. Are there really no limitations on man's power to mold the universe? And what about the world before man appeared? Is there a "subjective" as well as an "objective" making? Or do men rather "find" reality? Some of the implications of this metaphysics (e.g., hylozoism, the aliveness of inanimate matter) will strike us as, shall we say, romantic.

However, in noting these imaginative excesses, we must likewise indicate the appropriateness of this philosophy to modern science. For we know now that the outcome of scientific activity is an *inter*action between a knower and a known. What the physicist calls "real" depends in part on what he does, and on the questions he asks. The postulate of at least the partial plasticity of the universe is implicit in what man does to understand and master his surroundings.

Schiller's metaphysics, like Dewey's, thus has a biological matrix. But while both take the process of knowing as fundamental, Dewey, like James, was a realist, whereas Schiller gave his philosophy an idealistic and personalistic gradient. He said, "Humanism forms a third alternative to Realism and Idealism." Dewey, unlike Schiller, built upon the objective and social aspects of James's psychology. James wrote:[1]

> Schiller's doctrine and mine are identical, only our expositions follow different directions. He starts from the subjective pole of the chain, the individual with his beliefs, as the more concrete and immediately given phenomenon . . . I begin with the abstract notion of an objective reality.
>
> Schiller, remaining with the fallible individual, and treating only of reality-for-him, seems to many of his readers to ignore reality-in-itself altogether. But that is because he seeks only to tell us how truths are attained, not what the contents of those truths, when attained, shall be.

But when James received Schiller's *Studies in Humanism*, he wrote him,[2] "The essays on Freedom and the Making of Reality seem to be written with my own heart's blood—it's startling that two people should be found to think so exactly alike."

Peirce believed that what we call "the reality of the external world," while not "made" in Schiller's usage, resulted from the human activity of selection and emphasis by which we reduce the chaos about us to order. He wrote:[3]

> If all things are continuous, the universe must be undergoing a continuous growth from non-existence to existence. There

1 *The Meaning of Truth*, pp. 242–43.
2 On April 19, 1907. *Selected Letters*, ed. Hardwick (New York, 1960), p. 230.
3 *Collected Papers*, I, par. 362.

is no difficulty in conceiving existence as a matter of degree. The reality of things consists in their persistent forcing themselves upon our recognition. If a thing has no such persistence, it is a mere dream. Reality, then, is persistence, is regularity. In the original chaos, where there was no regularity, there was no existence.

Let us now see Schiller's views in detail.

Chapter 1

The Ethical Basis of Metaphysics[1]

Argument

The place of conduct in philosophy: (1) The absolutist reduction of conduct to "appearance"; (2) the pragmatist reaction which makes conduct primary and thought secondary. Is Pragmatism Irrationalism? No, but it explains it by exposing the inadequacy of Intellectualism. Ways of reaching Pragmatism (1) by justification of "faith" against "reason," (2) historical, (3) evolutionary. The definition of Pragmatism. Its relation to psychological teleology. The supremacy of "Good" over "True" and "Real." Kant's *Copernican Revolution*, and the complication of the question of reality with that of our knowledge. A further similar step necessitated by the purposiveness of actual knowing. The function of the will in cognition. "Reality" as the response to a will to know, and therefore dependent in part on our action. Consequently (1) "reality" cannot be indifferent to us; (2) our relations to it quasi-personal; (3) metaphysics quasi-ethical; (4) Pragmatism as a tonic: the venture of faith and freedom; (5) the moral stimulus of Pragmatism.

[1] This essay, originally an Ethical Society address, is reprinted from the July, 1903, number of the *International Journal of Ethics* with some additions, the chief of which is the note on pp. 49–50. Its title seems of course to put the cart before the horse, but it is easy to reply that nowadays it is no longer impracticable to use a motorcar for the removal of a dead horse. The paradox is, moreover, intentional. It is a conscious inversion of the tedious and unprofitable disquisitions on "the metaphysical basis of" this, that, and the other, which an erroneous conception of philosophical method engenders. They are all wrong in method, because we have not *de facto* a science of first principles of unquestionable truth from which we can start to derive the principles of the special sciences. Plato certainly failed to deduce the principles of the sciences from his metaphysical Idea of Good, and it may be doubted whether anyone has ever really deduced anything from metaphysics. The fact is rather that our "first" principles are postulated by the needs, and slowly secreted by the labours, of the special sciences, or of such preliminary exercises of our intelligence as build up the common-sense view of life.

So what my title means is, not an attempt to rest the "final synthesis" upon a single science, but rather that among the contributions of the special sciences to the final evaluation of experience, that of the highest, viz., ethics, has, and must have, decisive weight.

WHAT HAS philosophy to say of conduct? Shall it place it high or low, exalt it on a pedestal for the adoration of the world or drag it in the mire to be trampled on by all superior persons? Shall it equate it with the whole or value it as nought? Philosophers have, of course, considered the matter, though not perhaps as carefully nor as successfully as they ought. And so the relations of the theory to the practice of life, of cognition to action, of the theoretical to the practical reason, form a difficult and complicated chapter in the history of thought. From that history one fact, however, stands out clearly, viz., that the claims on both sides are so large and so insistent that it is hardly possible to compromise between them. The philosopher is not on the whole a lover of compromise, despite the solicitations of his lower nature. He will not, like the ordinary man of sense, subscribe to a plausible platitude like, e.g., Matthew Arnold's famous dictum that "Conduct is three-fourths of Life." Matthew Arnold was not a philosopher, and the very precision of his formula arouses scientific suspicions. But anyhow the philosopher's imperious logic does not deal in quarters; it is prone to argue *aut Caesar aut nullus*; if conduct be not the whole life, it is naught. Which therefore shall it be? Shall conduct be the substance of the All, or the vision of a dream?

Now it would seem at first that latterly the second alternative had grown philosophically almost inevitable. For under the auspices of the Hegelizing "idealists," Philosophy has uplifted herself once more to a metaphysical contemplation of the Absolute, of the unique Whole in which all things are included and transcended. Now whether this conception has any logical meaning and value for metaphysics is a moot point, which I have elsewhere treated;[2] but there can hardly be a pretence of denying that it is the death of morals. For the ideal of the Absolute Whole cannot be rendered compatible with the antithetical valuations which form the vital atmosphere of human agents. They are partial appreciations, which vanish from the standpoint of the Whole. Without the distinctions of good and evil, right and wrong, pleasure and pain, self and others, then and now, progress and decay, human life would be dissolved into the phantom flow of an unmeaning mirage. But in the Absolute the moral distinctions must, like all others,

2 *Riddles of the Sphinx*, ch. X; *Formal Logic*, p. 129 *n.*

be swallowed up and disappear. The All is raised above all ethical valuation and moral criticism: it is "beyond good and evil"; it is timelessly perfect, and therefore incapable of improvement. It transcends all our antitheses, because it includes them. And so to the metaphysician it seems an easy task to compose the perfection of the whole out of the imperfections of its parts: he has merely to declare that the point of view of human action, that of ethics, is not and cannot be final. It is an illusion which has grown transparent to the sage. So, in proportion as his insight into absolute reality grows clearer, his interest in ethics wanes.

It must be confessed, moreover, that metaphysicians no longer shrink from this avowal. The typical leader of this philosophic fashion, Mr. F. H. Bradley, never attempts to conceal his contempt for ethical considerations, nor omits a sneer at the pretensions of practice to be heard in the High Court of Metaphysics. "Make the moral point of view absolute," he cries,[3] "and then realize your position. You have become not merely irrational, but you have also broken with every considerable religion."

And this is how he dismisses the appeal to practice:[4] "But if so, what, I may be asked, is the result in practice? That I reply at once is not my business"; it is merely a "hurtful[5] prejudice" if "irrelevant appeals to practical results are allowed to make themselves heard."

Altogether nothing could be more pulverizing to ethical aspiration than chapter XXV of Mr. Bradley's *Appearance and Reality*.[6]

And the worst of it all is that this whole treatment of ethics follows logically and legitimately from the general method of philosophizing which conducts to the metaphysical assumption of the Absolute.

Fortunately, however, there appears to be a natural tendency when the consequences of a point of view have been stated with-

[3] *Appearance and Reality*, pp. 500–1.
[4] *Ibid.*, p. 450.
[5] But does not this "hurtful" reaffirm the ethical valuation which Mr. Bradley is trying to exclude?
[6] That such is the ethical purport of this philosophic teaching is confirmed by the ingenious but somewhat flippant exposition of the same doctrine in Prof. A. E. Taylor's *Problem of Conduct*. The real problem of this book would appear to be why anyone should trouble about such a theoretic absurdity as morals at all.

out reserve, and become plain to the meanest intelligence, to turn round and try something fresh. By becoming openly immoralist, metaphysic has created a demand for its moral reformation. So quite recently, there has become noticeable a movement in a diametrically opposite direction, which repudiates the assumptions and reverses the conclusions of the metaphysical criticism of ethics which we have been considering. Instead of regarding contemplation of the Absolute as the highest form of human activity, it sets it aside as trivial and unmeaning, and puts purposeful action above purposeless speculation. Instead of supposing that Action is one thing and Thought something alien and other, and that there is not, therefore, any reason to anticipate that the pure contemplations of the latter will in any way relate to or sanction the principles which guide the former, it treats every judgment as an act and Thought as a mode of conduct, as an integral part of active life. Instead of regarding practical results as irrelevant, it makes Practical Value an essential ingredient and determinant of theoretic truth. And so far from admitting the claim to independence of an irresponsible intelligence, it regards knowledge as derivative from conduct and as involving distinctively moral qualities and responsibilities in a perfectly definite and traceable way. In short, instead of being reduced to the nothingness of an illusion, conduct is reinstated as the all-controlling influence in every department of life.

It may be admitted, however, that all effective ethical effort ultimately demands a definite attitude towards life as a whole, and it therefore becomes an urgent need to find a philosophy which will support, or at least will not paralyse, moral effort. The new method of philosophizing will supply this desideratum in an almost perfect way. It has been called Pragmatism by the chief author of its importance, Professor William James, whose *Varieties of Religious Experience* so many others besides the professional readers of philosophic literature have been enjoying. But the name in this case does even less than usual to explain the meaning, and as the nature of Pragmatism has been greatly and conspicuously misunderstood, we must try to put it in a clearer light.

We may best begin by mentioning a few of the ways in which Pragmatism may be reached, before explaining how it should be defined. For many have conceived a considerable prejudice against it by reason of the method by which William James approached it.

James first unequivocally advanced the pragmatist doctrine in connexion with what he called the "will-to-believe."[7] Now this will-to-believe was put forward as an intellectual *right* (in certain cases) to decide between alternative views, each of which seemed to make a legitimate appeal to our nature, by other than purely intellectual considerations, viz., their emotional interest and practical value. Although James laid down a number of conditions limiting the applicability of his will-to-believe, the chief of which was the willingness to take the risks involved and to abide by the results of subsequent experience, it was not perhaps altogether astonishing that his doctrine should be decried as rank irrationalism.

Irrationalism seemed a familiar and convenient label for the new doctrine. For irrationalism is a permanent or continually recrudescent attitude of the moral consciousness, the persistent vogue of which it has always been hard to explain. It is ably and brilliantly exemplified at the present day by Mr. Balfour's *Foundations of Belief,* and, in a less defensible form, by Mr. Benjamin Kidd. And if, instead of denouncing it, we try to understand it, we shall not find that it is entirely absurd. At bottom, indeed, it indicates little more than a defect in the current rationalism, and a protest against the rationalistic blindness towards the nonintellectual factors in the foundation of beliefs. Common sense has always shown a certain sympathy with all such protests against the pretensions of what is called the pure intellect to indicate to man's whole complex nature. It has always felt that there are "reasons of the heart of which the head knows nothing," postulates of a faith that surpasses mere understanding, and that these possess a higher rationality which a bigoted Intellectualism has failed to comprehend.

If, then, one had to choose between Irrationalism and Intellectualism, the former would undoubtedly have to be pre-

---

[7] He had, however, laid the foundation of his doctrine long before in an article in *Mind* (1879). And, though the name is new, anticipations of the *thing* run through the whole history of thought. Indeed, this was to be expected, seeing that the actual procedure of the human mind has always been (unconsciously) pragmatist.

ferred. It is less inadequate to life, a less violent departure from our actual behaviour, a less grotesque caricature of our actual procedure. Like common sense, therefore, Pragmatism sympathizes with Irrationalism in its blind revolt against the trammels of a pedantic Intellectualism. But Pragmatism does more; it not only sympathizes, it explains. It vindicates the rationality of Irrationalism, without becoming itself irrational; it restrains the extravagance of Intellectualism, without losing faith in the intellect.[8] And it achieves this by instituting a new analysis of the common root both of the reason and of the emotional revulsion against its pride. By showing the "pure" reason to be a pure figment, and a psychological impossibility, and the real structure of the actual reason to be essentially pragmatical, and permeated through and through with acts of faith, desires to know, and wills to believe, to disbelieve, and to make believe, it renders possible, nay unavoidable, a reconciliation between a reason which is humanized and a faith which is rationalized in the very process which shows their antithesis to be an error.

That, however, Pragmatism should have begun by intervening in the ancient controversy between Reason and Faith was something of an accident. Itself it might equally well have been arrived at by way of a moral revolt from the unfruitful logic-chopping and aimless quibbling which is often held to be the sum total of philosophy.

Or again, it might be reached, most instructively, by a critical consideration of many historic views, notably those of Kant and Lotze,[9] and of the unsolved problems which they leave on our hands. Or, once more, by observing the actual procedure of the various sciences and their motives for accepting, maintaining, and modifying the "truth" of their various propositions, we may come to realize that what works best in practice is what in actual knowing we accept as "true."

But to me personally the straightest road to Pragmatism is one which the extremest prejudice can scarce suspect of truckling to the encroachments of theology. Instead of saying, like

---

[8] This passage has actually been quoted by a critic as cogent evidence that Pragmatism is Irrationalism! Cp. *Mind*, No. 75, p. 431, and No. 71, p. 426.
[9] Or, as James suggested, and as Prof. A. W. Moore has actually done in the case of Locke (see his *Functional Versus the Representational Theory of Knowledge*), by a critical examination of the English philosophers.

James, "so all-important is it to secure the right action that
(in cases of real intellectual alternatives) it is lawful for us to
adopt the belief most congenial with our spiritual needs and
to try whether our faith will not make it come true," I should
rather say "the traditional notion of beliefs determined by pure
reason alone is wholly incredible. For is not 'pure' reason a
myth? How can there be such a thing? How, that is, can we
so separate our intellectual function from the whole complex
of our activities that it can operate in real independence of
practical considerations? I cannot but conceive the reason as
being, like the rest of our equipment, a weapon in the struggle
for existence and a means of achieving adaptation. It must follow that the use, which has developed it, must have stamped
itself upon its inmost structure, even if it has not moulded it
out of prerational instincts. In short, a reason which has not
practical value for the purposes of life is a monstrosity, a
morbid aberration or failure of adaptation, which natural selection must sooner or later wipe away."

It is in some such way that I should prefer to pave the
way for an appreciation of the aims of Pragmatism. Hence
we may now venture to define it as the thorough recognition that the purposive character of mental life generally
must influence and pervade also our most remotely cognitive
activities.[10]

In other words, it is a conscious application to the theory
of life of the psychological facts of cognition as they appear
to a teleological Voluntarism. In the light of such a teleological psychology, the problems of logic and metaphysics are
rejuvenated by the decisive weight given to the conceptions
of Purpose and End. Or again, it is a systematic protest
against the practice of ignoring in our theories of Thought
and Reality the purposiveness of all our actual thinking, and
the relation of all our actual realities to the ends of our practical life. It is an assertion of the sway of human valuations
over every region of our experience, and a denial that such
valuation can validly be eliminated from the contemplation
of any reality we know.

Now inasmuch as such teleological valuation is also the

[10] For a further discussion of the definition of Pragmatism, cp. my article in
the *Encyclopædia Britannica*, 11th ed.

special sphere of ethical inquiry, Pragmatism may be said to assign metaphysical validity to the typical method of ethics. At a blow it awards to the ethical conception of Good supreme authority over the logical conception of True and the metaphysical conception of Real. The Good becomes a determinant both of the True and of the Real, and their secret inspiration. For from the pursuit of the latter we may never eliminate the reference to the former. Our apprehension of the Real, our comprehension of the True, is always effected by beings who are aiming at the attainment of some Good, and *choose* between rival claimants to reality and truth according to the services they render. Is it not then a palpable absurdity to deny that this fact makes a stupendous difference?

Pragmatism then has taken a further step in the analysis of our experience which amounts to an important advance in that self-knowledge on which our knowledge of the world depends. Indeed, this advance seems to be of a magnitude comparable with, and no less momentous than, that which gave to the *epistemological* question priority over the *ontological*.

It is generally recognized as the capital achievement of modern philosophy to have perceived that a solution of the ontological question—*What is reality?*—is not possible until it has been decided how reality can come within our ken. Before there can be a real for us at all, the real must be *knowable*, and the notion of an unknowable reality is useless, because it abolishes itself. The true formulation therefore of the ultimate question of metaphysics must become: *What can I know as real?* Thus the effect of what Kant (very infelicitously) called the Copernican Revolution in philosophy is that ontology, the theory of reality, comes to be conditioned by epistemology, the theory of our knowledge.

But this truth is incomplete until we realize all that is involved in the knowledge being *ours* and recognize the real nature of our knowing. Our knowing is not the mechanical operation of a passionless "pure" intellect, which

> Grinds out Good and grinds out Ill,
> And has no purpose, heart, or will.

Pure intellection is not a fact in nature; it is a logical fiction which will not really serve even the purposes of technical logic. In reality our knowing is driven and guided at every step by our subjective interests and preferences, our desires, our needs, and our ends. These form the motive powers also of our intellectual life.

Now what is the bearing of this fact on the traditional dogma of an absolute truth and ultimate reality existing for themselves apart from human agency? It must utterly debar us from the cognition of "reality as it is in itself and apart from our interests"; if such a thing there were, it could not be known, nor rationally believed in.

For our interests impose the conditions under which alone reality can be revealed. Only such aspects of reality can be revealed as are (1) knowable and (2) objects of an actual desire, and consequent attempt, to know. All other realities or aspects of reality, which there is no attempt to know, necessarily remain unknown, and for us unreal, because there is no one to look for them. Reality, therefore, and the knowledge thereof, essentially presuppose a definitely directed effort to know. And, like other efforts, this effort is purposive; it is necessarily inspired by the conception of some good ("end") at which it aims. Neither the question of Fact, therefore, nor the question of Knowledge can be raised without raising also the question of Value. Our "facts" when analysed turn out to be "values," and the conception of "value" therefore becomes more ultimate than that of "fact." Our valuations thus pervade our whole experience, and affect whatever "fact," whatever "knowledge" we consent to recognize. If, then, there is no *knowing* without *valuing*, if knowledge is a form of Value, or, in other words, a factor in a Good, Lotze's anticipation[11] has been fully realized, and the foundations of metaphysics have actually been found to lie in ethics.

In this way the ultimate question for philosophy becomes: What is reality *for one aiming at knowing what?* "Real" means real for what *purpose?* to what *end?* in what *use?* in what context? in preference to what alternative belief? The answers always come in terms of the will to know which puts the question. This at once yields a simple and beautiful explanation of the different accounts of reality which are given

11 *Metaphysics* (Eng. tr.), II, 319.

in the various sciences and philosophies. The purpose of the questions being different, so is their purport, and so must be the answers. For the direction of our effort, itself determined by our desires and will to know, enters as a necessary and ineradicable factor into whatever revelation of reality we can attain. The response to our questions is always affected by their *character*, and *that* is in our power. For the initiative throughout is ours. It is for us to consult the oracle of Nature or to refrain; it is for us to formulate our demands and to put our questions. If we question amiss, Nature will not respond, and we must try again. But we can never be entitled to assume either that our action makes no difference or that nature contains no answer to a question we have never thought to put.[12]

12 That the real has a determinate nature which the knowing reveals but does not affect, so that our knowing makes no difference to it, is one of those sheer assumptions which are incapable not only of proof, but even of rational defence. It is a survival of a crude realism which can be defended only, *in a pragmatist manner*, on the score of its practical convenience, as an avowed fiction. In this sense and as a mode of speech, we need not quarrel with it. But as an ultimate analysis of the fact of knowing, it is an utterly gratuitous interpretation. The plain fact is that we can come into contact with any sort of reality only in the act of "knowing" or experiencing it. As *unknowable*, therefore, the real is *nil;* as *unknown*, it is only potentially real. What is there in this situation to sanction the assumption that what the real *is* in the act of knowing, it is also outside that relation? One might as well argue that because an orator is eloquent in the presence of an audience, he is no less voluble in addressing himself. The simple fact is that we know the real *as it is when we know it*; we know nothing whatever about what it is apart from that process. It is meaningless, therefore, to inquire into its nature as it is in itself. And I can see no reason why the view that reality exhibits a rigid nature unaffected by our treatment should be deemed theoretically more justifiable than its converse, that it is utterly plastic to our every demand—a travesty of Pragmatism which has attained much popularity with its critics. The actual situation is, of course, a case of interaction, a process of cognition in which the "subject" and the "object" determine each other, and both "we" and "reality" are involved, and, we might add, *evolved*. There is no warrant, therefore, for the assumption that either of the poles between which the current passes could be suppressed without detriment. What we ought to say is that when the mind "knows" reality, both are affected, just as we say that when a stone falls to the ground, both it and the earth are attracted.

We are driven, then, to the conviction that the "determinate nature of reality" does *not* subsist "outside" or "beyond" the process of knowing it. It is merely a half-understood lesson of experience that we have enshrined in the belief that it does so subsist. Things behave in similar ways in their reaction to modes of treatment, the differences between which seem to us important. From this we have chosen to infer that things have a rigid and unalterable nature. It might have been better to infer that therefore the differences between our various manipulations must seem unimportant to the things.

The truth is rather that the nature of things is not *determinate* but *determinable*, like that of our fellow men. Previous to trial it is indeterminate, not merely for our ignorance, but really and from every point of view, within limits which it is our business to discover. It grows determinate by our experiments, like human character. We all know that in our social relations we frequently

It is no exaggeration, therefore, to contend, with Plato, that in a way the Good, meaning thereby the conception of a final systematization of our purposes, is the supreme controlling power in our whole experience, and that in abstraction from it neither the True nor the Real can exist. For whatever forms of the latter we may have "discovered," some purposive activity, some conception of a good to be attained, was involved as a condition of the discovery. If there had been no activity on our part, or if that activity had been directed to ends other than it was, there could not have been discovery, or *that* discovery.

We must discard, therefore, the notion that in the constitution of the world we count for nothing, that it matters not what we do, because reality is what it is, whatever we may do. It is true on the contrary that our action is essential and indispensable, that to some extent the world (our world) is of our making, and that without us nothing is made that is made. To what extent and in what directions the world is plastic and to be moulded by our action we do not know as yet. We can find out only by trying; but we know enough for Pragmatism to transfigure the aspect of existence for us.

It frees us in the first place from what constitutes perhaps the worst and most paralysing horror of the naturalistic view of life, the nightmare of an *indifferent* universe. For it proves that at any rate nature cannot be indifferent to us and to our

---

put questions which are potent in determining our own answers, and without the putting would leave their subjects undetermined. "Will you love me, hate me, trust me, help me?" are conspicuous examples, and we should consider it absurd to argue that because a man had begun social intercourse with another by knocking him down, the hatred he had thus provoked must have been a pre-existent reality which the blow had merely elicited. All that the result entitles us to assume is a capacity for social feeling variously responsive to various modes of stimulation. Why, then, should we not transfer this conception of a determinable indetermination to nature at large, why should we antedate the results of our manipulation and regard as unalterable facts the reactions which our ignorance and blundering provoke? To the objection that even in our social dealings not all the responses are indeterminate, the reply is that it is easy to regard them as having been determined by earlier experiments.

In this way, then, the notion of a "fact-in-itself" might become as much of a philosophic anachronism as that of a "thing-in-itself," and we should conceive the process of knowledge as extending from absolute chaos at the one end (before a determinate response had been established) to absolute satisfaction at the other, which would have no motive to question the absolutely factual nature of its objects. But in the intermediate condition of our present experience all recognition of "fact" would be provisional and relative to our purposes and inquiries.

doings. It may be hostile, and something to be fought with all our might; it may be unsuspectedly friendly, and something to be cooperated with with our whole heart; it *must* respond in varying ways to our various efforts.

Now inasmuch as we are most familiar with such varying responsiveness in our personal relations with others, it is, I think, natural, though not perhaps necessary, that a pragmatist will tend to put a personal interpretation upon his transactions with nature and any agency he may conceive to underlie it. Still, even ordinary language is aware that things behave differently according as you "treat" them that, e.g., *treated* with fire, sugar burns, while *treated* with water, it dissolves. Thus in the last resort the anthropomorphic "humanism" of our whole treatment of experience is unavoidable and obvious; and however much he wills to disbelieve it, the philosopher must finally confess that to escape anthropomorphism he would have to escape from self. And further, seeing that ethics is the science of our relations with other persons, i.e., with our environment *qua* personal, this ultimateness of the personal construction we put upon our experience must increase the importance of the ethical attitude towards it. In other words, our metaphysics must in any case be *quasi-ethical*.

It may fairly be anticipated, secondly, that Pragmatism will prove a great tonic to reinvigorate a grievously depressed humanity. It sweeps away entirely the stock excuse for fatalism and despair. It proves that human action is always a perceptible, and never a negligible, factor in the ordering of nature, and shows cause for the belief that the disparity between our powers and the forces of nature, great as it is, does not amount to incommensurability. And it denies that any of the great questions of human concern have been irrevocably answered against us. For most of them have not even been asked in a pragmatic manner, i.e., with a determination to test the answers by the value of the consequences, and in no case has there been that systematic and clear-sighted endeavour which extorts concessions, or at least an answer, from reluctant nature. In short, no doctrine better calculated to stir us to activity or more potent to sustain our efforts has ever issued from the philosophic study.

It is true that to gain these hopes we must make bold to take some risks. If our action is a real factor in the course of events, it is impossible to exclude the contingency that if we act wrongly it may be an influence for ill. To the chance of salvation there must correspond a risk of damnation. We select the conditions under which reality shall appear to us, but this very selection selects us, and if we cannot contrive to reach a harmony in our intercourse with the real, we perish.

But to many this very element of danger will but add to the zest of life. For it cannot but appear by far more interesting than the weary grinding out of a predetermined course of things which issues in meaningless monotony from the unalterable nature of the All. And the infinite boredom with which this conception of the course of nature would afflict us must be commingled with an equal measure of disgust when we realize that on this same theory, the chief ethical issues are eternally and inexorably decided against us. Loyal cooperation and Promethean revolt grow equally unmeaning. For man can never have a ground for action against the Absolute. It is eternally and inherently and irredeemably perfect, with a "perfection" which has lost all meaning for humanity, and so leaves no ground for the hope that the "appearances" which make up our world may somehow be remoulded into conformity with our ideals. As they cannot now impair the inscrutable perfection of the Whole, they need not ever alter to pander to a criticism woven out of the delusive dreams of us poor creatures of illusion.

It is a clear gain, therefore when Pragmatism holds out to us a prospect of a world that can become better, and even has a distant chance of becoming perfect, in a sense which we are able to appreciate. The only thing that could be preferred to this would be a universe whose perfection could not only be metaphysically deduced, but actually experienced; but such a one our universe emphatically is *not*.

Hence the indetermination which, as William James has urged,[13] Pragmatism introduces into our conception of the world is essentially a gain. It brings out a connexion with the ethical conception of freedom and the old problems involved in it, which we need not here consider. When we do, we may

13 *The Will to Believe*, p. ix.

see that while determinism has an absolutely indefeasible status as a scientific postulate, and is the only assumption we can use in our practical calculations, we may yet have to recognize the reality of a certain measure of indetermination. It is a peculiarity of ethics that this indetermination is forced upon it, but in itself it is probably universal. In its valuation, however, we may differ somewhat from James, regarding it neither as good nor as ineradicable. Our indeterminism, moreover, cannot have the slightest ethical value unless it both vindicates and emphasizes our moral responsibility.

This brings us to our last point, viz., the stimulus to our feeling of moral responsibility which must accrue from the doctrine of Pragmatism. It contains such a stimulus, alike in its denial of a mechanical determination of the world which is involved in its partial determination by our action, and in its admission that by wrong action we may evoke a hostile response, and so provoke our ruin. But in addition it must be pointed out that if every cognition, however theoretical, be an *act*, and so must have a practical purpose and value, it is potentially a moral act. We may incur indeed the gravest responsibilities in selecting the aims of our cognitive activities. We may become not merely wise or foolish but also good or bad by willing to know the good or the bad; nay, our very will to know may so alter the conditions as to evoke a response congenial with its character.

It is a law of our nature that what we seek, that we shall, in some measure, find. Like a rainbow, life glitters in all the colours; like a rainbow also it adjusts itself to every beholder. To the dayflies of fashion life seems ephemeral; to the seeker after permanence, it strikes its roots into eternity. To the empty, it is a yawning chasm of inanity; to the full, it is a source of boundless interest. To the indolent, it is a call to despairing resignation; to the strenuous, a stimulus to dauntless energy. To the serious, it is fraught with infinite significance; to the flippant, it is all a somewhat sorry jest. To the melancholic, each hope is strangled in its birth; to the sanguine, two hopes spring from every grave of one. To the optimistic, life is a joy ineffable; to the pessimistic, the futile agony of an atrocious and unending struggle. To love it seems that in the end all must be love; to hate and envy it becomes a hell. The

cosmic order, which to one displays the unswerving rigour of
a self-sufficient mechanism, grows explicable to another only
by the direct guidance of the hand of God. To those of little
faith the heavens are dumb; to the faithful, they disclose the
splendours of a beatific vision.

So each sees life as what he has it in him to perceive, and
variously transfigures what, without his vision, were an un-
seen void. But all are not equally clear-sighted, and which
sees best, time and trial must establish. We can but stake our
little lives upon the ventures of our faith. And, willing or unwilling, this we do and must.

In conclusion let us avow that after professing to discuss the
relations of philosophy and practice, we seem to have allotted
an undue share of our time to the former, and to have done
little more than adumbrate the practical consequences of the
new philosophy. In extenuation we may urge that the stream
of Truth which waters the fertile fields of Conduct has its
sources in the remote and lonely uplands, *inter apices philo-
sophiae,* where the cloud-capped crags and slowly grinding
glaciers of metaphysics soar into an air too chill and rare for
our abiding habitation, but keenly bracing to the strength of
an audacious climber. Here lie our watersheds; hither lead the
passes to the realms unknown; hence part our ways, and here
it is that we must draw the frontier lines of Right and Wrong.
It would seem, moreover, that in the depths of every soul there
lurks a metaphysic aspiration to these heights, a craving to
behold the varied patterns that compose life's whole spread out
in their connexion. With the right guides, such ascents are
safe, and even though at first twinges of mountain sickness
may befall us, yet in the end we shall return refreshed from
our excursion and strengthened to endure the drudgery and
commonplace that are our daily portion.

Chapter 2

The Definition of Pragmatism and Humanism

Argument

The need of definitions. I. Importance of the problem of error. Truth as the evaluation of claims. The question begged and burked by Intellectualism. The value of the consequences as the humanist test. Why "true" consequences are "practical" and "good." Impossibility of a "purely intellectual" satisfaction. First definition of Pragmatism: *truths are logical values.* II. Necessity of "verification" of truth by use or application; the second definition, *the truth of an assertion depends on its application;* and the third, *the meaning of a rule lies in its application;* the fourth, *all meaning depends on purpose.* Its value as a protest against the divorce of logic from psychology. Fifth definition, *all mental life is purposive,* a protest against Naturalism, as is the sixth, *a systematic protest against ignoring the purposiveness of actual knowing.* No alien reality. Finally this leads to a seventh definition as a conscious application to logic of a teleological psychology, implying a voluntaristic metaphysic. III. Humanism as the spirit of Pragmatism, and like it a natural method, which will not multilate experience. Its antagonism to pedantry. It includes Pragmatism, but is not necessitated by the latter, nor confined to epistemology. IV. Neither is as such a metaphysic, both are methods, metaphysical syntheses being merely personal. But both may be conceived metaphysically and have metaphysical affinities. Need of applying the pragmatic test to metaphysics.

REAL DEFINITIONS are a standing difficulty for all who have to deal with them, whether as logicians or as scientists, and it is no wonder that dialectical philosophers fight very shy of them, prefer to manipulate their verbal imitations, and count themselves happy if they can get an analysis of the acquired meaning of a word to pass muster instead of a trouble- some investigation of the behaviour of a thing. For a real definition, to be adequate, really involves a complete knowl- edge of the nature of the thing defined. And of what subject of scientific interest can we flatter ourselves to have complete knowledge?

The difficulty, moreover, of defining adequately is indefi- nitely increased when we have to deal with subjects of which our knowledge, or their nature, is rapidly developing, so that our definitions grow obsolete almost as fast as they are made. Nevertheless, definitions of some sort are psychologically needed: we must know what things are, enough at least to know what we are discussing. It is just in the most progres- sive subjects that definitions are most needed to consolidate our acquisitions. In their absence the confusion of thought and the irrelevance of discussion may reach the most amazing proportions. And so it is the duty of those who labour at such subjects to avail themselves of every opportunity of ex- plaining what they mean, to begin with, and never to weary of redefining their conceptions when the growth of knowledge has enlarged them, even though they may be aware that how- ever assiduously they perform this duty, they will not escape misconception, nor, probably, misrepresentation. The best definitions to use in such circumstances, however, will be genetic ones, explaining how the matters defined have come into the ken of science, and there assumed the shape they have.

All these generalities apply with peculiar force to the funda- mental conceptions of the new philosophy. The new ideas have simultaneously broken through the hard crust of aca- demic convention in so many quarters, they can be approached in such a multitude of ways, they radiate into so many possi- bilities of application, that their promoters run some risk of failing to combine their labours, while their opponents may be pardoned for losing their tempers as well as their heads amid the profusion of uncoordinated movements which the lack of formal definition is calculated to encourage.

Even provisional definitions of Pragmatism and Humanism, therefore, will possess some value if they succeed in pointing out their central conceptions.

I

The serious student, I dare not say of formal logic, but of the cognitive procedures of the human intelligence, whenever he approaches the theory of actual knowing, at once finds himself confronted with the problem of error.[1] All "logical propositions," as he calls them, make the same audacious claim upon him. They all claim to be "true" without reservations or regard for the claims of others. And yet, of course, unless he shuts his eyes to all but the most "formal" view of "truth," he knows that the vast majority of these propositions are nothing but specious impostors. They are not really "true," and actual science has to disallow their claim. The logician, therefore, must take account of this rejection of claims, of this selection of the really "true" from among apparent "truths." In constituting his science, therefore, he has to condemn as "false" as well as to recognize as "true," i.e., to evaluate claims to truth.

The question therefore is: How does he effect this? How does he discriminate between propositions which claim to be true, but are not, and claims to truth which are good, and may be shown to be valid? How, that is, are valid truths distinguished from mere claims which may turn out to be false? These questions are inevitable, and no theory of knowledge which fails to answer them has any claim on our respect. It avows an incompleteness which is as disgraceful as it is inconvenient.

Now from the standpoint of rationalistic intellectualism there is no real answer to these questions, because a priori

---

1 Contrast with this the putting of the question in an absolutist logic, e.g., Mr. Joachim's instructive *Nature of Truth,* which I had not seen when this was written. Mr. Joachim begins at the opposite end with "the Ideal," and avoids the consideration of error as long as he can. But when he does come to it, he is completely worsted, and his system is wrecked. Thus the difference between the absolutist and the humanist theory lies chiefly in the standpoint; the facts are the same on either view. The question, in fact, resolves itself into this, whether or not "logic" is concerned with *human* thought. This the humanist affirms, while the absolutist is under the disadvantage of not daring to deny it *wholly.* Hence the incoherence and inevitable collapse of his theory.

inspection cannot determine the value of a claim, and experience is needed to decide whether it is good or not.[2] Hence the obscurity, ambiguity, and shiftiness, the general impotence and unreality, of the traditional logic is largely a consequence of its incapacity to deal with this difficulty. For how can you devise any practicable method of evaluating "truths," if you decline (1) to allow practical applications and the consequences of the working out of claims to affect their validity, if you decline (2) to recognize any intermediate stage in the making of truth between the mere claim and a completed ideal of absolute truth, and, if, moreover, (3) you seek to burke the whole question of the *formation* of ideals by assuming that prior to all experience and experiment there exists one immutable ideal towards which all claims *must* converge?

Pragmatism, on the other hand, essays to trace out the actual "making of truth,"[3] the actual ways in which discriminations between the true and the false are effected, and derives from these its generalizations about the method of determining the nature of truth. It is from such empirical observations that it derives its doctrine that when an assertion claims truth, *its consequences are always used to test its claim.* In other words, what follows from its truth for any human

---

[2] The complete failure of intellectualism to apprehend even the most obvious aims of Pragmatism is amusingly illustrated by Mr. Bradley's fulminations against us on the ground that we cannot possibly distinguish between a random claim and an established truth. He pontifically declares (*Mind*, XIII, 322) that "the Personal Idealist . . . if he understood his own doctrine must hold any end, however perverted, to be rational, if I insist on it personally, and any idea, however mad, to be the truth, if only some one will have it so." Again, on p. 329, he ludicrously represents us as holding that "I can make and I can unmake fact and truth at my caprice, and every vagary of mine becomes the nature of things. This insane doctrine is what consistency demands," but Mr. Bradley graciously concedes that "I cannot attribute it even to the protagonist of Personal Idealism." Of course, if there is one subject which pragmatist logicians may be said to have made their own from the days of Protagoras downwards, it is that of the evaluation of individual claims and their gradual transformation into "objective" truths. Intellectualists, on the other hand, have ever steadfastly refused to consider the discrepancies arising from the existence of psychological variations in human valuations, or lazily preferred to attribute to "the human," or even to "the absolute," mind whatever idiosyncrasies they discovered in themselves. Thus inquiry into the actual making of truth has been tabooed, the most important questions have been begged, and both the extent and the limitations of the "common" world of intersubjective social agreement have been left an unaccountable mystery, sometimes further aggravated by the metaphysical postulation of a superhuman mind conceived as "common" to all human minds, but really incompetent to enter into relation with any of them, and *a fortiori* incapable of accounting for their individual differences.

[3] Cp. Chapter 9.

interest, and more particularly and in the first place, for the interest with which it is directly concerned, is what established its real truth and validity. This is the famous "Principle of Peirce," which ought to be regarded as the greatest truism, if it·had not pleased Intellectualism to take it as the greatest paradox. But that only showed, perhaps, how completely intellectualist traditions could blind philosophers to the simplest facts of cognition. For there was no intrinsic reason why even the extremest intellectualism should have denied that the difference between the truth and the falsehood of an assertion must show itself in some visible, observable way, or that two theories which led to precisely the same practical consequences could be different only in words.

Human interest, then, is vital to the existence of truth; to say that a truth has consequences and that what has none is meaningless means that it has a bearing upon some human interest. Its "consequences" must be consequences *to* someone engaged on a real problem *for* some purpose. If it is clearly grasped that the "truth" with which we are concerned is truth *for man* and that the "consequences" are human too, it is, however, superfluous to add either (1) that the consequences must be *practical,* or (2) that they must be *good,*[4] in order to distinguish this view sharply from that of rationalism.

For (1) all consequences are "practical," sooner or later, in the sense of affecting our action. Even where they do not immediately alter the course of events, they alter our own nature, and cause its actions to be different, and thus lead to different operations on the world.

Similarly (2) if an assertion is to be valuable, and therefore "true," its consequences must be "good." They can only test the truth it claims by forwarding or baffling the interest, by satisfying or thwarting the purpose, which led to the making

---

[4] In *Mind,* N.S. No. 54, XIV, 236, I tried to draw a distinction between a narrower and a wider "pragmatism," of which I attributed only the former to Mr. Peirce. In this I was following James's distinction between the positions that "truths should have practical consequences," and that they "consist in their consequences," and that these must be "good." Of these he seemed to attribute only the former to Mr. Peirce, and denominated the latter Humanism. But Humanism seems to me to go further still, and not to be restricted to the one question of "truth." If, as Mr. Peirce has privately assured me, he had from the first perceived the full consequences of his dictum, the formulation of the whole pragmatic principle must be ascribed to him. But he has also exhibited extensive inability to follow the later developments, and now calls his own specific form of Pragmatism "pragmaticism." See *Monist,* XV, 2.

of the assertion. If they do the one, the assertion is "good," and *pro tanto* "true"; if they do the other, it is "bad" and "false." For whatever arouses an interest or forwards an end is judged to be (so far) "good"; whatever baffles or thwarts is judged to be "bad." If, therefore, the consequences of an assertion turn out to be in this way "good," it is valuable for our purposes and, provisionally at least, establishes itself as "true"; if they are "bad," we reject it as useless and account it "false," and search for something that satisfies our purpose better, or in extreme cases accept it as a provisional truth concerning a reality we are determined to unmake. Thus the predicates "true" and "false" are nothing in the end but indications of logical value, and *as values* akin to and comparable with the values predicated in ethical and aesthetical judgments, which present similar problems of the validation of claims.[5]

The reason, therefore, why truth is said to depend on its consequences is simply this, that if we do not imagine truths to exist immutably and a priori in a supercelestial world, and to descend magically into a passively recipient soul, as rationalists since Plato have continually tried to hold, they must come into being by winning our acceptance. And what rational mode of verification can anyone suggest other than this testing by their consequences?

Of course, the special nature of the testing depends on the subject matter, and the nature of the "experiments" which are in this way made in mathematics, in ethics, in physics, in religion, may seem very diverse superficially.

But there is no reason to set up a peculiar process of verification for the satisfying of a "purely intellectual" interest, different in kind from the rest, superior in dignity, and autocratic in authority. For (1) there is no pure intellect. If "pure intellect" does not imply a gross blunder in psychology, and this is probably what it too often meant until the conception was challenged, it means an abstraction, an intellect conceived as void of function, as not applied to any actual problem, as satisfying no purpose. Such an intellect, of course, would be absurd. Or is it possibly conceived as having the end of amusing its possessor? As achieving this end it may claim somewhat more regard, but apart from its value as exercise, the

[5] Chapter 7, § 3.

mere play of the intellect, which is meant for serious work, does not seem intrinsically venerable; it is certainly just as liable to abuse as any other game. And (2) if we exclude morbid or frivolous excesses, the actual functioning of the intellect, even in what are called its most "purely intellectual" forms, is only intelligible by reference to human ends and values.

All testing of "truth," therefore, is fundamentally alike. It is always an appeal to something beyond the original claim. It always implies an experiment. It always involves a *risk* of failure as well as a prospect of success. And it always ends in a valuation. As Professor Mach has said:[6] "knowledge and error flow from the selfsame psychic sources; the issue alone can discriminate between them." We arrive, therefore, at our first definition of Pragmatism as the doctrine that (1) *truths are logical values*, and as the method which systematically tests claims to truth in accordance with this principle.

II

It is easily apparent that it directly follows from this definition of truth that all "truths" must be verified to be properly true. A "truth" which will not (or cannot) submit to verification is not yet a truth at all. Its truth is at best potential, its meaning is null or unintelligible, or at most conjectural and dependent on an unfulfilled condition. On its entry into the world of existence, a truth claim has merely commended itself (perhaps provisionally) to its maker. To become really true it has to be tested, and it is tested by being *applied*. Only when this is done, only, that is, when it is *used*, can it be determined what it really means, and what conditions it must fulfil to be really true. Hence all real truths must have shown themselves to be useful; they must have been applied to some problem of actual knowing, by usefulness in which they were tested and verified.

Hence we arrive at a second formulation of the pragmatic principle, on which Mr. Alfred Sidgwick has justly laid such

6 *Erkenntnis und Irrtum*, p. 114. The German word *Erfolg*, translated "issue," covers both "consequence" and "success"; it is, in fact, one of many words by which language spontaneously testifies to the pragmatic nature of thought. Cp. fact—made,—true—trow—trust, false—fail, verify, come true, object = aim, judgment = decision; and in German *wirklich—wirken, wahr—bewähren, Wahrnehmung, Tatsache*, etc.

stress,[7] viz., that (2) *the "truth" of an assertion depends on its application.* Or, in other words, "abstract" truths are not fully truths at all. They are truths out of use, unemployed, craving for incarnation in the concrete. It is only in their actual operations upon the world of immediate experience that they cast off their callous ambiguity, that they mean, and live, and show their power. Now in ordinary life men of ordinary intelligence are quite aware of this. They recognize that truth depends very essentially upon context, on who says what, to whom, why, and under what circumstances; they know also that the point of a principle lies in the application thereof, and that it is very hazardous to guide oneself by abstract maxims with a doctrinaire disregard of the peculiarities of the case. The man of science similarly, for all the world-embracing sweep of his generalizations, for all his laudations of inexorable "law," is perfectly aware that his theoretic anticipations always stand in need of confirmation in fact, and that if this fails his "laws" are falsified. They are not true, unless they "come true."

The intellectualist philosopher alone has blinded himself to these simple facts. He has dreamt a wondrous dream of a truth that shall be absolutely true, self-testing, and self-dependent, icily exercising an unrestricted sway over a submissive world, whose adoration it requites with no services, and scouting as blasphemy all allusion to use or application. But he cannot point to any truth which realizes his ideal. Even the abstract truths of arithmetic, upon which alone he seems to rest his case, now that the invention of metageometries has shown the "truth of geometry" to involve also the question of its application, derive their truth from their application to experience. The abstract statement, e.g., that "two and two make four," is always incomplete. We need to know to what "twos" and "fours" the dictum is applied. It would not be true of lions and lambs, nor of drops of water, nor of pleasures and pains. The range of application of the abstract truth, therefore, is quite limited. And conceivably it might be so restricted that the truth would become inapplicable to the outer world altogether. Nay, though states of consciousness could always be counted, so long as succession was exper-

7 *The Application of Logic,* p. 272, and ch. IX, § 43.

ienced, it is impossible to see how it could be true to an eternal consciousness. The gods, as Aristotle would have said, seeing that they cannot count, can have no arithmetic.

In short, truths must be used to become true, and (in the end) to stay true. They are also *meant* to be used. They are rules for action. And a rule that is not applied, and remains abstract, rules nothing, and means nothing. Hence we may, once more following Mr. Alfred Sidgwick, regard it as the essence of the pragmatic method that (3) *the meaning of a rule lies in its application.* It rules, that is, and is true, within a definite sphere of application which has been marked out by experiment.

Perhaps, however, it is possible to state the pragmatic character of truth still more incisively by laying it down that ultimately (4) *all meaning depends on purpose.* This formulation grows naturally out of the last two. The making of an assertion, the application of an alleged truth to the experience which tests it, can only occur in the context of and in connexion with some purpose, which defines the nature of the whole ideal experiment.

The dependence of meaning on purpose is beginning to be somewhat extensively recognized, though hardly as yet what havoc this principle must work among the abstractions of intellectualist logic. For it is one of the most distinctive ways in which the pragmatic view of truth can be enunciated, and guards against two of the chief failings of Intellectualism. It contains an implicit protest against the abstraction of logic from psychology; for purpose is as clearly a psychological conception as meaning is professedly a logical one.[8] And it negatives the notion that truth can depend on how things would appear to an all-embracing, or "absolute," mind. For such a mind could have no purpose. It could not, that is, select part of its content as an object of special interest to be operated on or aimed at. In human minds, on the other hand, meaning is always selective and purposive.

It is, in fact, a biological function, intimately related to the welfare of the organism. Biologically speaking, the whole mind, of which the intellect forms part, may be conceived as a typically human instrument for effecting adaptations, which

[8] See Chapter 8, § 9.

has survived and developed by showing itself possessed of an efficacy superior to the devices adopted by other animals. Hence the most essential feature of Pragmatism may well seem its insistence on the fact that (5) *all mental life is purposive.* This insistence in reality embodies the pragmatic protest against Naturalism, and as such ought to receive the cordial support of rationalistic idealisms. But it has just been shown that absolutist idealisms have their own difficulties with the conception of purpose, and besides, it is an open secret that they have for the most part long ago reduced the "spiritual nature of reality" to a mere form, and retired from the struggle against Naturalism.[9] A "spiritual nature of reality" which accepts all the naturalistic negations of human activity and freedom, and leaves no room for any of the characteristic procedures and aspirations of the human spirit, is a more dangerous foe to man's spiritual ambitions than the most downright materialism.

Pragmatism, therefore, must enter its protest against both the extremes that have so nearly met. It must constitute itself into (6) *a systematic protest against all ignoring of the purposiveness of actual knowing,* alike whether it is abstracted from for the sake of the imaginary "pure" or "absolute" reason of the rationalists, or eliminated for the sake of an equally imaginary "pure mechanism" of the materialists. It must insist on the permeation of all actual knowing by interests, purposes, desires, emotions, ends, goods, postulations, choices, etc., and deny that even those doctrines which vociferate their abhorrence of such things are really able to dispense with them. For the human reason is ever gloriously human, even when most it tries to disavow its nature, and to misconceive itself. It mercifully interposes an impenetrable veil between us and any truth or reality which is wholly alien to our nature. The efforts, therefore, of those who ignore the nature of the instruments they use must ever fail, and fail the more flagrantly the more strenuously they persist in thinking to the end.

If, however, we have the courage and perseverance to persist in thinking to the end, i.e., to form a metaphysic, it is likely that we should arrive at some sort of Voluntarism. For

9 Cp. Chapter 3, § 5.

Voluntarism is the metaphysic which most easily accords and harmonizes with the experience of activity with which all our thinking and all our living seem to overflow. Metaphysics, however, are in a manner luxuries. Men can live quite well without a conscious metaphysic, and the systems even of the most metaphysical are hardly ever quite consistent, or fully thought out. Pragmatism, moreover, is not a metaphysic, though it may, somewhat definitely, point to one. It is really something far more precious, viz., an epistemological method which really describes the facts of actual knowing.

But though it is only a method in the field of logic, it may well confess to its affinities for congenial views in other sciences. It prides itself on its close connexion with psychology. But it clearly takes for granted that the psychology with which it is allied has recognized the reality of purposes. And so it can be conceived as a special application to the sphere of logic of standpoints and methods which extend far beyond its borders. So conceived, we may describe it as (7) *a conscious application to epistemology (or logic) of a teleological psychology, which implies, ultimately, a voluntaristic metaphysic.*

These seven formulations of the essence of Pragmatism look, doubtless, very different in words; but they are nevertheless very genuinely equivalent. For they are closely connected, and the "essence," like the "definition," of a thing is relative to the point of view from which it is regarded.[10] And the problems raised by Pragmatism are so central that it has points of contact with almost every line of philosophical inquiry, and so is capable of being defined by its relation to this. What is really important, however, is not this or that formulation, but the spirit in which it approaches, and the method by which it examines, its problems. The method we have observed; it is empirical, teleological, and concrete. Its spirit is a bigger thing, which may fitly be denominated Humanism.

III

Humanism is really in itself the simplest of philosophic standpoints; it is merely the perception that the philosophic problem concerns human beings striving to comprehend a world of human experience by the resources of human minds.

10 Cp. *Formal Logic*, pp. 53–4.

Not even Pragmatism could be simpler or nearer to an obvious truism of cognitive method. For if man may not presume his own nature in his reasonings about his experience, wherewith, pray, shall he reason? What prospect has he of comprehending a radically alien universe? And yet not even Pragmatism has been more bitterly assailed than the great principle that man is the measure of his experience, and so an ineradicable factor in any world he experiences. The Protagorean principle may sometimes seem paradoxical to the uninstructed, because they think it leaves out of account the "independence" of the "external" world. But this is mere misunderstanding. Humanism has no quarrel with the assumptions of common-sense realism; it does not deny what is popularly described as the "external" world. It has far too much respect for the pragmatic value of conceptions which *de facto* work far better than those of the metaphysics which despise and try to supersede them. It insists only that the "external world" of realism is still dependent on human experience, and perhaps ventures to add also that the data of human experience are not completely used up in the construction of a real external world. Moreover, its assailants are not realists, though, for the purpose of such attacks, they may masquerade as such.

The truth is rather that Humanism gives offence, not because it leaves out, but because it leaves in. It leaves in a great deal Intellectualism would like to leave out, a great deal it has no use for, which it would like to extirpate, or at least to keep out of its sight. But Humanism will not assent to the mutilations and expurgations of human nature which have become customary barbarisms in the initiation ceremonies of too many philosophic schools. It demands that man's integral nature shall be used as the whole premiss which philosophy must argue from wholeheartedly, that man's complete satisfaction shall be the conclusion philosophy must aim at, that philosophy shall not cut itself loose from the real problems of life by making initial abstractions which are false, and would not be admirable, even if they were true. Hence it insists on *leaving in* the whole rich luxuriance of individual minds, instead of compressing them all into a single type of "mind," feigned to be one and immutable; it leaves in also the psychological wealth of every human mind and the complexities of its interests, emotions, volitions, aspirations. By so doing it sacrifices, no doubt, much illusory simplicity in abstract formulas, but it appreciates and explains vast masses of what before had had to be slurred over as unintelligible fact.[11]

The dislike of Humanism, therefore, is psychological in origin. It arises from the nature of certain human minds who have become too enamoured of the artificial simplifications, or too accustomed to the self-inflicted mutilations, and the self-imposed torments, whereby they hope to merit absorption in absolute truth. These ascetics of the intellectual world must steadfastly oppose the free indulgence in all human powers, the liberty of moving, of improving, of making, of manipulating, which Humanism vindicates for man, and substitutes for the old ideal of an inactive contemplation of a static truth. It is no wonder that the Simeons Stylitae of the old order, hoisted aloft each on the pillar of his metaphysical "system," resent the disturbance of their restful solitude, "alone with the Alone," by the hoots of intrusive motorcars; that the Saint Antonys of the deserts of Pure Thought are infuriated by their conversion into serviceable golf links; and that the Juggernaut Car of the Absolute gets fewer and fewer votaries to prostrate themselves beneath its wheels every time it is rolled out of the recesses of its sanctuary—for when man has grown conscious of his powers he will prefer even to chance an encounter with a useful machine to being run over by a useless "deity."

The active life of man is continuously being transformed by the progress of modern science, by the knowledge which is power. But not so the "knowledge" which is "contemplation," which postpones the test of action, and struggles to evade it. Unfortunately, it is hard to modernize the academic life, and it is this life which is the fountainhead of Intellectualism. Academic life naturally tends to produce a certain intellectualistic bias, and to select the natures which incline to it. Intellectualism, therefore, in some form will always be a congenial philosophy which is true to the academic life.

Genuine wholehearted Humanism, on the other hand, is a singularly difficult attitude to sustain in an academic atmosphere; for the tendencies of the whole mode of life are un-

11 Contrast Mr. Joachim's *Nature of Truth* throughout, especially pp. 167–78.

ceasingly against it. If Protagoras had been a university professor, he would hardly have discovered Humanism; he would more likely have constructed a Nephelococcygia of a system that laid claim to absolute, universal, and eternal truth, or spent his life in overthrowing the discrepant, but no less presumptuous, systems of his colleagues. Fortunately he lived before universities had been invented to regulate, and quench, the thirst for knowledge; he had to earn his living by the voluntary gratitude for instructions which could justify themselves only in his pupils' lives; and so he had to be human and practical, and to take the chill of pedantry off his discourses.

Just because Humanism, then, is true to the larger life of man, it must be in some measure false to the artificially secluded studies of a "seat of learning"; and its acceptance by an academic personage must always mean a triumph over the obvious temptation to idealize and adore the narrownesses of his actual life. However much it exalts the function of man in general, it may always be taken to hint a certain disparagement of the academic man. It needs a certain magnanimity, in short, in a professor to avow himself a humanist.

Thorough humanists, therefore, will always be somewhat rare in academic circles. There will always be many who will not be able to avoid convincing themselves of the truth of a method which works like the pragmatic one (and indeed in another twenty years pragmatic convictions will be practically universal), without being able to overcome the intellectualistic influences of their nature and their mode of life. Such persons will be psychologically incapacitated to advance in the path which leads from Pragmatism to Humanism.

Yet this advance is in a manner logical as well as psychological. For those whose nature predisposes them towards it will find it reasonable and satisfying, and when they have reached the humanist position and reflect upon the expansion of Pragmatism which it involves, there will seem to be a "logical" connexion. Pragmatism will seem a special application of Humanism to the theory of knowledge. But Humanism will seem more universal. It will seem to be possessed of a method which is applicable universally, to ethics, to aesthetics, to metaphysics, to theology, to every concern of man, as well as to the theory of knowledge.

Yet there will be no "logical" compulsion. Here, as always when we come to the important choices of life, we must be free to stop at the lower level, if we are to be free to advance to the higher. We can stop at the epistemological level of Pragmatism (just as we can stop short of philosophy on the scientific plane, and of science on the plane of ordinary life), accepting Pragmatism indeed as the method and analysis of our cognitive procedure, but without seeking to generalize it, or to turn it into a metaphysic. Indeed, if our interest is not keen in life as a whole, we are very likely to do something of the kind.

IV

What, then, shall be said of metaphysics? As Pragmatism and Humanism have been defined, neither of them necessitates a metaphysic.[12] Both are methods; the one restricted to

---

12 Hence the criticism to which both have frequently been subjected on the ground that they were not metaphysically complete philosophies (e.g., by Dr. S. H. Mellone in *Mind*, XIV, pp. 507–29) involves a certain misconstruction. I can refer the curious to a (or rather *my*) humanist metaphysic in *Riddles of the Sphinx* (new ed., 1910). But the essay on "Axioms as Postulates" in *Personal Idealism* was epistemological throughout; so were the pragmatic parts of *Humanism*. "Activity and Substance" does indeed contain some metaphysical construction, but it is not distinctively pragmatic. When, therefore, Dr. Mellone (*l.c.*, p. 528) ascribes to me the assumption of an absolute chaos as the prius of experience, condemns it as unthinkable, and finally complains of feeling a "collapse" when "this incredible metaphysical dogma is suddenly transformed into a methodological postulate," he has made his difficulty by construing my epistemology as metaphysics. Antecedently this misinterpretation would never have seemed possible to me, and so I thought it unnecessary to insert a warning against it. But that several able critics have fallen into this error shows the extent of the confusion of thought induced by the deliberate blurring of the boundaries between logic and metaphysics which we owe to Hegelizing philosophers. If, however, Dr. Mellone will do me the honour of rereading my doctrine as purely epistemological, he will see that both the difficulty and the "collapse" were in his own preconceptions. In itself the conception of knowledge as developing by the progressive determination of a relatively indeterminate and plastic "matter" never pretended to be more than an analysis of knowledge. It does indeed point to the conceptual limit of a "first matter" in which as yet no determinations have been acquired, but it does not affirm its positive existence, and it is quite conceivable (1) that our analysis may be brought up against some irreducible datum of fact, and (2) that it should never actually get back to the metaphysical origin of things. Anyhow, the question of the proper metaphysical interpretation of the conceptions used in pragmatic epistemology was not raised. Epistemologically, however, the conception of a determinable plastic "matter" seems useful enough as descriptive of our knowing, and as innocent and at least as valid as the Aristotelian notion that knowledge always arises out of pre-existent knowledge. Of course, such notions get into difficulties when we try to extract from them accounts of the absolute origin of knowledge. But is it so sure that absolute origins can ever be traced? They are certainly not to be had for the asking. For they always seem to involve a demand for the derivation of something out of nothing. And I am not aware that any theory has up to

the special problem of knowing, the other more widely applicable. And herein lies their value; for methods are necessities of scientific progress, and therefore indispensable. Metaphysics, on the other hand, are really luxuries, personal indulgences that may be conceded to a lifelong devotion to science, but of no coercive objective validity. For there is an immense discrepancy between the ideal claims of metaphysics and the actual facts. By definition metaphysics is (i.e, tries to be) the science of the final synthesis of *all* the data of our experience. But *de facto* these data are (1) insufficient, and (2) individual. Hence (1) the metaphysical synthesis is lacking in cogency: it is imaginative and conjectural. It is the ideal completion of an image of reality which is rough-hewn and fragmentary; it is the reconstruction of a torso. Whoever therefore prefers to remain within the bounds of actual knowledge is entitled to refrain from pledging himself to a metaphysic. He may recognize any realities, he may employ any conceptions and methods he finds necessary or expedient, without affirming their ultimate validity.

(2) And so those whose spirits crave for an ideal completion and confirmation of knowledge by a metaphysical construction must abate their pretensions. They must renounce the pretence of building what is universal, and eternal, and compulsory, and "valid for intelligence as such." In view of the actual facts, does it not argue an abysmal conceit and stupendous ignorance of the history of thought to cherish the delusion that of all philosophies one's own alone was destined to win general acceptance *ipsissimis verbis,* or even to be reflected, undimmed and unmodified, in any second soul? Every metaphysic, in point of fact, works up into its structure large masses of subjective material which is individual, and drawn from its author's personal experience. It always takes its final form from an idiosyncrasy.

And, furthermore, this is quite as it should be. If it really is the duty of metaphysics to leave out nothing, to undo abstractions, to aspire to the whole of experience, it *must* have this personal tinge. For a man's personal life must contribute

---

date answered these questions. But I am hopeful that humanist metaphysics will not be so widely irrelevant to actual life as in the past metaphysical attempts have mostly been.

largely to his data, and his idiosyncrasy must colour and pervade whatever he experiences. It is surely the most sinister and fatal of abstractions to abstract from the variety of individual minds, in order to postulate a universal substance in which personal life is obliterated, because one is too ignorant or indolent to cope with its exuberance. Two men, therefore, with different fortunes, histories, and temperaments, *ought not* to arrive at the same metaphysic, nor can they do so honestly; each should react *individually* on the food for thought which *his personal life* affords, and the resulting differences *ought not* to be set aside as void of ultimate significance. Nor is it true or relevant to reply that to admit this means intellectual anarchy. What it means is something quite as distasteful to the absolutist temper, viz., toleration, mutual respect, and practical cooperation.

It means also that we should deign to see facts as they are. For in point of fact, the protest against the tyrannous demand for rigid uniformity is in a sense superfluous. No two men ever really think (and still less feel) alike, even when they profess allegiance to the selfsame formulas. Nor does the universe appear to contain the psychological machinery by which such uniformity could be secured. In short, despite all bigotry, a philosophy is always in the last resort the theory of *a* life, and not of life in general or in the abstract.

But though Pragmatism and Humanism are only methods in themselves, it should not be forgotten (1) that methods may be turned into metaphysics by accepting them as ultimate. Whosoever is wholly satisfied by a method may adopt it as his metaphysic, just as he may adopt the working conceptions of a science. Both Pragmatism and Humanism, therefore, may be held as metaphysics; this will induce no difference in their doctrines, but only in the attitude towards them.

(2) Methods may have metaphysical affinities. Thus our last definition of Pragmatism conceived it as derivative from a voluntarist metaphysic. Humanism, similarly, may be affiliated to metaphysical personalism.

(3) Methods may *point,* more or less definitely, to certain metaphysical conclusions. Thus Pragmatism may be taken to point to the ultimate reality of human activity and freedom,[13]

13 Cp. Chapter 4.

to the plasticity and incompleteness of reality,[14] to the reality of the world process "in time," and so forth. Humanism, in addition, may point to the personality of whatever cosmic principle we can postulate as ultimate, and to its kinship and sympathy with man.

Clearly, therefore, there is no reason to apprehend that the growth of the new methods of philosophizing will introduce monotonous uniformity into the annals of philosophy. "Systems" of philosophy will abound as before, and will be as various as ever. But they will probably be more brilliant in their colouring, and more attractive in their form. For they will certainly have to be put forward, and acknowledged, as works of art that bear the impress of a unique and individual soul. Such has always been their nature, but when this is frankly recognized, we shall grow more tolerant and more appreciative. Only we shall probably be less impressed, and therefore less tormented, than now, by unclear thinking and bad writing which try to intimidate us by laying claim to absolute validity. Such "metaphysics" we shall gently put aside.

It is clear, therefore, that metaphysic also must henceforth submit its pretensions to the pragmatic test. It will not be valued any longer because of the magniloquent obscurity with which it speaks of unfathomable mysteries which have no real concern with human life, or because it paints fancy pictures which mean nothing to any but their painters. It will henceforth have to test all its assumptions by their working, and above all to test the assumption that "intellectual satisfaction" is something too sacred to be analysed or understood. It will have to verify its conjectures by propounding doctrines which can be acted on, and tested by their consequences. And that not merely in an individual way. For subjective value any philosophy must of course have—for its inventor. But a valid metaphysic must make good its claims by greater usefulness than that. It need not show itself "cogent" to all, but it must make itself acceptable to reasonable men, willing to give a trial to its general principles.

Such a valid metaphysic does not exist at present. But there is no reason why it should not come into being. It can be built up piecemeal bit by bit, by the discovery that truths which

14 Cp. Chapter 5.

have been found useful in the sciences may be advantageously taken as ultimate, and combined into a more and more harmonious system. The opposite procedure, that of jumping to some vast uncomprehended generality by an a priori intuition,[15] and then finding that it does not connect up with real life, is neither scientifically tolerable nor emotionally edifying in the end. All experience hitherto has proved it a delusion. The procedure of a valid metaphysical construction must be essentially "inductive," and gradual in its development. For a perfect and complete metaphysic is an ideal defined only by approximation, and attainable only by the perfecting of life. For it would be the theory of such a perfect life, which no one as yet is contriving to live.

[15] It matters not at all what that intuition is. Whether we proclaim that All is "Matter," or "Spirit," or "God," we have said nothing, until we have made clear what "God," "Spirit," "Matter" *are in their application to our actual experience,* and wherein one practically differs from, and excels, the other. But it is just at this point that intuitions are wont to fail their votaries, and to leave them descanting idly on the superiority of one synonym of "the blessed word Mesopotamia" over the others.

Chapter 3

Absolutism and Religion

Argument

§ 1. The philosophic breakdown of Absolutism. But may it not really be a religion, and to be judged as such? § 2. The pragmatic value of religion, and academic need of a religious philosophy. § 3. The history of English Absolutism: its importation from Germany as an antidote to scientific naturalism. § 4. Its success and alliance with theology. Its treatment of its own "difficulties." § 5. Its revolt against theology. The victory of the left. § 6. The discrepancy between Absolutism and ordinary religion, exemplified in (1) its conception of "God," and (2) its treatment of evil. § 7. The psychological motives for taking Absolutism as a religion. § 8. Its claim to have universal cogency compels us, § 9, to deny its rationality to our minds. (1) The "craving for unity" criticized. (2) The guarantee of cosmic order unsatisfactory. (3) An a priori guarantee illusory. (4) The meaninglessness of monism. An "infinite whole" a contradiction. The inapplicability of absolutist conceptions. § 10. The inability of Absolutism to compromise its claim to universality leads it to institute a *Liberum Veto* and to commit suicide.

§ 1. WE HAVE constantly had occasion to criticize the peculiar form of rationalistic intellectualism which styles itself Absolute Idealism and may conveniently be called Absolutism, and to observe how it has involved itself in the most serious difficulties. It has been shown, for example that the proof of the Absolute as a metaphysical principle, and its value when assumed, were open to the gravest objections. It has been shown that the absolutist theory of knowledge has completely broken down, and must always end in scepticism. It has been shown that if

74

the idealistic side of the theory is insisted on, it must develop into solipsism. It has been shown that if a serious attempt is made to derive the Many from the One, to deduce individual existences from the Absolute, the result inevitably is that the Absolute is either "dissociated," or mad, or defunct, because it has committed suicide in a temporary fit of mental aberration.

In short, if a tithe of what we have now and formerly had to urge against the Absolute be well founded, Absolutism must be one of the most gratuitously absurd philosophies which has ever been entertained. And if so, how comes it that men professedly and confessedly pledged to the pursuit of pure unadulterated truth can be found by the dozen to adhere to so indefensible a superstition?

To answer this question will be the aim of this essay.

It is not enough to reply, in general terms, what at once occurs to the student of human psychology, viz., that intellectual difficulties are hardly ever fatal to an attractive theory, that logical defects rarely kill beliefs to which men, for psychological reasons, remain attached. This is doubtless true, but does not enable us to understand the nature of the attraction and attachment in this case. Nor can it be reconciled with the manifest acumen of many absolutist thinkers to suppose that they have simply failed to notice, or to understand, the objections brought against their theory. If, therefore, they have failed to meet them with a logical refutation, the reason must lie in the region of psychology.

This reflection may suggest to us that we have, perhaps, unwittingly misunderstood Absolutism, and done it a grave injustice.

For we have treated it as a *rational* theory, resting its claim on rational grounds, and willing to abide by the results of logical criticism. But this may have been a huge mistake. What if this assumption was wrong? What if its real appeal was not logical, but psychological, not to the "reason" but to the feelings, and more particularly to the religious feelings? Does not Mr. Bradley himself hint that philosophy (his own, of course) may be "a satisfaction of what may be called the mystical side of our nature"?[1]

---

[1] *Appearance and Reality*, p. 6.

If so, a fully developed case of Absolutism would never yield to merely philosophic treatment. It might be driven to confess the existence of logical difficulties, but these would not dismay it. It would go on believing in what to its critics seemed the absurd and impossible, with a pathetic and heroic faith that all would "some day"[2] be explained "somehow."[3]

§ 2. This possibility, at any rate, deserves to be examined. For religions are as such deserving of respectful and sympathetic consideration from a humanist philosophy. They are pragmatically very potent influences on human life, and the religious instinct is one of the deepest in human nature. It is also one of the queerest in the wide range of its manifestations. There are no materials so unpromising that a religion cannot be fashioned out of them. There are no conclusions so bizarre that they cannot be accepted with religious fervour. There are no desires so absurd that their satisfaction may not be envisaged as an act of worship, lifting a man out of his humdrum self.

There is, therefore, no antecedent absurdity in the idea that Absolutism is at bottom a religious creed, a development of, or a substitute for, or perhaps even a perversion of, some more normal form of religious feeling, such as might well be fomented in an academic atmosphere.

Once this theory is mooted, confirmations pour in on every side. The central notion of Absolutism, the Absolute itself, is even now popularly taken to be identical with the "God" of theism. It seems, at any rate, grand and mysterious and all-embracing enough to evoke, and in a way to satisfy, many of the religious feelings, as being expressive of the all-pervasive mystery of existence.

There is, moreover, in every university, and especially in Oxford, a standing demand for a religious, or quasi-religious, philosophy. For, rightly or wrongly, established religions always cater in the first place for the unreflective. They pass current, and are taught, in forms which cannot bear reflection, as youthful minds grow to maturity. Consequently, when reflection awakens, they have to be transformed. This is what gives his opportunity to the religious philosopher. And also to

[2] Cp. Dr. McTaggart's *Hegelian Dialectic*, ch. V.
[3] Cp. Mr. Bradley's *Appearance and Reality, passim.*

the irreligious philosopher, who "mimics" him. They both offer to the inquiring minds of the young a general framework into which to fit their workaday beliefs—a framework which in some respects is stronger and ampler, though in others more meagre and less lovely, than the childlike faith which reflection is threatening to dissolve, unless it is remodelled. Hence the curious fascination, at a certain stage of mental development, of some bold "system" of metaphysics, which is accepted with little or no scrutiny of its wild promises, while in middle age the soul soon comes to crave for more solid and less gaseous nutriment. It is proper, then, and natural, that an absolutist metaphysic should take root in a university, and flourish parasitically on the fermentation of religious instincts and beliefs.

§ 3. The history of English Absolutism distinctly bears out these anticipations. It was originally a deliberate importation from Germany, with a purpose. And this purpose was a religious one—that of counteracting the antireligious developments of Science. The indigenous philosophy, the old British empiricism, was useless for this purpose. For though a form of Intellectualism, its sensationalism was in no wise hostile to Science. On the contrary, it showed every desire to ally itself with, and to promote, the great scientific movement of the nineteenth century, which penetrated into and almost overwhelmed Oxford between 1850 and 1870.

But this movement excited natural, and not unwarranted, alarm in that great centre of theology. For Science, flushed with its hard-won liberty, ignorant of philosophy, and as yet unconscious of its proper limitations, was decidedly aggressive and overconfident. It seemed naturalistic, nay, materialistic, by the law of its being. The logic of Mill, the philosophy of evolution, the faith in democracy, in freedom, in progress (on material lines), threatened to carry all before them.

What then was to be done? Nothing directly; for on its own ground Science seemed invulnerable, and had a knack of crushing the subtlest dialectics by the knockdown force of sheer scientific fact. But might it not be possible to change the venue, to shift the battleground to a region *ubi instabilis terra innabilis unda,* where the land afforded no firm footing, where the frozen sea could not be navigated, where the very air was thick with mists, so that phantoms might well pass for realities

—the realm, in short, of metaphysics? Germany in those days was still the promised land of the metaphysical mystery-monger, where everything was doubted, and everything believed, just because it had been doubted, and the difference between doubt and belief seemed to be merely a question of the point of view; it had not yet become great by the scientific exploitation of "blood and iron" (including organic chemistry and metallurgy).

Emissaries accordingly went forth, and imported German philosophy, as the handmaid, or at least the governess, of a distressed theology. Men began to speak with foreign tongues, and to read strange writings of Kant's and Hegel's, whose very uncouthness was awe-inspiring and terrific. Not that, however, it should be supposed that the Germanizers were all consciously playing into the hands of clericalism, as Mark Pattison insinuated. T. H. Green, for example, was, by all accounts, sincerely anxious to plunge into unfathomed depths of thought, and genuinely opposed to the naturalistic spirit of the age; and if there was anything transparent about his mind, it was assuredly its sincerity. His philosophy—so it was commonly supposed by Balliol undergraduates in the eighties—was encouraged by the Master (Jowett) on the ground that, inasmuch as metaphysics was a sort of intellectual distemper incidental to youth, it was well that it should assume a form not too openly divergent from the established religion.[4]

Others, again, welcomed the new ideas on pedagogical grounds, being haunted by the academic dread lest Mill's *Logic* should render philosophy too easy, or at least contrast too markedly with the crabbed hints of the *Posterior Analytics.* So German Absolutism entered the service of British theology, soon after its demise in its native country.

§ 4. The results at first seemed excellent, theologically speaking. The pressure of "modern science" was at once relieved. It soon began to be bruited abroad that there had been concocted in Germany a wonderful "metaphysical criticism of science," hard to extract and to understand, but marvellously efficacious. It was plain, at any rate, that the most rabid scientists could make no reply to it—because they had insuper-

4 In reality, however, he seems latterly to have deplored Green's influence as tending to draw men away from the practical pursuits of life.

able difficulties in comprehending the terms in which it was couched. Even had they learnt the lingo, the coarse fibre of their minds would have precluded their appreciating the subtleties of salvation by Hegelian metaphysics. So it was rarely necessary to do more than recite the august table of the a priori categories in order to make the most audacious scientist feel that he had got out of his depth; while at the merest mention of the Hegelian Dialectic, all the "advanced thinkers" of the time would flee affrighted.

The only drawback of this method was that so few could understand it, and that, in spite of the philosophers, the besotted masses continued to read Darwin and Spencer, Huxley and Haeckel. But even here there were compensations. What can never be popularized, can never be vulgarized. What cannot be understood, cannot be despised or refuted. And it is grateful and comforting to feel oneself the possessor of esoteric knowledge, even when it does not go much beyond ability to talk the language and to manipulate the catchwords.

As regards the *direct* support German philosophy afforded to Christian theology, on the other hand, it would be a mistake to lay too much stress on it. Kant's threefold postulation of God, Freedom, and Immortality could not add much substance to an attenuated faith. And besides, the agnostic element in Kant, which had seemed well enough so long as Mansel used it to defend orthodoxy, was recognized as distinctly dangerous when Spencer, soon afterwards, proceeded to elaborate it into his doctrine of the Unknowable. Hegel's "philosophy of religion," indeed, promised more. It professed to identify God the Father with the "thesis," God the Son with the "antithesis," and God the Holy Ghost with the "synthesis" of a universal "Dialectic," and thus to provide an a priori rational deduction of the Trinity. But it could hardly escape the acuteness of the least discerning theologians that, though such combinations might seem "suggestive" as "aids to faith," they were not quite demonstrative or satisfactory. The more discerning realized, of course, the fundamental differences between Hegelian philosophy and Christian theology. They recognized that the Hegelian Absolute was not, and could not be, a personal God, that its real aim was the self-development, not of the Trinity, but of an immanent "Absolute Idea," and that the world, and not the Holy Ghost, was entitled to the dignity of the Higher Synthesis. They felt also the awkwardness of supporting a religion which rested its appeal on a unique series of historical events by a philosophy which denied the ultimate significance of events in time.

So, on the whole, Absolutism did not prove an obedient handmaid to theology, but rather a useful ally; their association was not service so much as symbiosis, and even this was eventually to develop into hostile parasitism.

The gains of theology were chiefly *indirect*. Philosophy instituted a higher, and not yet discredited, court for the trial of intellectual issues, to which appeal could be made from the decisions of science. And it checked, and gradually arrested, the flowing tide of science, if not among scientific workers, yet among the literary classes.

It supported theology, moreover, by a singularly useful parallel. Here was another impressive study of the abstrusest kind, with claims upon life as great and as little obvious as those of theology, and yet not open to the suspicion of being a pseudoscience devised for the hoodwinking of men. For was not philosophy a purely intellectual discipline, a self-examination of Pure Reason? If it was abstract, and obscure, unprofitable, hard to understand, and full of inherent "difficulties," why condemn theology as irrational and fraudulent for exhibiting, though to a less degree, the like characteristics?

Thus could theologians use the defects of philosophy to palliate those of theology, and to assuage the doubts of pupils, willing and anxious to clutch at whatever would enable them to retain their old beliefs, by representing them as inevitable, but not fatal, imperfections incidental to the makeup of a "finite" mind.

These services, moreover, were largely mutual. It was the religious interest, and the need of studying theology, which brought young men to college, and so provided the philosophers with hearers and disciples.

Theology reciprocated also by infusing equanimity into philosophy with regard to its own intrinsic "difficulties." For, alas, nothing human is perfect, not even our theories of perfect knowledge! The new philosophy soon developed most formidable difficulties, which would have appalled the unaided reason. It was taught to "recognize" these "difficulties" (when they could no longer be concealed), and to plead the frankness of this recognition as an atonement for the failure to remove them, to analyse their grounds, or to reconsider the assumptions which had led to them. Or, if more was demanded, it was shown that they were old, that similar objections had been brought ages ago (and remained similarly unanswered); and, finally, the philosophic exposition of the nature of Pure Reason would end in an exhortation to a reverent agnosticism, based on a recognition of the necessary limitations of the human mind! Only very rarely did bewildered pupils note the discrepancy between the mystical conclusion and the initial promise of a completely rational procedure; after a protracted course of abstract thinking the exhausted human mind is only too apt to acquiesce in a confession of failure, which seems to equalize the master's and the pupil's intellect. Lest we should seem, however, to be talking in the air, let us adduce a notorious example of such a "philosophic" treatment of a "difficulty."

It has now for more than a quarter of a century been recognized by absolutist philosophy that there exists at its core a serious gap between the human and the superhuman "ideal" which it deifies, and that it possesses no logical bridge by which to pass from the one to the other. Thus T. H. Green professes to discover that knowledge is only possible if the human consciousness is conceived as the "reproduction" in time of an Eternal Universal Consciousness out of time. But as to the nature of the connexion and interaction between them, as to how the Eternal Consciousness renders human minds its "vehicles," he can, of course, say nothing. Nay, he is finally driven to confess that these two "aspects" of consciousness, *qua* human and *qua* eternal, "cannot be comprehended in a single conception."[5] In other words, "consciousness" is merely a *word* used to cover the fundamental discrepancy between two incompatible conceptions, and an excuse for shirking the most fundamental of philosophic problems.

[5] *Prolegomena to Ethics*, § 68. Capt. H. V. Knox has drawn attention to the vital importance of this extraordinary passage (*Mind*, N.S. No. 33, IX, 64), and Mr. Sturt has also commented on it in *Idola Theatri*, p. 238.

This being so, it is interesting to see what his friends and followers have made of a situation which ought surely to be intolerable to a rational theory. Has its rationalistic pride been in any way abated? Not a whit. Has its doctrine ceased to be taught? Not at all. Has it been amended? In no wise. Have attempts been made to bridge the chasm? No; but its existence has repeatedly been "recognized." Mr. Bradley "recognizes" it as the problem how the Absolute "transmutes appearances" (= the world of our experience) into "reality" (= his utopian ideal); but his answer is merely that the trick is achieved by a gigantic "somehow." Mr. Joachim "recognizes" it as "the dual nature of human experience," but will not throw over it even a mantle of words. Professor J. S. Mackenzie "recognizes" it by remarking "that a truly conceptual object cannot, properly speaking, be contained in a divine mind, any more than in a human mind, unless the divine mind is *something wholly different from anything* that we understand by a mind."[6] Has the difficulty led to any analysis of its grounds, or revision of its assumptions? Not to my knowledge. It has been "recognized," and is now recognized as "old"[7] and familiar and venerable; and what more would you have? Surely not an answer? Surely not a Rationalism which shall be rational? It is, and remains, a "difficulty," and that is the end of it!

§ 5. But though in point of intellectual achievement our "Anglo-Hegelian" philosophy must be pronounced to be stationary, its mundane history has continued, and its relations to theology have undergone a startling change. As it has become more firmly rooted, and as, owing to the reform of the universities, the tutorial staff of the colleges has ceased to be wholly clerical, the alliance between Absolutism and theology has gradually broken down. Their cooperation has completely disappeared. It now sounds like an untimely reminiscence of a bygone era when Mr. Bradley vainly seeks to excite theological odium against his philosophic foes.

In part, no doubt, the need for the alliance has grown less. Science is far less aggressive towards theology than of yore. It has itself probed into unsuspected depths of being, which make blatant materialism seem a shallow thing, and have

---

6 *Mind*, N.S. No. 59, XV, 326 n. Italics mine.
7 As we have seen, it is essentially as old as Plato.

destroyed the illusion that it knows all about "matter." It has become humble, and begun to wonder whether, after all, its whole knowledge is more than "a system of differential equations which work"; in other words, it has ceased to be dogmatic, and is discovering that its procedure is, in truth, *pragmatic*.

Absolutism, on the other hand, has grown secure and strong and insolent. It has developed a powerful "left wing," which, as formerly in Germany, has triumphed within the school, and quarrelled with theology. Mr. F. H. Bradley, Dr. McTaggart, Professor B. Bosanquet, Professor A. E. Taylor, Mr. H. H. Joachim, Professor J. S. Mackenzie are among its best-known representatives. The "right wing" seems to have almost wholly gone from Oxford, though it still appears to flourish in Glasgow. As for the "centre," it is silent or ambiguous.[8]

But about the views of the left there can be no doubt. It is openly and exultingly antitheological. It disclaims edification. It has long ago made its peace with Naturalism, and boasts that it can accept all the conclusions of the latter, and reproduce them in its own language. It has now swallowed Determinism whole and without a qualm.[9] As a whole, it has a low opinion of ethics, and it has even lapsed into something remarkably resembling hedonism.[10] In short, its theological value has become a formidable *minus* quantity, which is mitigated only by the technicality of its onslaughts, which in their usual form can be appreciated only by the few. Still, even this consolation fails in dealing with Dr. McTaggart's most recent and entertaining work, *Some Dogmas of Religion,* which puts the case against Christianity quite popularly, with a lucidity which cannot be surpassed, and a cogency which can be gainsaid only by extensive reliance on the pragmatic considerations which Dr. McTaggart has conspicuously neglected. He has, indeed, relented in some few respects, and no longer defines "God," as an *impossible* being, as he did in his *Hegelian Cosmology,* and now admits that a finite God is thinkable; but he still prefers to call himself an atheist, and there is no saying

8 Prof. J. A. Stewart's invitation to the school to refute Mr. Bradley before continuing the use of edifying phrases has met with no response whatever (see *Mind,* N.S. XI, 376).
9 T. H. Green was a "soft" determinist.
10 Cp. F. H. Bradley's *Appearance and Reality,* ch. XXV; A. E. Taylor's *Problem of Conduct;* and J. M. E. McTaggart's *Hegelian Cosmology.*

how much mischief his popular style might not do among the masses were not his book published at half-a-guinea net.

All this is very sad in many ways; but one could pardon these attacks on theology if only they advanced the cause of truth. For we, of course, in no wise hold a brief for theology, which we have reason to regard as in the main an intellectualistic corruption of an essentially pragmatic religion. Unfortunately, however, the prosperity of Absolutism does not mean an end to our intellectual troubles. We have already seen that, when consistently thought out, it ends in scepticism. And it has not merely quarrelled with theology, but is undermining a far greater thing, namely, religion, in its ordinary acceptance, as we must now try to understand.

§ 6. Absolutism may be itself a religion, but it diverges very widely from what is ordinarily known as such, and relies on motives which are not the ordinary religious feelings. This may be shown as regards the two most crucial cases—the problem of "God" and the problem of evil.

(1) As regards the conception of "God," the absolutist and the religious man differ essentially. The term "God" is used by philosophers, perhaps unavoidably, with a great latitude of meanings, and so disputants too often finish with the confession "your 'God' is my 'devil'!" But still, if we apply the pragmatic test, it must be possible to discover some points in which the consequences of a belief in a God differ from those of a belief in no God. "God," that is, if we really and honestly mean something by the term, must stand for something which has a real influence on human life. And in the ordinary religious consciousness "God" does in point of fact stand for something vital and valuable in this pragmatic way. In its most generalized form "God" probably stands for two connected principles. It means (a) a human moral principle of Help and Justice; and (b) an aid to the intellectual comprehension of the universe, sometimes supposed to amount to a complete solution of the world problem. In the ordinary religious consciousness, however, these two (rightly) run together, and coalesce into the postulate of a Supreme Being, because no intellectual explanation of the world would seem satisfactory, if it did not also provide a moral explanation, and a response to human appeals.

But in Absolutism these two sides of "God" fall hopelessly asunder. In vain does T. H. Green, after conceiving God as a purely intellectual principle, declare that God for religious purposes must *also* be such as to render morality possible.[11] For Absolutism conceives pure intellectual satisfaction as self-sufficing, and puts it out of relation to our moral nature, nay, to all *human* interests. But if so, the moral side of God must wholly disappear. If the Absolute is God, God cannot be personal, or interested in persons as such. Its relation to persons must be a *purely logical* relation of inclusiveness. The Absolute includes everything, of course, and ex officio. But the Whole cannot be *partial*, in either sense of the term. It must sustain *all* its "parts" impartially, because it approves of them all alike—inasmuch as it maintains them in existence.

The ordinary religious consciousness, on the other hand, definitely postulates a partial God, a God to succour and to sympathize with us poor "finite" fragments of a ruthless Whole. As Mr. Bradley scornfully but quite truly puts it,[12] "the Deity, which they want, is of course finite, a person much like themselves, with thoughts and feelings mutable in the process of time.[13] They desire a person in the sense of a self, among and over against other selves, moved by personal relations and feelings towards these others—feelings and relations which are altered by the conduct of the others. *And, for their purpose, what is not this, is really nothing.* Of course for us to ask seriously if the Absolute can be personal in such a way would be quite absurd." The absolutist God, therefore, is no *moral* principle. Neither has it *scientific* value, even when taken as an intellectual principle. For it is not the explanation of anything in particular, just because it is the explanation of everything in general; and what is the meaning of a general explanation which explains nothing in particular, is apparently a question it has not yet occurred to our absolutists to ask.

It is quite clear, however, that the Absolute is not God in the ordinary sense, and many of our leading absolutists are now quite explicit in avowing this, and even in insisting on it. As we have already seen what Dr. McTaggart thinks (§ 5),

11 *Works*, II, p. 74 *n.*
12 *Appearance and Reality*, p. 532. Italics mine.
13 Cp. Plato's description of an "Idea" which should be really human in the *Sophist*, 249.

let us once more consult Mr. Bradley's oracle. "We may say that God is not God, till he has become all in all, and that a God which is all in all, is not the God of religion." "We may say that the God, which could exist, would most assuredly be no God." "Short of the Absolute, God cannot rest, and having reached this goal, he is lost and religion with him." Nor has any theologizing absolutist ever dared to question these responses.[14]

(2) The problem of evil is probably the most fundamental, and certainly the most pressing, of religious problems; it is also that most manifestly baffling to ordinary religious feeling. It is, however, divisible into a practical and a theoretic problem. The former of these is simply the problem of how *de facto* to get rid of evils. This is a difficult, but not a desperate or irrational, endeavour. The theoretic problem, on the other hand, has been mainly manufactured by theology. It arises from the impossibility of reconciling the postulated goodness with the assumed omnipotence of God. This problem troubles the religious consciousness only in so far as it assents to these two demands. Now this in a manner it may certainly be said to do. The postulate of God's goodness is, as we have seen, essential. But the assent to the notion of divine omnipotence is never more than verbal. In practice no real religion can ever work with a single, unrestricted principle. Without a duality, or plurality, of principles the multiplicity of the cosmic drama cannot be evolved. Hence the religious consciousness, and all but the most "philosophic" forms of theology, do in point of fact conceive evil as due to a power which is not God, and somehow independent; it is variously denominated "matter," "free will," or "the devil." The more "philosophic" theologians try to conceive a "self-limitation" either of the divine power or of the divine intellect; in the latter case following Leibniz's suggestion that in creating the world God chose the best universe he could think of. But on the whole the theoretic explanation of evil is acknowledged to form a serious "difficulty."

What now has Absolutism to say on the subject? It cannot, of course, construe God's omnipotence with the amiable laxity of popular religion; it must insist on the strictest interpretation. Its God must be really all in all; the Whole cannot be con-

14 *Op. cit.,* pp. 448, 449, 447.

trolled or limited by anything, either within it or without it. It must be perfect; its seeming imperfection must be an illusion of imperfect finite beings—though, to be sure, that illusion again would seem to be necessary and essential to the perfection of the Whole.

It is clear that such a theory—which at bottom coincides with that of Eleaticism—must make short work of the religious attempts to understand the existence of evil. Human "free will" it has long schooled itself to regard as "a mere lingering chimera";[15] the resistance of "matter" it gaily consigns to "the devil," who in his turn is absorbed with "God" in the "Higher Synthesis" of the Absolute. Evil, therefore, is not ultimately and metaphysically real. It is "mere appearance," "transcended," "transmuted," etc., in the Absolute along with all the rest.

All this is very pretty and consistent and "philosophical." But it is hardly a solution of the problem, either practically or theoretically. Not practically because it throws no light on the question why anything in particular should be as it is; nor yet theoretically, because it is avowedly a mystery *how* the Absolute contrives to transcend its "appearances."

Thus the net outcome is that the religious consciousness, so far from obtaining from "philosophy" any alleviations of its burdens, not to speak of a solution of the problem of evil, is driven forth with contumely and rebuked for having the impudence to ask such silly questions! Assuredly Mr. Bradley does well to remark that (absolutist) "metaphysics has no special connexion with genuine religion."[16]

§ 7. How, then, can Absolutism possibly be a religion? It must appeal to psychological motives of a different sort, rare enough to account for its total divergence from the ordinary religious feelings, and compelling enough to account for the fanaticism with which it is held and the persistence with which the same old round of negations has been reiterated through the ages. Of such psychological motives we shall indicate the more important and reputable.

(1) It is decidedly flattering to one's spiritual pride to feel oneself a "part" or "manifestation" or "vehicle" or "repro-

15 *Ibid.*, p. 435 n.
16 *Ibid.*, p. 454.

duction" of the "Absolute Mind," and to some this feeling affords so much strength and comfort and such exquisite delight that they refrain from inquiring what these phrases mean, and whether the relation they indicate would seem equally satisfactory if regarded conversely from the standpoint of the Absolute Mind. It is, moreover, chiefly the strength of this feeling which explains the blindness of absolutists towards the logical defects of their theory. It keeps them away from "Plato's Chasm," the insuperable gap between the human and the ideal; for whenever they imagine that they have "advanced towards a complete solution" by approaching its brink, they find that the glow of feeling is chilled.

(2) There is a strange delight in wide generalization merely as such, which when pursued without reference to the ends which it subserves, and without regard to its actual functioning, often results in a sort of logical vertigo. This probably has much to do with the peculiar "craving for unity" which is held to be the distinctive affliction of philosophers. At any rate, the thought of an all-embracing One or Whole seems to be regarded as valuable and elevating, quite apart from any definite function it performs in knowing, or service it does, or light it throws on any actual problem.

(3) The thought of an Absolute Unity is cherished as a guarantee of cosmic stability. In face of the restless vicissitudes of phenomena it seems to secure us against falling out of the universe. It assures us a priori—and that is its supreme value —that the cosmic order cannot fall to pieces, and leave us dazed and confounded among the debris of a universe shattered, as it was compounded, by the mere chance comings and goings of its fortuitous constituents. We want to have an absolute assurance of the inherent coherence of the world; we want to have an absolute assurance a priori concerning the future; and the thought of the Absolute seems designed to give it. It is probably this last notion that, consciously or unconsciously, weighs most in the psychology of the absolutist creed.

§ 8. Such, if we are not mistaken, are the essential foundations of the absolutist's faith—the things which he "believes upon instinct" and for which he proceeds to "find bad reasons," to quote Mr. Bradley's epigram about (his own?) metaphysics.[17] And we, of course, to whom human instincts are interesting and precious and sacred, should naturally incline to respect them, whether or not we shared them, whether or not the reasonings prompted by them struck us as logically cogent. We should respect Absolutism, like any other religion, if we were allowed to

Unfortunately, however, Absolutism is absolutism, and will not let us. It will not tolerate freedom of thought, and divergence of opinion, and difference of taste. It is not content to rest on widespread feelings which appeal to many minds; it insists on its *universal cogency*. All intelligence as such must give its assent to its scheme; and if we will not or cannot, we must either be coerced or denied intelligence. Differences of opinion and tastes and ideals are not rationally comprehensible; hence it is essentially intolerant, and where it can, it persecutes.

We are compelled, therefore, to fight it in self-defence, and to maintain that its contentions are *not* logically cogent. For unless we can repulse its tyrannical pretensions, we lose all we cared for, viz., our liberty to think our experience in the manner most congenial to our personal requirements.

§ 9. But in order that we may not imitate its bad example, let us not contend that because Absolutism fails of being a rational system cogent for all minds, it collapses into incoherent self-contradictory nonsense; but let us merely, quite mildly, explain why and where it falls short of perfect rationality *to our individual thinking*. For then, even if we succeed in making good our case, we shall not have attacked the absolutist's *amour propre*, which is the *"amor intellectualis Dei"*; he can still escape defeat by the unassailed conviction that *to his mind* his case remains unanswerable. And so we shall both be satisfied; if only he will recognize a plurality of types of mind, and consequent thereon, a possibility of more than one "rational" and "logically cogent" system of philosophy.

Armed, then, with the consoling assurance that our "logical" criticism is at bottom *psychological*, and cannot, therefore, in defending our own disputed rationality, hurt the religious feelings of the absolutist, let us proceed to declare roundly that the grounds of Absolutism are (*to our minds*) logically quite inadequate.

17 *Ibid.*, p. xiv.

(1) In pragmatic minds the emotional "craving for unity" described in § 7 (2) is not an all-absorbing passion. It is rationally controlled by calm reflection on its functional value. Merely to be able to say that the universe is (in some sense) one, affords them no particular delight. Before they grow enthusiastic over the unity of the universe, they want to know a good deal more about it; they want to know more precisely what are the consequences of this unity, what good accrues to anything merely in virtue of its inclusion in a universe, how a world which is one is superior as such to a congeries of things which have merely come to act together. All these matters can doubtless be explained, only Absolutism has not yet condescended to do so; it will be time to welcome it when it has. Moreover, when these questions have been answered, it will be asked further as to why it feels justified in ascribing its ideal of unity to our experience, and how it proposes to distinguish between the two cases of a real and a pseudo-unity. How, in short, can it be ascertained whether a world, of which unity can be predicated in some respects, possesses also, and will evermore continue to manifest, all the qualities which have been included in our ideal of unity?

(2) We shall further be desirous of inquiring what is the value of the apparent guarantee of cosmic order by the "systematic unity," the "self-fulfilling" coherence of the Absolute? What precisely are (a) its benefits, and (b) the grounds of the guarantee?

(a) From a human point of view the benefits of the postulate of cosmic order, though great, are not nearly enough fully to rationalize existence. And they have to be paid for. On the one hand, there can be no indeterminism in the rigid real. Absolutism is absolute determinism. And there can be no intervention of a higher power in the established order of nature. That is, there can be neither "free" choice nor "miracle." Both are the acme of irrationality from the absolutist's point of view, and would put him to intellectual confusion. On the other hand, this sacred "order" of the Absolute does not exclude the most stupendous vicissitudes, the most appalling catastrophes, in the phenomenal world.

Let us, therefore, take a concrete case, viz., (1) the total volatilization of the earth and all that creeps upon it, in consequence of the sun's collision with another star; and (2) an opportune miracle which enables those who will avail themselves of it to escape, say, to Mr. H. G. Wells's "Utopian double" of our ill-starred planet. Now it is clear that *intellectually* (1) would not be a catastrophe at all. The established laws of the "perfect" universe provide such "catastrophes" in regular course. They happen one or two a year. And *we* do not mind. We think them rather pretty, if the "new stars" flare up brilliantly enough, and are gratified to find that the "reign of law" obtains also in "distant parts of the stellar regions"; (2), on the other hand, would be intellectually a real disaster. An irruption of miracle, however beneficent, destroys the (conception of a) system of nature. A consistent absolutist, therefore, would not hestitate to choose. (He has no freedom of choice anyhow!) He would decline to be saved by a miracle. He would refuse to be put to intellectual confusion. He would prefer to die a martyr's death in honour of an unbroken order of nature.

A Humanist would not be so squeamish. He would reflect that the conception of an "order of nature" was originally a human device for controlling human experience, and that if at any time a substitute therefor turned up, he was free to use it. He would have no ingrained objection even to a miraculous disorder, provided that it issued in a sequence of events superior to that which "inexorable laws" afforded. And he would marvel that the absolutist should never, apparently, have thought of the possibility that his whole martyrdom might be stultified by his *ignorance* of what the cosmic order included or excluded; so that if he had known more, he might have seen that the "miracle" he had scouted was really part of a higher and more humanly "rational" order, while the collision he had so loyally accepted was nothing of the kind, but in truth an "accident." And in either case is it not clear that each man's choice would be determined, not by the pure rationality of the alternatives and an irresistible logic of the situation, but by the preferences of his individual idiosyncrasy?

(3) (*b*) We have already often hinted that our ignorance and the difficulties of identifying our actual knowledge with the ideal truth are continually undermining the value of rationalistic assumptions and defeating the aims it sets out to attain.

So in this case. When the a priori guarantee of the coherence and predictability of the universe by means of the Absolute comes to be examined, it turns out to be of the flimsiest kind.

It rests on three assumptions: (1) that the order of nature which we have postulated, and which has, for the last few hundreds or thousands of years, shown itself (more or less) conformable to our demand, is really adequate to our "ideal" and will fully realize it. This assumption manifestly rests in part on nonintellectual considerations, in part on the dubious procedure of the ontological proof, in part on the assumed correctness of the "ideal." (2) It is assumed that we know (a) the Whole, (b) the world, and (c) our own minds, well enough to know that we shall continue to make the same demands and to find that reality will continue to conform to them. Now it seems to be distinctly hazardous to affirm that even the human mind must continue to make even its most axiomatic demands to all eternity: that even the known world contains many more surprises for us, seems quite probable; while it seems fantastic to claim that we know the total possibilities of existence well enough to feel sure that nothing radically new can ever be evolved. Yet any irruption of novelty from any of these three sources would be enough to invalidate our present Absolutism, and to put it to intellectual confusion. It is false, therefore, to assume (3) that what would now seem to be "irrational," and to put us to "intellectual confusion," may not really be part of a larger design, and possessed of a higher rationality. Hence the rationalist's protest against irrationalism must always fail, if the latter chooses to claim a higher (and other) rationality.

Now all these assumptions may be more or less probable, but it cannot be asserted that their acceptance is obligatory, and that their rejection entails intellectual suicide. Hence there remains, in Absolutism, as in all other philosophies, an empirical element of risk and uncertainty, which "the Absolute" only conceals, but does nothing to eradicate.

(4) Lastly, and perhaps most fundamentally and cogently, what sense is there in calling the universe a universe at all? How, that is, can the notion be *applied* at all? To call our world "the universe" is to imply that it is somehow to be conceived as a whole. But we could never actually treat it as such.

For we could never know it well enough. It might be of such a kind as not to be a completed whole, and never to become one, either because it was not rigid, but unpredictably contained within itself inexhaustible possibilities of new developments, or because it was really a mere fragment, subject to incalculable influxes and influences from without, which, if reality were truly infinite, might never cease. But either of these possibilities would suffice entirely to invalidate reasonings based on the assumed identity of *our* world with *the* universe.

It is somewhat remarkable that this difficulty should not, apparently, have been perceived by absolutists, and it is significant of the emotional character of their whole faith, that they should habitually delight in the collocation of "infinite" with "whole," without suspecting the gross contradiction this implies. The "infinite" is that which cannot be got together into a whole, and the whole is that which must be complete. But the truth is that, as used by Absolutism, neither term is used with much precision. Both are mainly labels for emotions.

It would be possible, but not very instructive, to go through the whole series of absolutist catchwords, to expose their vagueness and ambiguity, and to show that in the end they are all meaningless, because *they are all inapplicable to our actual experience.* Inapplicable, that is, *without risk.* But if they are once admitted to involve risks, they are in the first place *empirical,* and in the second *lacking in complete intellectual cogency.* Whoever wills may decline to take the risks, and by so doing renounce the absolutist interpretation of experience. And his procedure may be *for him* quite as rational as that of the absolutist. But is not this to have shown that Absolutism can *rationally* be rejected?

§ 10. This conclusion is all we need, and if only it can be similarly accepted by the absolutist, will constitute a true eirenicon. This is the last possibility we have to examine.

Our arguments were satisfactory to us because they seemed rational to us. We only undertook to show that we could make out a rational case *for ourselves.* Of course, however, in calling them rational we implied a claim that all similar minds would assent to them. We did not dogmatize about *all* minds, because, for all we can know a priori, there may be minds differently constituted from our own. Only, if there are, they are not "similar" minds (for our present purposes). The differences in functioning and constitution between these minds and ours are worthy of examination, and may (or may not) be capable of explanation. But it is at any rate useless to *argue* with them. That is all.

But the case looks materially different from the absolutist's standpoint. He was, *ex hypothesi*, unable to combat our case with arguments which seemed rational to us. But, at the same time, he does not accept the arguments which seem rational to us. They seem to him as little "cogent" as his do to us. To resolve this deadlock, he is offered the suggestion that in some respects there exist intrinsic differences in the logical texture of human minds, and that consequently we may, and must, agree to differ. Thus if he accepts this, he too is secured against attack, and peace must ensue.

But can the absolutist content *himself* with this solution? If he does, will he not debar himself from his original claim that his theory is absolutely cogent and valid for intelligence as such? For was it not part of his theory that such complete cogency existed, and was possessed by his arguments? He cannot therefore compromise his claim. He must insist on proving his case *literally to every one of his adversaries,* and similarly on disproving theirs to *their* own complete (logical) satisfaction, and not merely to his! It is evident that this imposes on him a stupendous burden of proof. To fail to admit the logical cogency of a single step in his argument is to shake the whole structure to its foundations. To renounce it, is to refute it. A single dissentient, therefore, will be not merely a theoretical impeachment and a practical nuisance, but actually an unanswerable argument against the truth of the theory, of which it will be at all costs necessary to persuade him! Is it a wonder that absolutists are irritated by the mildest of protests against the least of their beliefs? Their whole view of the universe is imperilled; they are put to intellectual confusion, if the objector is not "somehow" silenced or removed.

But have they anyone to thank for their dilemma but themselves? Why did they devise a theory which, by its very hostility to individual liberty, by its very insistence on absolute conformity, is finally forced to sanction the *Liberum Veto* in philosophy, and thereby to ensure its own destruction? It was not prudent. Nor is it a wise theory which offers such facilities for its own refutation. The situation might move to compassion the most relentless enemy. But we are helpless. The equitable compromise we offered has been rejected. Absolutism has foisted upon us the *Liberum Veto,* and forced us to exercise it. It has thrust the sword into our hands upon which it proceeds to fall. And we, after all, shall not be inconsolably afflicted. It saves much argument when one's opponent commits the happy dispatch.

Chapter 4

Freedom

Argument

§ 1. IT IS one of the most striking features of a new philosophy that it not only breaks fresh ground but also brings up
old issues in a new form, and exhibits them in a new light.
Accordingly, it is natural enough that Humanism should have
something distinctive to say about the old puzzle concerning
freedom and determination. It is in fact under obligation to
treat this subject, because it has implicitly committed itself,

as its chief exponents have of course been perfectly aware.[1] It has assumed that human action is endowed with real agency and really makes a difference alike to the system of truth and to the world of reality. Without this assumption, all the talk about the "making" of truth and reality would be meaningless absurdity. And the assumption itself would be equally absurd, if all human actions were the completely determined products of a rigidly necessary order of events.

It is obvious, therefore, that unless the selections and choices which are shown to pervade our whole cognitive function are real, the system of our science will collapse as surely as our conception of moral agency, and that there can be no real making of either truth or reality. And conversely, if a philosophy finds it necessary to recognize choices and selections *anywhere,* it must provide for their ultimate reality and collide with a theory which declares them to be ultimately illusory. Our trust in an immediate experience which presents us at least with an appearance of alternatives and choices stands in need of vindication, and if we distrusted this appearance, we should engender a scepticism about our cognitive procedure to which it would be hard to set limits. Thus our immediate experience plainly suggests the reality of an indetermination which seems irreconcilable with the assumption of Determinism; and immediate experience our Humanism dare not disavow.

Humanism, therefore, has to defend and establish the reality of this indetermination, and so to conceive it that it ceases to conflict with the postulates of science, and fits harmoniously into its own conception of existence. It has, in other words, to make good its conception of a determinable indetermination and to show that it is involved in the assertion of a really evolving, and therefore as yet incomplete, reality. This it can do by showing that the indetermination, though real, is not dangerous, because it is not unlimited, and because it is determinable, as the growth of habit fixes and renders deter-

---

1 See James's "Dilemma of Determinism" in *The Will to Believe,* which is the only profitable thing written on the whole subject in English for the last thirty years. My aim in this essay is merely to carry a little further and to render a little more explicit the consequences of James's principles. Prof. R. F. A. Hoernle has detected the vital importance of this criticism of determinism, and gives an excellent account of the humanist attitude towards it in *Mind,* N.S. No. 56, pp. 462–67.

minate reactions which were once indeterminate. But no one who is at all acquainted with the complexities of human thought will suppose that this goal of humanist endeavour will be easily attained.

§ 2. What we must mean by "freedom" should be clear from what has been said, and it will be unnecessary to delay the discussion by examining attempts to conceive "freedom" in any less radical fashion. There have been, of course, a variety of attempts to conceive freedom as a sort of determinism, and these have been admirably classified by William James as "soft" determinisms. But under sufficient pressure they always harden into the most adamantine fatalism, and a "soft" determinism usually betokens only the amiable weakness of an intelligence seeking for a compromise.

Thus the notion of "self-determination," for example, when thought out, will be found to involve that of self-creation, and it may be doubted whether any being, actual or imagined, could completely satisfy its requirements, if we except the jocose paradoxes of a few Indian creation myths in which the Creator first lays the World Egg, and then hatches himself out of it. In all the ordinary exemplifications of the notion, the being which is supposed to determine itself is ultimately the necessary product of other beings with which it can no longer identify itself. We are made by a long series of ancestors, and these in their turn were inevitably generated by non-human forces—of a purely physical kind, if science is to be trusted. Nor do we escape this derivation of the "self-determining" agent from a not-self by postulating a non-natural cosmic consciousness, and trusting to it to break through the chains of natural necessity. For such a being must be conceived either as itself the imponent of the natural necessity to which we are enslaved, or, if it escapes therefrom itself, as abrogating it so thoroughly as to invalidate our whole faith in a stable order of nature. Moreover, in neither case would such a being be our "self" any more than is the stellar nebula, among the last and least of whose differentiations we are bidden to enroll ourselves. Any "universal consciousness" must be common to us all, and cannot therefore be that which is peculiar to each, and the source of our unique individuality. It is better, therefore, to accept the doctrine of our "self-determination" by identification with the Absolute as sheer dogma than to try to think it out.

We shall dismiss, therefore, from consideration any use of "freedom" which does not primarily involve the possibility of real alternatives, between which real choices have to be made, which are not merely illusory.

§ 3. Now the difficulty of the question of freedom arises from the fact that it lies in the focus where two of the great postulates that guide our actions meet and collide. But herein also lies its interest and its instructiveness for the theory of knowledge. For nothing is better calculated to reveal the nature of our postulation than the way in which we treat such cases.

The two postulates in question are the scientific postulate of determinism and the ethical postulate of freedom. The first demands that all events shall be conceived as fully determined by their antecedents, in order that they may be certainly calculable once these are known; the second demands that our actions shall be so conceived that the fulfilment of duty is possible in spite of all temptations, in order that man shall be responsible and an agent in the full sense of the term.

It is clear, however, that these postulates conflict. If the course of events really conforms to the determinist postulate, no alternatives are possible. No man, therefore, can act otherwise than he does act. Nor is there any sense in bidding him do otherwise than he does or be other than he is; for good or for evil his predestined course seems to be inevitably marked out for him, down to the minutest detail, by forces that precede and transcend his individual personality. To speak of responsibility or agency in respect to such a being seems a mockery; man is but a transitory term in an infinite series of necessitated events which recedes into the past, and portends its extension into the future, without end; so that at no point can any independence or initiative be ascribed to him.

We are confronted, then, by this dilemma, that if the course of events is wholly determined, the whole of the ideas and beliefs and phraseology which imply the contrary must rest upon illusion. There are not really in the world any alternatives, disjunctions, contingencies, possibilities; hypotheses, doubts, conditions, choices, selections are delusions of our ignorance, which could not be harboured by a mind which saw existence as it really is, steadily and as a whole. If per contra the course of events is not determined, we seem to reject the sole assumption on which it can be known and calculated, and to reduce nature to a chaos. We must sacrifice either our knowledge or ourselves. For what alternative can be found to these imperious postulates? If all things are determined, all are irredeemably swept along in one vast inhuman flow of Fate; if anything is undetermined, we have sold ourselves to a demon of caprice who can everywhere disrupt the cosmic order.

It speaks well for the levelheadedness of humanity that it has not allowed itself to be scared to death by the appalling pretensions of these philosophic bogies; and that on the whole mankind has exhibited an equanimity almost equal to the *sang-froid* of Descartes when he set himself to doubt methodically everything that existed, but resolved meanwhile not to change his dinner hour.

In point of fact determinists and indeterminists for all practical purposes get on quite well with each other and with uncritical common sense. They profess to think the universe a very different thing, but they all behave in very much the same way towards it.

Still it is worth while to try to account for so strange a situation. And if we have the patience to analyse precisely the nature of the conflicting postulates, and of the immediate consciousness of freedom, we shall perhaps perceive how the puzzle is constructed.

§ 4. Determination is an indispensable postulate of science as such. Its sway extends not merely over the natural sciences, in which it is nowadays often thought to originate because its somewhat discreditable ethical origin has been forgotten,[2] but quite as cogently over theology and ethics. Unpredictable mir-

---

[2] This very prettily exemplifies the divergence between the origin of a belief and its validity. For as a matter of history Determinism was devised as an excuse for the bad man, and arose out of Socratic Intellectualism. We see from Aristotle's *Ethics* (*Eth. Nic.* III, ch. 5) that in his time the moralist had to contend against the view that vice is involuntary while virtue is voluntary. Aristotle meets it by showing that the argument proves virtue to be as involuntary as vice. This inference has merely to be accepted to lead to full-blown Determinism. Accordingly we find that in the next generation this was done, and the "free-will" controversy was started between the Stoics and the Epicureans.

acles and incalculable choices are just as disconcerting and subversive as interruptions of the mechanical sequence of happenings.

The reason is that, always and everywhere, we are interested in predicting the future behaviour of things, because we wish to adjust our conduct accordingly. We welcome, therefore, an assumption which will constitute a general justification of our habitual procedure, and encourages us to try to predict the future of all things from their known antecedents.

The assumption of Determinism, therefore, has primarily a *moral* significance; it is an encouragement and not a revelation. It does not in itself enable us to predict how anything will behave; to discover this we have to formulate the special "laws" of its behaviour. But it gives us a general assurance to counteract the primary impression of confusion with which the universe might otherwise afflict us. It justifies us in looking for special laws and rejecting a priori the attribution of events to lawless and incalculable chance. Whenever experience confronts us with "facts" which exhibit such a character, we feel emboldened to declare them to be mere "appearances." The facts, we affirm, are really law-abiding, only we do not yet know their laws. And to a perfect knowledge all events would be completely calculable. In short, by making the determinist assumption, we nerve human science to carry on from age to age its heroic struggle against the brute opacity, the bewildering variety, of the presented sequence of events.

But there is nothing in all this to carry the assumption out of the realm of methodology into that of metaphysics. By conceiving Determinism as a postulate, we go a very little way towards showing that determination is actual and complete and an ultimate fact. For it is quite easy to accept it as a methodological assumption without claiming for it any ontological validity. So long as we restrict ourselves to the methodological standpoint, any postulate is good while it is serviceable; its ultimate validity is not required or inquired into: nay, it may continue to be serviceable even after it has been discovered to be false.

This point may be illustrated by an instructive example suggested by the late Professor Henry Sidgwick.[3] He supposes

[3] *Methods of Ethics,* bk. I, ch. V, § 3.

that "we were somehow convinced that the planets were endowed with Free Will," and raises the question how far this would reasonably impair our confidence in the stability and future of the solar system. Now, according to the ordinary account of the matter as given by a dogmatic and metaphysical rendering of Determinism, the consequences should be terrible. The fatal admission of indetermination should carry with it the death knell of astronomy, and ultimately of all science. For of course we should always have to face the contingency that the planets might depart incalculably from their orbits, and so our most careful calculations, our most cogent inferences, could always be refuted by the event. "What use, therefore, is it any longer," a convinced determinist might exclaim, "to try to know anything when the very basis of all knowing is rendered fundamentally unknowable?"

But a practical man of science would decline to concur in so alarmist an estimate of the situation. He would wait to see whether anything alarming happened. He would reflect that after all the planets might not exercise their freedom to depart from their courses, and might abstain from whirling the solar system headlong to perdition, at least in his time. And even if they did vary their orbits, their vagaries might prove to be so limited in extent that they would not be of practical importance. In fact, the divergences might be so small as to be cloaked by the discrepancies between the calculated and the observed orbits, which until then had been ascribed to the imperfection of our knowledge. It would only be if *de facto* he found himself a horrified spectator of heavenly bodies careering wildly across the sky that he would renounce the attempt to predict their behaviour. Until then he would continue to make his calculations and to compile his nautical almanacs, hoping and praying the while that the sun's influence would prevent Mars and Venus from going wrong. For however much his inward confidence in the practical value of his labours might be abated, his methods would be affected not one jot. So long as it was worth while to calculate the planets' orbits, he would have to assume methodologically that they were determined according to the law of gravitation, just as before. He would realize, that is, that the methodological use of his deterministic principle could survive the discovery of its metaphysical falsity. For since the "free" act was *ex hypothesi* incalculable, the truth of freedom as a metaphysical fact could yield no method by which calculations could be made and behaviour predicted, and hence science would unavoidably ignore it.

We see, then, (1) that in whatever way the metaphysical question is decided, the methodological use of the determinist principle is not interfered with, and that science in consequence is safe, whatever metaphysics may decree. And (2) the principle, and with it science, in so far as it depends on the principle and not on actual experience, is practically safe whatever the actual course of events. For however irregularly and intricately things might behave, they could not thereby force us to renounce our postulate. We should always prefer to ascribe to our ignorance of the law what might really be due to inherent lawlessness. The postulate would only be abandoned in the last resort, when it had ceased to be of the slightest practical use to anyone, even as a merely theoretic encouragement in attempting the control of events. (3) It should follow from this that the scientific objection to a doctrine of freedom was strictly limited to its introduction of an unmanageable contingency into scientific calculations. It would hold against an indeterminism which rendered events incalculable, but not against a belief in freedom as such. A conception of freedom, therefore, which allowed us to calculate the "free" event, would be scientifically quite permissible. And a conception of freedom which issued in a plurality of calculable alternatives would be scientifically unobjectionable, even though it would smother metaphysical Determinism with kindness and surfeit it with an *embarras de richesses*. We should prepare ourselves, therefore, to look out for such a conception of freedom.

§ 5. In considering the moral postulate of freedom, we should begin by noting that the moralist has no direct objection to the calculableness of moral acts and no unreasoning prejudice in favour of indeterminism. He seems to need it merely in order to make real the apparent alternatives with which the moral life confronts him. But he would have as much reason as the determinist to deplore the irruption into moral conduct of acts of freedom, if they had to be conceived as destructive of the continuity of moral character;

he would agree that if such acts occurred, they could only be regarded as the irresponsible freaks of insanity. But he might question whether his dissatisfaction with Determinism necessarily committed him to so subversive a conception of moral freedom. He would deny, in short, that rigid determination or moral chaos were the only alternatives.

The moralist, moreover, if he were prescient, would admit that he could perfectly conceive a moral life without indetermination. Nay, he might regard a moral agent as possessed of the loftiest freedom whose conduct was wholly calculable and fully determined, and therefore absolutely to be trusted. For whether or not he regarded a course of conduct as objectionable would naturally depend on its moral character, and a good life is all the better for resting on a staunch basis of fixed habits.

As compared with such a life, it would of course have to be admitted that an indetermination in moral action which implied a possibility of wrongdoing was a stain upon the agent's character, and indicative of a defect or incomplete development of the intelligence or moral nature. The moralist, therefore, would agree with Aristotle that the divine ideal would be that of a "necessary" being, fully determined in its actions by its own nature, and therefore "free" to follow its promptings, and to realize without impediment its own perfections. Why then, and where, does the moralist come into conflict with Determinism? It is only when we have to deal practically with the bad man that it becomes morally necessary to insist that an alternative to his bad life must be really possible. The bad man's life may be habitually bad, but his case is not hopeless, unless he is necessitated to go on in the way he is going. If alternatives are possible, his redemption is possible. But his redemption is hopeless if there never was but one way for him and all the world. The moralist, therefore, demands an alternative to the bad man's foredoomed badness, in order to rationalize the moral universe.

He wants to be able to say to the bad man: "You need not have become the leper you are. You might have moulded yourself otherwise. Your villainous instincts and unhappy circumstances do not exculpate you. You might have resisted your temptations. Even now your case is not quite hopeless.

Your nature is not wholly rigid. In God's universe no moral lapses are wholly irretrievable. Occasions therefore will present themselves in which, even for you, there will be real alternatives to evil-doing, and if you choose to do right, you may yet redeem yourself." But he does *not* need or desire to say analogously to the good man: "In spite of the deeply ingrained goodness of your habits, you are still free to do evil. May I live to see the day when you commit a crime and vindicate thereby your moral freedom!"

The moralist, in short, insists on the reality of the alternative in the one case only; he has no objection to a freedom which transcends itself and is consolidated into impeccable virtue. In other words, he does not wish to conceive all moral acts as indeterminate, but only some; and he has no need whatever to conceive them as indeterminable. This alone suffices to constitute an essential difference between the real demand for moral freedom and the bogey of indeterminism which determinists seek to put in its place.

It should further be observed that there is no moral need to insist on an unlimited indetermination even in order to impress the bad man. A very slight degree of plasticity will suffice for all ethical demands. And in point of fact no moralist or indeterminist has ever denied the reality of habits. Any notable alteration of habit or sudden conversion is always regarded as more or less miraculous, if it tends in the right direction, or as morbid, if it does not. We see, therefore, that the moral postulate of freedom is by no means in itself an absurd or extreme one, even though it is not yet apparent how it can scientifically be satisfied.

§ 6. We may, however, obtain light on this subject by next considering the empirical consciousness of freedom. Consciousness certainly appears to affirm the existence of real alternatives, and of real choices between them. But it can hardly be said to testify to a freedom which is either unceasing or unrestricted.

(1) What we feel to be "free" choices are comparatively rare events in a moral life of which the greater part seems to be determined by habits and circumstances leaving us neither a real, nor even an apparent, choice. Empirically our free choices occur as disturbances in the placid flow of experiences,

as distinctly upsetting to the equilibrium of our lives as the crises in which we feel "unfree" and constrained to do what we would rather not. Both felt freedom and felt necessity, in short, are symptoms of a crisis, and mark the turning points of a life. They are in a sense correlative and indicative of a certain (specifically human) stage in moral development.[4]

(2) The alternatives which we empirically encounter never seem to be unlimited. We never feel "free" to do anything and everything. Intellectually our choice seems always to be one between alternative ways of achieving an end, of realizing a good. Morally it seems always to be a choice between "duty" and "inclination," "right" and "wrong." We feel "free" to choose, but not at random; the alternatives are definitely labelled "wrong but pleasant" and "right but repugnant."

(3) These alternatives do *not* seem unconnected with our character. So far from appearing to be so, it is of the essence of our "choice" that *both* alternatives should appeal to us. Alike if our sense of duty had grown strong enough, and we had no inclination to do anything but what is right; and if evil indulgences had utterly destroyed our sense of duty, and we retained no inkling of what was right, our choice would disappear, and with it the feeling that we were "free."

Our moral "freedom," therefore, seems to indicate a moral condition intermediate between that of the angel and that of the devil. It seems to lie in the indeterminateness of a character which is not yet fixed in its habits for good or evil, but still sensitive to the appeals of both. Similarly, the intellectual alternatives would disappear for intelligences either vastly more perfect or vastly less perfect than our own. A mind that could unerringly pick out the best means for the realization of its ends would not be perplexed by alternatives, any more than a mind that was too stupid to perceive any but the one most obvious course. In either case, therefore, the reality of the alternatives and the feeling of "freedom" which accompanies our choice seem to be relative to definite moral and intellectual states which occur at a definite stage of habituation. A mind to which the truths of arithmetic are still contingent, which sometimes judges 12×12 to be 144 and sometimes not, is not yet decided in its habits of arithmetical calculation. A will to

4 As I pointed out long ago in *Riddles of the Sphinx,* pp. 445–46.

which moral alternatives are contingent, which when entrusted
with a bottle of whiskey doubts whether to get drunk or to
stay sober, is not yet established in its virtue.

In both cases, no doubt, the contigency of our reaction betokens a defect. To a perfect knowledge the best course would
allow no inferior alternative to be entertained; a perfect will
would not be tempted by an alternative to the right course. To
a combination, therefore, of perfect will with perfect knowledge no alternatives of any sort could exist, and no act could
ever be "contingent."

But why should this prevent us from recognizing the alternatives that seem to exist for us? It only renders them relative
to the specific nature of man. It does not render them unintelligible. They are not irruptions from nowhere. They spring
from a character in which they are naturally rooted, because
that character is still contingent.

When, therefore, the determinist attempts to represent our
freedom as incalculably upsetting the continuity of character,
he is stooping to sheer calumny. If I am perplexed to choose
between a number of possible means to my end, it is because
just my intelligence presents just those alternatives to me under
just those circumstances. A mind whose makeup, knowledge,
and training were even slightly different might have quite different alternatives, or none at all, or be puzzled in cases when I
should not feel the slightest hesitation. So too our moral
choices are personal; they presuppose just the characters and
circumstances they arise from.

§ 7. It is extremely important to observe the precise character of these empirical appearances, because if this is done,
it is easy to perceive in them the real solution of the whole
crux. They directly suggest a way of reconciling the scientific
and the ethical postulate; a way so simple that it would seem
incredible that no one should have perceived it before, had
we not learnt from long and sad experience that the simplest
solutions are usually the last which the philosophic mind is
able to hit upon or willing to accept, especially if such solutions happen also to be empirically obvious. And yet what
could be simpler than the inferences from the facts we have
described? If it is true that empirically the "free" acts always
seem to spring from the given situation, if the alternatives

always seem to exist for a particular mind under particular circumstances, does it not follow at once that *whichever of the alternatives is chosen, it will appear to be rationally connected with the antecedent circumstances?* There will be no break, and no difficulty of transition from the act to its antecedents and back again.

If, therefore, the actual course of events is contemplated ex post facto, it will always be possible to argue that it is intelligible because it sprang from character and circumstances. And if our purpose is deterministic, it can always be maintained that no other course could have been adopted; that because *it* was intelligible, no other course would have been. But this is manifestly false; the alternative, had it been adopted, would have seemed equally intelligible, just because it was such as to be really entertained by the agent under the circumstances, and as naturally rooted in them. After the event, therefore, the determinist is in the position to argue "heads I win, tails you lose"; whatever the issue, he can claim it as a confirmation of his view. Before the event, on the other hand, he was always impotent; he could always modestly disclaim prediction (and therewith avoid refutation) on the ground of insufficient knowledge. His position, therefore, seems inexpugnable.

And yet what has happened has really utterly upset him; for we have come upon a sort of third alternative to determinism and indeterminism. The determinists had argued that if the course of events was not rigidly determined it must be wholly indeterminable; that if it was not uniquely calculable, it could not be calculated at all. But here we appear to have a case in which alternative courses are equally calculable, and to be confronted with a nature which is really indeterminate and really determinable in alternative ways which seem equally natural and intelligible. The determinist, therefore, is really baffled. It no longer follows from the rejection of his theory that we must give up calculating and understanding the course of things. If their nature is such that at various points they engender real alternatives, they will engender a plurality of intelligible possibilities, and the choice between them will constitute a real "freedom," without entailing any of the dreadful consequences with which determinism and indeterminism both

seemed to menace us. Thus we need neither overturn the altar
of science, nor sacrifice ourselves upon it; the freedom which
seemed lost so long as only one course of nature seemed rational, intelligible, and calculable is restored when we recognize that two or more may seem intelligible, because equally
natural and calculable. We can satisfy, therefore, the scientific
postulate of calculability, without denying the reality of the
alternatives which our moral nature seems both to require and
to attest. For we can confidently lay it down that no event
will ever occur which will not seem intelligibly connected with
its antecedents *after it has happened*. It will, therefore, be
judged to have been calculable, even though this inference
will contain a certain modicum of illusion. For though, no
doubt, if we had known enough, we might have calculated it
out as a real possibility, we could not have made sure that
just this possibility and not any of its alternatives would actually be realized. But practically this is more than enough for
science, and would admit of far greater success in calculation
than the deficiencies of our knowledge now actually concede
to us.

It must not be thought, however, that the conception of
freedom we have thus arrived at constitutes a refutation of
Determinism. Methodological postulates as such cannot be
refuted; they can only be disused. And metaphysical dogmas
also, that is, ultimate attitudes of thought, cannot be refuted;
they can only be chosen or rejected; for they form the foundations on which our demonstrations rest. Determinism, then, as
a scientific postulate, has not been endangered; as a metaphysical creed it reduces itself, like all such ultimate assumptions,
to a matter of free choice. And herein, in this case, lies a paradox, perhaps; for as we cannot vindicate our freedom unless
we are determined to be free, so we cannot compel those to
be free who are free to be determined, and prefer to think it
so.[5]

§ 8. But though this paradox may be left to the careful consideration of determinists, we can now resolve another—that
which was noted in § 5—as to the charming agreement which

[5] As William James well says, freedom "ought to be freely espoused by men
who can equally well turn their backs upon it. In other words, our first act of
freedom, if we are free, ought in all inward propriety be to affirm that we are
free" (*The Will to Believe*, p. 146).

obtains between determinists, libertarians, and ordinary folk, in their practical behaviour. For if the postulates are really methodological necessities, everyone in his practice will have to use them, however he may think about them metaphysically, and whether or not he thinks about them at all. The theoretic divergences, therefore, in our views will make no practical difference; both parties will use both postulates, and will have a right to do so.

(1) Everyone has to take it for granted that the course of events is calculable in so far as he is interested in forecasting it. This, indeed, is merely a periphrasis of the statement that Determinism is a methodological postulate. The libertarian, therefore, has the same right as anyone else to treat events as calculable, to try to calculate all he can and knows. He may be conscious that this aim can never be fully realized, that things are not wholly calculable; but while he calculates he must hope that they will behave as if they were determined, and will not frustrate his efforts by exhibiting their freedom. Even if he fails, it will be his interest to attribute his lack of success not to the real contingency he has admitted into nature, but rather to the defects of his knowledge. He will wholly agree, therefore, with the determinist that if he had known more, his calculation would have succeeded. And he would defend himself by urging that anyhow the contingency introduced into our world by our ignorance must vastly exceed that due to any real indetermination in the nature of things.

In dealing, on the other hand, with cases which evoke the moral postulate of freedom, the libertarian will, of course, recognize the reality of the freedom he has assumed. But this will not debar him from calculating. He will assume the indetermination in the nature he is studying to be real, and calculate the alternative courses to which it can be supposed to lead. And if he has a pretty clear conception of the nature of his "free" fellowmen, his success in forecasting their behaviour will not fall sensibly short of his success in calculating that of more remote natures which he takes to be fully determined.

(2) The determinist regards the scientific postulate as the expression of an ultimate truth about reality. But in practice it reduces itself to the expression of a pious hope. "If I knew all the antecedents, I could calculate all the consequences,"

is an aspiration and a wish rather than a postive achievement. This was why we treated it in § 4 as essentially a moral encouragement to endeavour. Even the determinist, moreover, must be dimly conscious that his wish will never be granted him, that the whole course of events never will be calculated by him. Why, then, should he repine at learning that the impossibility of his ideal rests ultimately on the inherent nature of reality rather than on the ineradicable weakness of his mind? Practically it makes no difference. He finds *de facto* that he cannot calculate all events. He tries them all, just like the libertarian. But he is baffled in just the same way. Both, therefore, must agree that contingencies exist in their common world which *they* cannot calculate. To deny their ultimate reality is no practical assistance; it only adds the annoyance that we must conceive ourselves to be subject to illusion and incapable of perceiving things as they really are.

On the other hand, in dealing with moral contingencies the determinist has to treat them as just as real as the libertarian. However firmly he may be convinced that his neighbour's acts are rigidly determined, he does not always feel certain that he knows his nature sufficiently to predict them. He is fortunate if he can feel sure what alternatives are most likely to appeal to him, and calculate the consequences and adjust his own course accordingly. In practice, therefore, he will do just as the libertarian did: he will have to recognize, that is, real but calculable alternatives which exist, at all events for him.

In other words, the pragmatic difference between the rival theories tends to be evanescent; in practice both parties have to pocket their metaphysics and to act sensibly; in theory the differences are such that their influence on practice is very remote, and mainly emotional. For common sense, again, there are no practical alternatives; the whole metaphysical controversy, therefore, seems nugatory, and is regarded with the utmost equanimity. And is not this all as it should be in a universe in which thought is secondary to action?

§ 9. We have, however, pushed forward our doctrine of freedom somewhat rapidly, and shall do well to analyse its nature in order to secure our ground.

We should realize, in the first place, that we took a risk in declaring the immediate consciousness of freedom to contain the solution of the puzzle. There is always a risk in taking appearances to contain ultimate truth. But it is not so serious as to take them as containing no truth at all. And to our Humanism it will naturally seem a better risk to take to trust appearances than to invalidate them for no sufficient reason. Let us therefore bravely accept the risk and pose our critics by asking, Why, after all, should the alternatives which seem to be real not be really real? Because to regard them as real renders science impossible and life chaotic? That allegation we have shown to be untrue. Science is in no danger from our doctrine, and for the purposes of life we all assume the reality of contingencies. Because we do not yet understand the positive nature of freedom, beyond this that it involves indetermination? And because a real indetermination ultimately leads to a metaphysically unthinkable view of the universe?

These latter suggestions are more deserving of consideration. And so let us first explore the positive nature of the sort of freedom we have seemed to find, considering it empirically and psychologically, before attempting to evaluate its metaphysical significance.

There does not seem to be any reason why we should not accept the empirical reality of psychological indetermination, once we have really disabused our minds of the prejudice engendered by a misconception of the scientific postulate. Such indetermination, indeed, appears to be a natural incident in the growth of a habit, and the capacity for retaining a certain plasticity and growing new habits seems to be essential to existence in a universe which has, on the one hand, acquired a certain stability and order, and yet, on the other, is still evolving new conditions, to which novel adjustments are from time to time required. A nature, therefore, which was entirely indeterminate in its reactions, and one which was entirely rigid and determinate, would alike be inefficacious and unsuited to our world. To live in it we need a certain degree of plasticity and the intelligence to perceive when better adjustments can be effected by varying our habits of reaction. This power, indeed, seems to be the essence of our "reason."[6] Why then

6 Cp. Chapter 10, § 4.

should philosophy insist on regarding this plasticity as quite illusory?

It appears, further, to be a misapprehension when this plasticity of habit is regarded as conflicting with the conception of "law." Law, subjectively regarded from the standpoint of a knower trying economically to conceive the universe, means regularity, and therefore calculableness and trustworthiness. Phrasing it intellectualistically, this constitutes the "intelligibility" of the natural order. Regarded objectively, however, "law" means nothing but habit. The "laws of nature," however they may be thought to originate, are *de facto* the established habits of things, and their constancy is an empirical fact of observation. It is from experience alone that we learn that nature in general conforms itself to our postulate of regularity and renders it so applicable that we can take it to be "true."

But experience never fully warrants the assertion that the habits of nature are absolutely fixed and constant. For all we can prove to the contrary, even the most fundamental laws may be changing—let us hope "evolving" into something better. Over large tracts of nature—wherever we can trace the working of intelligence—the laws do not even appear to have an absolute constancy. All this, however, will not interfere with our methodological assumption of constancy unless the changes in habits are very rapid; as rapid, say, as the changes in the fashions. Nor will it necessarily render the course of things unintelligible. On the contrary, we have seen that adaptive innovations in habits, intelligent divergences from law, are the very essence of "reason," and if the changes of fashions are irrational in their frequency, they are at the same time rational, as satisfying the desire to display one's credits with one's dressmaker or tailor.

There is then no real psychological difficulty about the idea that the plasticity of habit carries with it a certain indetermination, which, however, is intelligible and calculable and salutary. The only difficulty really involved lies in conceiving a nature which is, as it were, divided against itself and advancing at different rates in different parts, in such a way that the "desires" may engender internal friction by persistently hankering after ingrained habits of behaviour long after the "reason" has condemned their inappropriateness under the now altered circumstances. And this difficulty no doubt deserves more attention than psychologists and moralists have yet bestowed upon it. But in whatever way it may be explicable, it can hardly be denied that something of the sort actually exists; and for our present purpose this suffices.

Metaphysically, on the other hand, the difficulty which the existence of indetermination involves is a very big one. If, that is, it is admitted to exist at all, it touches the last problems of ontology. For it resolves itself into the question of the possibility of thinking a really incomplete reality, a world which is really plastic and growing and changing. And the a priori sort of metaphysics has always found the reality of change an insuperable stumbling block. We, on the other hand, may think the reality of change too evident to argue over, we may deem the objections raised against it silly quibbles, we may see that to deny it only leads to phantom universes having no relation to our own; but we must recognize the reality of a formidable prejudice. It will be more prudent, therefore, to postpone the final tussle with this prejudice till we have considered (1) how far the consequences of the human freedom we have conceived may be traced throughout the world; (2) how far something analogous can be attributed to the other existences in the world; and (3) how we should value a world whose nature is ultimately "free."

§ 10. *If human freedom is real, the world is really indeterminate.* This is easily demonstrable. For if we really have the power to choose between alternatives, the course of things will necessarily differ according as we do one thing or an other. This follows alike whether we conceive the rest of the world to be fully determined, or to have itself some power of spontaneous choice. If a single variable factor is introduced among a mass of invariable antecedents, the consequents will needs be different. If it is introduced amid a mass of antecedents which themselves are variable, the final outcome may indeed remain the same, but only if these other factors set themselves intelligently to counteract and thwart the first. Thus the intermediate course of events will yet be different, seeing that it will have been altered to encounter the first variable. In either case, therefore, there will be alternative courses of history, and a real indetermination in a universe which harbours a free agent.

Humanly speaking, the first case seems clearly to be congruous with the facts. Human purposes have not all been thwarted; they have left their mark upon the earth, and made it a very different place from what it would otherwise have been. Of course, however, we may hold that their realization has occurred only in so far as it has not thwarted an ulterior and diviner purpose which has a countermove to every human sin and error.[7]

This consequence, then, of human freedom is too clear to be denied. It can only be minimized. After all, it may be said, what does human freedom come to? It can only effect infinitesimal changes on the surface of the earth. It cannot divert the stars in their courses, it cannot even regulate the motions of the earth, it cannot ward off the ultimate collapse of the solar system.

To which it may be replied (1) that our agency is not necessarily negligible because it cannot control the cosmic masses; (2) that our interests are chiefly confined to the earth's surface, and that it matters not a little whether or not we can manipulate that; (3) that the extent to which we can alter the course of things depends on the extent to which we can render things plastic to our purposes; (4) that with audacity and study we may find the world far more plastic than as yet we dare to think. Science is as yet only beginning, and mankind is only beginning to trust itself to science, which as yet hardly dares to speculate about all that it might possibly attempt. Lastly, (5) even differences of choices which at first seem infinitesimal may lead to growing divergences, and ultimately constitute all the differences between a world in which we are saved and one in which we are damned.

On the whole, therefore, we shall do well not to think too meanly of our powers, but to reflect rather on the responsibilities involved even in our most trivial choices. If we can really make our "fate" and remake our world, it behooves us to make sure that they shall not be made amiss.

§ 11. It will next be politic to face an objection which has probably long been simmering in our readers' minds. "Is it

[7] Cp. James, *The Will to Believe,* pp. 181–82.

credible," they will incline to ask, "that man alone should be free and form an exception to the rest of the universe? And if the rest of the universe is determined, is it not probable that man will be likewise?"

Now it cannot be admitted that our view of man should necessarily be falsified in order to accommodate it to our beliefs about the rest of the universe. But at the same time the human mind finds exceptions irksome, and is disposed to question them. We can, however, get rid of this "exception" in another way. Instead of sacrificing our freedom to cosmic analogies, let us try to trace something analogous to our freedom throughout the universe.

It is evident, in the first place, that a higher and more perfect being than man, if the intelligent operations of such a one are traceable in the world, would be both "freer" than man, that is, more able to achieve his ends and less often thwarted, and also more determinate in his action, and more uniform and calculable in the execution of his purposes. It is clear, therefore, that a "God" would work by "law" rather than by "miracle," in proportion as he really controlled the world, and that consequently it would be very easy to misinterpret his agency, and to ascribe it to a mechanical necessity; which of course is what has usually been done.

Turning next to beings lower in the scale than ourselves, we have of course good reason to attribute to the higher animals a mental constitution very like our own. And that should carry with it something very like our sense of freedom. A dog, for example, appears to be subject to conflicting impulses, to doubt and hesitate, to attend selectively and choose, and sometimes to exhibit a spontaneity which baffles calculation almost as completely as that of his master. We can indeed imagine the great motives that broadly determine his conduct, but in some respects his motives are harder to appreciate, because his mind is remoter from our own.

As we descend the scale of life these difficulties grow more marked; our spiritual sympathy with, and inward understanding of, the conduct we observe grow less and less. The feelings which prompt, and the motives which impel, to the spontaneous acts we notice grow ever more mysterious. But externally we can still predict the lower animal's behaviour. We do not understand the why of its spontaneous, random motions. But we observe that these variations lie between certain narrow limits, which are narrowed down as intelligence is lowered. An amoeba never does anything startling to shock the biologist. Hence as intelligence diminishes or grows alienated from our own, conduct becomes more uniform, and therefore in a way more calculable. Only it is in another way. We have become external spectators of acts to which we have lost the inner clue.

Nevertheless, when we descend to the inanimate, and meet apparently perfect regularity, we feel that we have reached the true home of mechanical "law" which knows no breaking, disturbed by no intelligence, and varied by no vestige of spontaneous choice. But we have no inward comprehension whatever of the processes we watch. Why should material masses gravitate inversely as the square of the distance? What satisfactions can they derive from this ratio in particular? Why should atoms dance just in the mazy rhythms they severally choose? Why should electrons carry just the "charges" they empirically bear? All this is sheer, brute, uncomprehended fact, of which no philosophy since Hegel's has had the folly to essay an a priori explanation. But little we care, or scientifically need care, so long as it all happens with a "mechanical" regularity which can be accurately calculated.

It is convenient, therefore, to assume that the inorganic is the realm of rigid mechanism and devoid of every trace of spontaneous spirit. But this is an assumption which is strictly indemonstrable. The regularity to which we trust is no adequate proof. For, taken in large masses, human actions show a similar constancy. Averages remain regular and calculable, even though their individual components may vary widely and incalculably from the mean. Under stable and normal conditions of society, the statistics of births, marriages, and deaths do not vary appreciably from year to year. Yet some of these events are usually set down to individual choices.

Now in observing the inorganic we are dealing with the world's constituents in very large numbers. Physical and chemical experiments operate with many thousands and millions of millions at a time. The least speck visible under the microscope is composed of atoms by the million. Consequently the regularity we observe may very well be that of an average. If, then, a single atom here or there displayed its extraordinary intelligence or original perverseness by refusing to do as the rest, how, pray, should it ever be detected by us? How should we ever suspect that the process rested upon choice and was not utterly mechanical?

Thirdly, it must be borne in mind that we may fail to observe the differences in the behaviour of individual atoms or electrons merely because our experiments are too ignorant and clumsy to discriminate between them, so as to tempt some, without alluring others. Their complete qualitative identity is inferred from experiments which are as crude and barbarous as would be experiments which concluded to the nonexistence of human individuality from the fact that when men were hurled over a precipice in large quantities they were all equally dashed to pieces.

How coarse our methods are we usually discover only when they are improved. Thus it long seemed inexplicable how a grain of musk could retain its fragrance for years without sensibly losing weight, if this quality really rested on the emission of particles; but this mystery is now to a large extent solved by the discovery of radioactivity. It has turned out that the electroscope is a far more delicate instrument than the most sensitive balance, which remains unaffected by the violent propulsion of electrons which accompanies the disruption of atomic matter. And so the whole doctrine of the indestructibility of matter may be radically wrong, and its apparent proofs due merely to the roughness of our former measurements. In experimenting with radium we have managed to select those "atoms" which are nearing their explosive end, and to concentrate them until their death agonies grow visible to us; but concerning the generation of atoms we are still in the dark, though we suspect a good deal, enough at any rate to entertain the idea that the constancy of matter may be merely the stability of an average. Similarly it is possible that long-continued fractionations might sift out the chief individual differences in all the chemical "elements." It is therefore quite fallacious to infer that things have a rigid and unalterable nature, because they show their indifference to us by reacting alike to modes of treatment which to our eyes seem different. In view of our ignorance of their inner nature this may only show that differences which seem important to us do not seem important to them.[8]

Deficient as our observations are in delicacy, they are still more deficient in endurance. The evidence that the "laws" of nature remain really constant is hardly complete even for the last few centuries. The discrepancies, for example, between the historically recorded and the retrospectively calculated eclipses of the sun and the moon are too great to be compatible with existence of our present planetary orbits even a few centuries ago.[9] To explain them we have to choose between the assumptions that our records are false, that the moon is slowly escaping us, that the earth's diurnal rotation is slowing down, that the sun's motion or attraction is altering, or that the law of gravitation is changing, or whatever combination of these and other hypotheses we can devise to fit the facts more nearly. To guide that choice we have only the vague methodological maxim that it is well to try first such hypotheses as involve the least disturbance of the accepted system of science. But even the greatest readjustments may be needed. If now we supposed the primary laws of nature to be changing slowly and continuously, most of the evidence which is now held to imply their rigid constancy would be seen to be inconclusive. Thus even in the inorganic world habits might be plastic and "laws" might be gradually evolving.

If this be so, it is, moreover, clear that we ourselves might take a part in determining this evolution. Our operations might induce things to develop their habits in one way rather than another, and so we should literally be altering the laws of nature. It is even permissible to surmise that we may already sometimes have accomplished this. The chemist, for example, seems often so to play upon the acquired habits of his substances as to bring into existence compounds which but for him would never have existed, and never could have existed in a state of nature. And so he may induce new habits; for once these combinations have been formed, they may leave permanent traces on the natures that take part in them, and so alter their "affinities" for the future.

[8] Cp. Chapter 1, p. 49, *n.*
[9] See an article on "Ancient Eclipses" by Prof. P. H. Cowell in *Nature*, No. 1905.

The speculations whereby we have illustrated the possibility that individuality, plasticity, and freedom may pervade also the inorganic world will seem wild and unfamiliar. But they are such that science may someday verify them, if they are looked for. At present we blind ourselves to their possibility by making the methodological assumptions of determinism and mechanism. But it should be clearly confessed that it is entirely possible that the world may now be, and may always have been, such as to contain a certain indetermination throughout its structure, which we have only failed to discover because we have closed our eyes to it, in order to have a more easily calculable universe. If, however, this postulate is modified so that "free" acts also are conceived as calculable, our eyes may be opened, as it were by magic, and the evidences of "freedom" may everywhere pop up and stare us in the face.

§ 12. We come at last to the ultimate metaphysical advantages and disadvantages of the belief in freedom which we have developed. That it has its drawbacks is fairly obvious. Indeterminism, even when it has been tamed, i.e., limited, and rendered calculable and determinable, still means chance; and chance means risk; and risk, though it seems inseparable from life, means a possibility of failure. Our craven instincts, therefore, our indolence, our diffidence, will always demand an assurance of salvation, a universe which *cannot* go astray, but is predestined to be perfect.

The prejudices thus engendered are probably among the strongest of the secret motives which inspire the absolutist's aversion from Pragmatism. As Professor Muirhead opportunely confesses, the admission of contingency seems to turn the universe into "a joint-stock enterprise under God and Co., Limited, *without insurance against accident,*"[10] and this would be very much of a *pis aller* to predestinate perfection.

But is predestinate perfection possible or really thinkable? And what is the "insurance against accident" offered us by the agents of the Absolute really and truly worth?

If the universe as we know it is predestined to anything, it is predestined to go on as it is upon its fatal course. For the universe, we are assured, contains no free agents, human or divine, to work out beneficial transformations in its nature. It

[10] *Hibbert Journal,* IV, 460. Italics mine.

is predestined, therefore, to be an unmeaning dance of cosmic matter, diversified at intervals by catastrophes, as blind blundering suns go crashing into each other's systems and make holocausts of the values and polities which some powerless race of planetary pygmies has painfully evolved. It is predestined to a fate which nothing can avert, which no one can mitigate or improve.

And to make our "insurance" doubly sure, we are furthermore assured that this universe, which extorts its tribute of tears from every feeling breast, is *already perfect,* if only we could see it—which being necessarily "finite" we cannot! There is not, therefore, the slightest reason why, for finite minds, the universe should ever seem, or become, more satisfactory than now it is. The absolutist in his Determinism at bottom entirely agrees with Mephistopheles:

Glaub' unser einem dieses Ganze
Ist nur für einen Gott gemacht.

The only boon which his view "insures" us is that a world which with all its faults had seemed plastic and improvable becomes a hopeless hell for the wanton and superfluous torture of helpless "finite" beings, whose doom was predestined from all eternity!

For my part, I should prefer a universe marred by chance to such a certainty. For the "chance" in this case means a chance of improvement. Of course, a world that was really perfect in a simple and human way, and was incapable of declining from the perfection because it contained no indetermination, would be better still. But such a world ours plainly is not, though it has a chance of developing such perfection by becoming wholly harmonious and determinate. And is it not "assurance" enough for all reasonable requirements that in a world wholly harmonized, no one could upset its harmony nor have any motive for changing his habits and the way of the world?

There remains to be discussed the metaphysical objection to the conception of indetermination which was postponed in § 9. It is at bottom an objection to the reality of change in ultimate reality, to the notion of its incompleteness and development. It is, however, merely a survival of Eleatic prejudice, and the simplest way to dispose of it is by a demand for its credentials. For why should it be taken as certain a priori that the real cannot change? All we *know* about reality negatives this notion. And if our immediate experience is not to convince us of the reality of change, of what can anything convince us? Or if it is claimed that the impossibility of change can be made dialectically evident by a priori reasoning from ideas, our reply will be that, if so, the ideas in question must be faulty. For our ideas should be formed to understand experience, not to confute it. Ideas which are inapplicable are invalid. Ideas which contradict experience are either false, or in need of verification by the altering of the reality which contradicts them. In short, it is vain to threaten libertarians with the metaphysical terrors of what James calls "the block-universe." That conception is usually mystical, when it is not a materialistic corollary from an obsolescent physics; it can never be really thought out in metaphysics except into sheer, unmitigated Eleaticism. And, as in Zeno's time, the puzzle *"solvitur ambulando"* by those who really wish to know; we leave it aside and pass on.

To sum up: our freedom is really such as it appears; it consists in the determinable indetermination of a nature which is plastic, incomplete, and still evolving. These features pervade the universe; but they do not make it unintelligible. Nay, they are the basis of its perfectibility.

Chapter 5

The Making of Reality

Argument

§ 1. Hegel's great idea of a thought process which was to be also the cosmic process spoilt by his dehumanizing of the former. The false abstractions of the Dialectic from time and personality lead to its impotence to explain either process. § 2. Humanism renews Hegel's enterprise by conceiving the "making of truth" to be also a "making of reality." Its epistemological validity. § 3. The problem of a metaphysical "making of reality." § 4. Its difficulties. (1) Can reality be wholly engendered by our operations? (2) Can the pragmatic method yield a metaphysic? § 5. Even epistemologically we must (1) distinguish between "discovering" and "making" reality. The distinction may mark the division between Pragmatism and Humanism. But it is itself pragmatic, and in some cases the difference between "making" and "finding" becomes arbitrary. § 6. (2) The great difference between original and final "truth" and "fact" in the process which validates "claims" and makes "realities." The pragmatic un-importance of starting points. Initial truth as "sheer claim" and initial fact as mere potentiality. Their methodological worthlessness. § 7. (3) The method-ological nullity and metaphysical absurdity of the notion of an "original fact." Ultimate reality some-thing to be looked forward, and not back, to. § 8. The transition of metaphysics. Humanism and meta-physics. § 9. Four admitted ways in which the "mak-ing of truth'" involves a "making of reality." A fifth, knowing, makes reality by altering the knowers, who are real. § 10. But is the object known also altered, and so "made"? Where the object known is not aware it is known, it is treated as "independent," because knowing seems to make no difference. Fallaciousness of the notion of mere knowing. Knowing as a prelude to doing. § 11. The apparent absence of response to our cognitive operations on the part of "things," due to their lack of spiritual communion with us. But really they do respond to us as physical bodies, and are affected by us as such. § 12. Hylozoism or panpsychism as a form of Humanism. "Catalytic action" and its human analogues. § 13. Hence there is real making of reality by us out of plastic facts. § 14. The extent of the plasticity of fact, practically and methodologically. § 15. Nonhuman making of reality. § 16. Two indispensable assumptions: (1) the reality of freedom or determinable indetermination. § 17. (2) The incompleteness of reality, as contrasted with the absolutist notion of an eternally complete whole, which renders our whole world illusory.

§ 1. IT WAS a great thought of Hegel's[1] that truth and reality, logic and metaphysics, belonged together and must not be separated, and that to make the world truly intelligible, the making of truth and the making of reality must be made to coincide. He tried, therefore, to conceive the cosmic process as one with the thought process, and to represent all the events which happened in the real evolution of the world in time as incidents in the self-development of a "dialectical process" in which the Absolute Idea arrived at a full logical comprehension of its own eternal meaning.

But, unfortunately, he spoilt this great idea (with which Dr. McTaggart alone of his English followers seems to concern himself) in the execution. He tried to conceive thought as out of time, and its "eternity" as higher than the time process of reality, and as containing the "truth" and meaning of the latter. But this equation of the *eternal* "logic process" with the *temporal* "cosmic process" did not work out to a real solution. The one was eternally complete, the other manifestly incomplete; and no real correspondence could be established between their respective terms. Moreover, the real events of the cosmic process stubbornly refused to be reduced to mere

1 Or rather of Fichte's; but Hegel appropriated it.

illustrations of a dialectical relation of "categories," and the desperate attempt of the Dialectic to declare the *surplus* of meaning, which the real possessed over the logical, to be really a *defect,* to be mere meaningless "contingency" which reason could not, and need not, account for, was really a covert confession of its fundamental failure.

This failure, moreover, was really an inevitable consequence of its own fundamental assumptions. It had begun by misconceiving the "thought process," which was to be its clue to reality. It had begun by abstracting from its concrete nature, from the actual thinking of human beings. It had begun, that is, by misconceiving the function of abstraction. It had begun, in short, by *dehumanizing* thought in order to make it more adequate to ultimate reality. But the result was that it destroyed the real link between reality and thought. For it is only as concrete human thinking that we know thought to be a real process at all. Once this link is severed, once the human side of thought is flung aside as meaningless and worthless, thought per se, however "absolute" and "ideal" and "eternal" we may call it, is wafted away from earth into the immense inanity of abstractions which have lost the touch with a reality to which they can never again be applied.

This fate has overtaken the Dialectic. The self-development of its "categories" is not the real development of any actual thought. It is not, consequently, the real explanation of any actual process. It still bears a sort of ghostly resemblance to our concrete thinking, to the body of incarnate truth from which it was abstracted; and, therefore, it can still claim a shadowy relevance to the real events of life. But it is too abstract ever to grasp either thoughts or events in their full concreteness. Thus its claim to predict events is very like the weather prophecies in *Zadkiel's Almanac*—so vaguely worded that almost anything may be said to confirm it. But it can never suggest any definite reason why definite persons at any definite time should think just those thoughts which they think, or use just the categories which they use, rather than any other. It can never allege any reason why events should exemplify the logical relations of the categories in the precise way they are said to do, rather than in a dozen other ways which would do equally well, or why, conversely, the categories should achieve exemplification by just the events which occur, rather than by a myriad others which would perform this function no less well. All such definite questions it waves aside as concerned merely with the impenetrable "contingency" of the phenomenal. Even, therefore, if we take the most favourable view of its claims, and admit it to be an explanation of everything in general, it still fails to satisfy the demands, either of science or of practice, by being too vague and too ambiguous to be the explanation of anything in particular. It is truly the "unearthly ballet of bloodless categories" Mr. Bradley has called it, a mere witches' sabbath of disembodied abstractions, from which the true seeker after the meaning of reality will no more distil spiritual satisfaction than Dr. Faustus did from the *Walpurgisnacht* on the Brocken. And even as an intellectual debauch, as a sowing of spiritual wild oats, it is better to avoid what may so seriously confuse and debilitate the mind.

It remains, however, to show that the points at which the Hegelian Dialectic's failure becomes patent are in direct connexion. It fails, practically on its own showing, to account for *the whole* of the time process, *because* it fails to account for *the whole* of the thought process. For it has in both cases made the same fatal abstraction. It has assumed that because *for the practical purposes of human knowing* it is convenient and possible and sufficient to abstract from the full concreteness ("particularity") of the real, what we neglect, and often have to neglect, is really meaningless. But this is not the case. There is nothing "accidental" and void of significance about the real, nothing which a *complete* theory of events can afford to ignore. The minutest "incident" has its meaning, every least shade of personality its importance, even though our limitations may practically force us to neglect them. Such concessions may be accorded to the humility of a pragmatic theory of knowledge; they cannot be rendered compatible with the all-embracing claims of a theory of absolute knowledge. Hence the pretensions of the Dialectic to absolute completeness do not entitle it to the arrogance of such abstractions. If it cannot or will not explain everything, it forfeits its claim to be "concrete" and to be valid. It has misunderstood, moreover, the nature of abstraction. The abstraction which occurs in actual thinking is human, and not absolute; it is relative to a restricted purpose, and can be rectified by altering the purpose whenever this is requisite or desirable. Abstraction, in other words, is an instrument of thought, and not a good per se. It should not be dehumanized any more than any other feature of our thinking. And if we refrain from dehumanizing our thought, we shall not be forced to "de-realize" reality in order to make it "intelligible."

§ 2. Let us try, therefore, to renew Hegel's enterprise of the identification of the making of truth and the making of reality, under the better auspices of a logic which has not disembowelled itself in its zeal to become true. That the pragmatic theory of knowledge does not start with any antithesis of "truth" and "fact," but conceives "reality" as something which, for our knowledge at least, grows up in the making of truth, and consequently recognizes nothing but continuous and fluid transitions from hypothesis to fact and from truth to truth we have already seen. It follows that the "making of truth" is also in a very real sense a "making of reality." In validating our claims to "truth" we really "discover" realities. And we really *transform* them by our cognitive efforts, thereby proving our desires and ideas to be real forces in the shaping of our world.

Now this is a result of immense philosophic importance. For it systematically bars the way to the persistent but delusive notion that "truth" and "reality" somehow exist apart, and apart from us, and have to be coaxed or coerced into a union, in the fruits of which we can somehow participate. The making of truth, it is plain, is anything but a passive mirroring of ready-made fact. It is an active endeavour, in which our whole nature is engaged, and in which our desires, interests, and aims take a leading part. Nevermore, therefore, can the *subjective* making of reality be denied or ignored, whether it be in the interests of rationalism, and in order to reserve the making of reality for an "absolute thought," or whether it be in the interests of realism, and in order to maintain the absoluteness of an "independent" fact. Taken strictly for what it professes to be, the notion of "truth" as a "correspondence" between our minds and something intrinsically foreign to them, as a mirroring of alien fact, has completely broken down. The reality to which truth was said to "correspond," i.e., which it has to know, is *not* a "fact" in its own right, which pre-exists the cognitive functioning. It is itself a fact *within* knowing, immanently deposited or "precipitated" by the functioning of our thought. The problem of knowledge, therefore is *not* "How can thought engender truth about reality?" It is rather "How can we best describe the continuous cognitive process which engenders our systems of 'truth' and our acceptance of 'reality' and gradually refines them into more and more adequate means for the control of our experience?" It is in this cognitive elaboration of experience that both reality and truth grow up *pari passu*. "Reality" is reality for us, and known by us, just as "truth" is truth for us. What we judge to be "true," we take to be "real," and accept as "fact." And so what was once the most vaporous hypothesis is consolidated into the hardest and most indubitable "fact." Epistemologically speaking, therefore, so far as our knowledge goes or can go, the making of truth and the making of reality seem to be *fundamentally one.*

§ 3. But how about metaphysics? Does this "making of truth" supply a final answer to all the questions we can ask? This is by no means obvious. Even on the epistemological plane the making of truth seemed to recognize certain limitations, the exact nature of which, being unable to pursue the subject into the depths of metaphysics, we were not able to determine. We had to leave it doubtful, therefore, how far a coincidence of our cognitive making of truth with the real making of reality could be traced, and whether ultimately both processes could be combined in the same conception. It seemed possible that our so-called making of reality would not in the end amount to a revelation of the ultimate essence of the cosmic process, and that the analogies between the two would finally prove fallacious or insufficient.

We postponed, therefore, the further consideration of these questions, and have been rewarded since then by lighting upon a number of truths which may be distinctly helpful in a renewed attack upon our problem of the "making of reality."

(1) We have seen that an evolutionist philosophy ought not prematurely to commit itself to a static view of reality, and that it is not an ineluctable necessity of thought, but a metaphysical prejudice, to believe that reality is complete and rigid

and unimprovable, and that real change is therefore impossible. We have thus gained the notion of a plastic, growing, incomplete reality, and this will permit us to conceive a "making of reality" as really cosmic.

(2) The examination of freedom in the last essay (§§ 9–12) brought us once more into contact with this idea of a really incomplete reality. For it seemed that there might after all be a vein of indetermination running through the universe, and that the behaviour and the habits of things could still be altered. This idea cropped up as a logical consequence of the reality of human freedom, which we found it possible to maintain on other grounds. This freedom and plasticity, moreover, would explain and justify our treatment of our ideas as real forces, and our claim that the "making of truth" was necessarily also a making of reality. For the plasticity of the real would explain how it was that our subjective choices could realize alternative developments of reality.

And (3) it appeared to be possible that this plasticity of things might involve not merely a passive acquiescence in our manipulations, but a modicum of initiative, and that thus "freedom" might not be confined to human nature, but might in some degree pervade the universe. If so, not only would the possibilities of "making reality" be vastly enlarged, but we should have established the existence of a very real and far-reaching identity in nature between human and nonhuman reality, which would justify the expectation of very considerable likeness in the processes by which they severally adjust themselves to their environment. Accordingly, we might feel entitled to look for analogues also to the human making of truth and reality, and these might help to render intelligible the vast masses of reality, which it seemed we could not humanly claim to have "made."

§ 4. Still, it will not do to underrate the difficulties of the situation. The pragmatic method, we have always admitted, has definitely postulated an initial basis of fact as the condition of its getting to work at all. And although any particular "fact" can always be conceived as having been "made" by a previous cognitive operation, this latter in its turn will always presuppose a prior basis of fact. Hence, however rightly we may emphasize the fact that *what we call reality* is bound up with our knowing and dependent on our manipulations, there will always seem to be an insuperable paradox in the notion that *reality can, as such and wholly, be engendered by the consequences of our dealings with it.*

Our pragmatic method, moreover, has so far fought shy of metaphysics. It has pleaded that originally it had professed to be merely epistemological in its scope, and has gravely doubted whether metaphysics were not for it *ultra vires.*[2] It may be well, therefore, to indulge the foibles of our method, to the extent at least of considering what more can be said about the making of reality on strictly epistemological ground, before we transform it, by claiming for it universal application and expanding it to cosmic dimensions, and thereby soar to metaphysics.

§ 5. In point of fact there is a good deal more to be said. For example, (1) the difficulty about conceiving the acceptance of fact as the basis of the pragmatically developed situation should be treated, not as an objection to the pragmatic method, but as a means of bringing out its full significance. For it can be made to bring out the important distinction between the reality which is "made" only for us, i.e, *subjectively,* or as we say, "discovered," and that which we suppose to be *really* "made," made objectively and in itself. That we make this distinction is obvious; but why do we make it? If both the subjective and the objective "making of reality" are products of the same cognitive process, of the same "making of truth" by our subjective efforts, how can this distinction arise, or, ultimately, be maintained?

Now it is clear, in the first place, that acceptance of the pragmatic method in no wise compels us to ignore this distinction. Nor does it as such compel us to assert the "making of reality" in the *objective* sense. It seems quite feasible to conceive the making as *merely subjective,* as referring only to our

---

2 I do not think that the text of *Axioms as Postulates* anywhere, even in isolated paragraphs, entitles critics to read it in a metaphysical sense. And certainly the whole method and purpose of that essay should have made it unmistakable that it was nowhere intended to be taken in any but an epistemological sense. If so, it is beside the point to object to §§ 3–7 as not giving a satisfactory account of the creation of the universe. Really that would have been too much to expect even from the untamed vigour of a new philosophy! That the question under discussion referred only to our cognitive making of reality was quite plainly stated in § 7.

knowledge of reality, without affecting its actual existence.[3] Nay, the existence of the distinction may itself legitimately be appealed to to show that common sense draws a clear line at this point. And so it may be denied that we "make" reality metaphysically, though not that we "make" it epistemologically.

The validity of this position may provisionally be admitted. Let it merely be observed that it is compatible with a full acceptance of Pragmatism *as a method,* and even with a very extensive "making of reality" by our efforts. For these efforts are still indispensable in order that reality may be "discovered." It is still true that our desires and interests must anticipate our "discoveries," and point the way to them—and that so our conception of the world will still depend on our subjective selection of what it interested us to discover in the totality of existence. And of course the "making of reality," in so far as we mould things to suit us, and in so far as social institutions are real forces to be reckoned with and potent in the moulding of men, is also unaffected by the refusal to conceive the ultimate making of reality as proceeding identically, or analogously, with our "making of truth." So that it is quite possible to be a good pragmatist without attempting to turn one's method into a metaphysic.

Secondly, it is clear that if the pragmatic method is true, the distinction between "discovering" and "making" reality must itself have a pragmatic ground. It must be evolved out of the cognitive process, and be validated by its practical value. And this we find to be the case. The distinction is a practical one, and rests on the various behaviours of things. A reality is said to be discovered, and not made, when its behaviour is such that it is practically inconvenient or impossible to ascribe its reality for us entirely to our subjective activity. And as a rule the criteria of this distinction are plain and unmistakable. To wish for a chair and find one, and to wish for a chair and make one, are experiences which it is not easy to confuse, and which involves very different operations and attitudes on our part. In the one case, we have merely to look

---

[3] Hence it seems possible to be, e.g., a pragmatist in epistemology, and a realist in metaphysics, like Prof. Santayana.

around, and our trusty senses present to us the object of our desire in effortless completion; in the other, a prolonged process of construction is required.

More verbally confusing cases arise when we have made a claim to reality which we cannot sustain, or denied a reality which we subsequently recognize. These cases seem to lend themselves to the belief in an "independent" reality, because in our dealings with them we do not seem to alter "reality," but only our beliefs about it. The confusion, however, is at bottom one between a reality (or truth) which is claimed, and one which is verified. If a claim is falsified, the new truth (or reality) which takes its place may always be antedated, and conceived as having existed independently of the claim which it refutes. But it cannot be said to be similarly independent of the process which has established it. The truth is that what in such a case we have made is not a reality, but a mistake. And a mistake is a claim to reality (or truth) which will not work, and has to be withdrawn. But the failure of a cognitive experiment is no proof that experimentation is a mistake. Nor does the fact that a reality existed, which we mistakenly denied, prove that it was not "made," even by ourselves.

In other cases the line is not so clear, and the "finding" seems to involve a good deal of "making." Our language itself often testifies to this. Thus we often "find" that when we have "made" mistakes, the precise amount of wilfulness involved in the "making" is difficult to gauge. Or consider our dealings with other beings spiritually responsive to our action. Our behaviour to them may really determine their behaviour to us, and make them what we believed or wanted them to be.[4] Thus "making love" and "finding love" are not in general the same. But you may make love, because you find yourself in love, and making love may really produce love in both parties to the suit. Few people, moreover, would really "find" themselves in love, if the object of their affections had done absolutely nothing to "make" them fall in love. And every married couple has probably discovered by experience that the reality and continuance of their affection depends on the behaviour of both parties.

It is clear then (a) that, roughly and in the main, there

4 Cp. Chapter 1, p. 49 n.

is a real pragmatic distinction between "discovering" and "making" reality. But (b) we also get some suggestive hints that this distinction may not be absolute, and that in our dealings with the more kindred and responsive beings in the world, our attitude towards them may be an essential factor in their behaviour towards us. If so, we shall have sufficient ground for the belief that our manipulations may really "make," and not merely "find" reality, and sufficient encouragement to pursue the subject farther.

§ 6. (2) In admitting that the pragmatic making of truth always presupposed a prior basis of fact, an important point was omitted. We neglected to notice also the great and essential difference between the nature of the truth and the reality as it enters the process at the beginning and as it emerges from it at the end. Both the truth and the reality have been transformed. Their originally tentative character has disappeared. The "truth," which entered the process as a mere claim, has now been validated. The "reality," which at first was a suspicion, a hope, a desire, or a postulate, is now fully substantiated, and an established fact. The difference wrought by the pragmatic verification, therefore, is as great in the case of the "reality" as in that of the truth, and it was surely worth the whole labour of rethinking the traditional formulas in pragmatic terms to have had our attention drawn to its existence.

For the pragmatic theory of knowledge, initial principles are literally ἀρχαί, mere starting points, variously, arbitrarily, casually selected, *from which we hope and try to advance to something better.* Little we care what their credentials may be provided that they are able to conduct us to firmer ground than that from which we were fain to start. We need principles that work, not principles that possess testimonials from the highest a priori quarters. Even though, therefore, their value was prospective and problematical, they were accepted for the services they proffered. For we knew better than to attach undue importance to beginnings, than to seek for principles self-evident, and realities undeniable to start with. We divined from the first that truth and reality in the fullest sense are not fixed foundations, but ends to be achieved.

Consequently, the question about the nature of initial truth and reality cannot be allowed to weigh upon our spirits. We have not got to postpone knowing until we have discovered them. For actual knowing always starts from the existing situation.[5] Even, therefore, if we fail to penetrate to such absolute beginnings, our theory can work. And it is not disposed to regard initial facts or truths as specially important, even if they could be ascertained. Indeed, our method must treat them as *conceptual limits* to which actual cognition points, but which it never rests on. Initial truth it will regard as *sheer claim,* unconfirmed as yet by any sort of experience, and undiscriminatingly inclusive of truth and falsehood. A really a priori truth, i.e., a claim which really preceded all experience, would be as likely to be false as true when it was applied. It has no value, therefore, for a theory of knowledge which is wishful to discriminate between true and false. Initial reality, similarly, would be *sheer potentiality,* the mere ὕλη of what was destined to develop into true reality. And whatever value metaphysics may attach to them, the theory of knowledge can make nothing of sheer claims and mere potentialities. Methodologically we may and must assume that every truth and every reality now recognized is to be conceived as evolved from the cognitive process in which we now observe it, and as destined to have a further history.

For if we declined to treat it so, we should lose much and gain nothing. We should gratuitously deprive ourselves of the right of improving on the imperfect and unsatisfactory realities and truths which we *now* have. By conceiving them as *rigid,* i.e., as fixed and unalterable from the beginning, we should merely debar ourselves from discovering that after all they were plastic, if such chanced to be their nature. If, on the other hand, they chanced to be rigid, we should not be put to shame; we should merely suppose that we had not yet found the way to bend them to our will. The sole methodological principle, therefore, which will serve our purpose and minister to a desire for progressive knowledge is that which conceives no reality as so rigid and no truth as so valid as to be constitutionally incapable of being improved on, when and where our purposes require it. We may be *de facto* quite unable to effect such an improvement. But why should that compel us to forbid effort and to close the door to hope for all eternity?

5 Cp. Chapter 9, § 3.

To sum up then: even though the pragmatic method implies a truth and a reality which it does not make, yet it does *not* conceive them as valuable. It conceives them only as indicating limits to our explanations, and not as revealing the solid foundations whereon they rest. All *effective* explanation, however, starts from the actual process of knowing, which is pragmatic, and not from hypothetical foundations, which are dubious. And all effective truth and reality result from the same pragmatic process.

§ 7. (3) It is clear, then, that we have, on methodological grounds, a certain right to demur to the demand for an explanation of the initial basis of fact. It is quite true that our method logically implies a previous fact as its datum. But it is also true that since any determinate character in a "fact" may be conceived, and must be assumed, to have been derived, this original datum is reduced for us in principle to a mere potentiality, an indeterminate possibility of what is subsequently made of it. And so methodologically, as we saw in the last section, it need not trouble us, because we are concerned not with presuppositions, but with ends.

It is only, however, when this notion of an original fact is translated into the language of metaphysics that its methodological nullity is fully revealed. When the doctrine of the making of reality out of a relatively indeterminate material is construed metaphysically, and pushed back to the "beginning," it seems to assert the formation of the Real out of a completely indeterminate Chaos, of which nothing can be said save that it was capable of developing the determinations it *has* developed under the operations which *were* performed upon it.

But how, it is asked, with a fine show of indignation, by philosophers who have forgotten Plato's δεξαμένη and the creation stories of all the religious mythologies from the book of Genesis downwards, can such a notion be put forward as a serious explanation? How can a wholly indeterminate "matter" be determined by experiment? What would any experiment have to go upon? By what means could it operate? And why should the "matter" react in one way rather than in any other? And then, without awaiting a reply or crediting us with any awareness of some of the oldest and least venerable of metaphysical puzzles, they hastily jump to the conclusion that

Pragmatism has no real light to throw on the making of reality, and that they may just as well revert to the cover of their ancient formulas.

It is, however, from their conclusion only that we should dissent. We may heartily agree that these questions should be put in a metaphysical sense, if only in order that it may be seen what their answers would involve. We may agree also to some of their terms. It is obvious, for example, that to derive reality from chaos is not seriously to explain it. But then we never said or supposed it was. On the other hand we should *not* admit, at least not without cause alleged, that because a thing is indeterminate it is necessarily indeterminable, or that if it is indeterminate, it must be conceived as *infinitely* so, merely because we are not able *before the event* to predict in what ways it will show itself determinable. We shall plead, in short, the doctrine that *the accomplished fact* has logical rights over the "original" fact.

Still, chaos is no explanation. This is just our reason for the methodological scruple about the whole notion of expecting a complete metaphysical explanation of the universe from the pragmatic analysis of knowledge. It may reasonably be contended that the whole question is invalid because it asks too much. It demands to know nothing less than how reality comes to be at all, how fact is made absolutely. And this is more than any philosophy can accomplish or need attempt. In theological language, it is to want to know how God made the world out of nothing. Nay, it includes a demand to know how God made himself out of nothing! But this is not only a question to which we are never likely to get an answer, but also one which, as Lotze wisely remarked, is logically inadmissible. For it ignores the facts that something must be taken for granted in all explanation, and that the world, just as we have it now, is the presupposition *de facto* of every question we ask about it, including those as to its past and its "origin." Thus in a methodological sense the existing world, with its pragmatic situation, is the necessary presupposition of the original datum from which it is held to be derived.

Moreover, even if *per impossibile* the demand could somehow be satisfied, and we could learn how the first fact was made, there is no reason to think that the procedure would strike us as particularly "rational" or enlightening, or that this "knowledge" would leave us any the wiser. It would certainly appear to have been a making of something out of nothing. And the first "something" would probably seem something despicable or disgusting. It would very likely look to us like the primordial irruption into the world we now have of that taint of corruption, evil, or imperfection which philosophers have tried so often to *think,* and so rarely to *do,* away.

The fact is that the conception of ultimate reality looks forward, and not back, and must do so (like Orpheus) if it is to rescue our life from the house of Hades. It cannot be separated from that of ultimate satisfaction. We can conceive ourselves, therefore, as getting an answer to the question about the beginning of the world process only at the end. And it will be no wonder if by that time we should have grown too wise and too well satisfied to want to raise the question. To us, at least, it is no paradox that a *psychological* inability or unwillingness to raise a problem may also be its only *logical* solution. When perfection has been attained, the universe, having at last become harmonious and truly *one,* will perforce forget its past in order to forget its sufferings. For us, meanwhile, it should suffice to think that perfection may be attained.[6]

To reject this would be to allow the validity of von Hartmann's objection to the existence of a God on the ground that, if he were conscious, he would go mad over trying to understand the mystery of his own existence. Von Hartmann infers that the Absolute must be unconscious; but even that does not apparently prevent it from going mad.

The objection, therefore, which has troubled us so long may now finally be put aside. Methodologically an original fact is unimportant, because it is unknowable, and because no actual fact need be treated as original. The demand to know it, moreover, is invalid, and cannot be satisfied by any philosophy in any real way. "Original fact" is a metaphysical impostor. For it could be the explanation of nothing, not even of itself. And, lastly, we now perceive that the way to satisfy what is legitimate in the demand is not by conceiving an original fact, but by conceiving a final satisfaction.

§ 8. The only obstacle, therefore, which can still impede

6 Cp. Chapter 9, § 12; *Personal Idealism,* p. 109; *Riddles of the Sphinx,* ch. XII.

our progress on our projected excursion into metaphysics is that which arises from the native reluctance of the pragmatic method itself to sanction such adventures. But at this point we may bethink ourselves that this method itself is not final. We have conceived it from the first as included in, and derivative from, a larger method, which may show itself more obliging. Our Pragmatism, after all, was but an aspect of our Humanism.[7] And Humanism, though itself only a method, must surely be more genial. It cannot but look favourably on an attempt thoroughly to humanize the world and to unify the behaviour of its elements, by tracing the occurrence of something essentially analogous to the human making of reality throughout the universe. Nor will it severely repress us, when we try to answer any question of real human interest, on the ground of its metaphysical character.

For "metaphysics," it will say, "though adventures, and so hazardous, are not unbecoming or unmanly. There is not really much harm in them, provided that they are not made compulsory, that no one is compelled to advance into them farther than he likes, and that everyone perceives their real character and does not allow them to delude him. The worst that can happen to you is that you should find yourself unable to advance, or to reach the summit of your hopes. If so, you can always retire with safety, and be no worse off than if you had never attempted an enterprise too great for your powers. So, too, if you grow tired. What alone renders metaphysics offensive and dangerous are the preposterous pretensions sometimes made on their behalf. For, so far from being the most certain of the sciences (as is their proud aspiration), they are *de facto* the most tentative, just because they ought to be the most inclusive. Every new fact and advance in knowledge, and every new variation of personality, may upset a system of metaphysics. You must not, therefore, grow fanatical about your metaphysical affirmations, but hold them with a candid and constant willingness to revise them, and to evacuate your positions when they become untenable. And after all, you have always a safe fortress to retire upon if the worst should come to the worst. If the objective 'making of reality' should prove illusory, you can take refuge with the subjective making of

---

[7] Cp. *Humanism*, Preface, § 3.

reality which the pragmatic method has quite clearly established."

Thus encouraged, let us see how far a real making of reality can be predicated of our world.

§ 9. Dare we affirm, then, that our making of truth really alters reality, that mere knowing makes a difference, that things are changed by the mere fact of being known? Or rather, to elicit more precise responses, let us ask *in what cases* these things may be affirmed?

For we will see[8] that in some cases these assertions are plainly true, and refer only to facts which should have been noticed long ago, and which the pragmatic method has now firmly established. Thus (1) our making of truth really alters "subjective" reality. It first "makes" real objects of interest and inquiry by judicious *selection* from a larger whole. This purposive analysis of the given flux is the most indispensable condition of all knowing, and has been wholly overlooked. It is of necessity "arbitrary" and "risky," as being *selective.* (2) It so thoroughly humanizes all knowing that any "realities" we "find" to satisfy our interests and inquiries are subtly pervaded and constituted by relations to our (frequently unconscious) preferences. (3) Our knowledge, *when applied,* alters "real reality," and is not real knowledge, if it cannot be applied. Moreover, (4), in some cases, e.g., in human intercourse, a subjective making is at the same time a real making of reality. Human beings, that is, are really affected by the opinion of others. They behave differently, according as their behaviour is observed or not, as e.g., in "stage fright," or in "showing off." Even the mere thought that their behaviour may be known alters it. As we saw in § 5, the difference between "making" and "discovering" reality tends in their case to get shadowy.

Still, none of this has amounted to what we must now proceed to point out, viz., (5) *that mere knowing always alters reality, so far at least as one party to the transaction is concerned.* Knowing always really alters the knower; and as the knower is real and a part of reality, *reality is really altered.* Even, therefore, what we call a mere "discovery" of reality involves a *real change* in us, and a real enlightenment of our

8 Chapter 9, § 13.

ignorance. And inasmuch as this will probably induce a real difference in our subsequent behaviour, it entails a real alteration in the course of cosmic events, the extent of which may be considerable, whilst its importance may be enormous.

§ 10. But what about the other party to the cognitive transaction, the "object" known? Can that be conceived as altered by being known and so as "made" by the process?

Common sense, plainly, may demur to asserting this, at least in the ordinary sense of "knowing." Often the objects known do not seem to be visibly altered by mere knowing, and we then prefer to speak of them as "independent" facts, which our knowing merely "discovers." This is the simple source of the notion of the "independent reality" which the metaphysics of Absolutism and Realism agree in misinterpreting as an absence of dependence upon human experience. But we have already seen (§ 5) that the distinction between "making" and "discovering" is essentially pragmatic, and cannot be made absolute; we must now examine further, when, and under what conditions, it may be alleged.

Whether a reality is called "independent" of our knowing, and said to be merely "discovered" when it is known, or not, seems to depend essentially on whether it is *aware of being known;* or rather on how far, and in what ways, it is aware of being known.

Beings who are in close spiritual communion with us, and thoroughly aware of the meaning of our operations, show great sensitiveness to our becoming aware of them. When we cognize them, and recognize their reality, they react suitably and with a more or less complete comprehension of our action. Such awareness is shown, e.g., by our fellow men and by such animals as are developed enough to take note of us, and to have their actions disturbed and altered by our knowing, or even by the thought that we may have noticed them. It is amusing to note, for example, how a marmot will show his perturbation and whistle his shrill warning, long before the casual intruder on his Alpine solitudes has suspected his existence.

But how does this apply to the lowest animals and to inanimate things? They surely are quite indifferent to our knowledge of them? To them mere knowing makes no difference.

This case looks, plainly, different, and language is quite right to distinguish them. But before we deal with it we must elucidate the notion of "mere knowing." Mere knowing does not seem capable of altering reality, merely because it is an intellectualistic abstraction, which, strictly speaking, does not exist. In the pragmatic conception, however, knowing is a prelude to doing. What is called "mere knowing" is conceived as a fragment of a total process, which in its unmutilated integrity always ends in an action which tests its truth. Hence to establish the bearing on reality of the making of truth, we must not confine ourselves to this fragmentary "mere knowing," but must consider the whole process as completed, i.e., as issuing in action, and as sooner or later altering reality.

Now that this pragmatic conception of knowing is the one really operative, the one which really underlies our behaviour, is shown by the actions of beings who display sensitiveness to our observation. The actor who exhibits stage fright is not afraid of *mere* observation. He is afraid of being hissed, and perhaps of being pelted. And the marmot who whistles in alarm is not afraid of merely having his procedures noted down by a scientific observer; he is afraid of being killed. Neither the one nor the other would care about a *mere spectator* who really did nothing but observe. If such a being really existed, and Plato's intellectualistic ideal were realized, he would be the most negligible thing in the universe. But knowing is pragmatic, and "mere" knowing is a fable. And, *therefore,* it is terrible and potent to make and unmake reality. It was not for nothing that the gods kept Prometheus chained; it is not for nothing, though it is in vain, that Intellectualism tries to muzzle Pragmatism.

§ 11. For one being to take note of another and to show itself sensitive to that other's operations, it must be aware of that other as capable of affecting its activities (whether for good or for evil), and so, as potentially intrusive into its sphere of existence. Man is sensitive to man because man can affect the life of man in so many ways. Hence the variety of our social reactions and the wealth of our social relations. But consider the relations of man and the domestic animals. The range of mutual response is very much contracted. Newton's dog Diamond, though no doubt he loved his master, had no reverence for the discoverer of gravitation. He in return had no appreciation of the rapture of a rabbit hunt. The marmot, similarly, conceives man only as a source of danger. Hence the simplicity of his reaction, just a whistle and a scurry. Why then should we search for anything more recondite in order to account for the apparent absence of response to our operations when we come to deal with beings who are no longer capable of apprehending us as agents? This would merely mean that they were too alien to us and our interests to concern themselves about us. Their indifference would only prove that we could not interfere with anything they cared about, and so that they treated us as nonexistent. We, too, treat their feelings, if they have any, as nonexistent, because we cannot get at them, and they seem to make no difference in their behaviour.

But is this absence of response absolutely real? A stone, no doubt, does not apprehend us as spiritual beings, and to preach to it would be as fruitless (though not as dangerous) as preaching to deaf ears. But does this amount to saying that it does not apprehend us at all, and takes no note whatever of our existence? Not at all; it is aware of us and affected by us on the plane on which its own existence is passed, and quite capable of making us effectively aware of its existence in our transactions with it. The "common world" shared in by us and the stone is not, perhaps, on the level of ultimate reality. It is only a physical world of "bodies," and "awareness" in it can apparently be shown only by being hard and heavy and coloured and space-filling, and so forth. And all these things the stone is, and recognizes in other "bodies." It faithfully exercises all the physical functions, and influences us by so doing. It gravitates and resists pressure, and obstructs ether vibrations, etc., and makes itself respected as such a body. And it treats us as if of a like nature with itself, on the level of its understanding, i.e., as bodies to which it is attracted inversely as the square of the distance, moderately hard and capable of being hit. That we may also be *hurt* it does not know or care. But in the kind of cognitive operation which interests it, viz., that which issues in a physical manipulation of the stone, e.g., its use in house-building, it plays its part and responds according to the measure of its capacity. Similarly, if "atoms" and "electrons" are more than counters of physical calculation, they too know us, after their fashion. Not as human beings, of course, but as whirling mazes of atoms and electrons like themselves, which somehow preserve the same general pattern of their dance, influencing them and reciprocally influenced. And let it not be said that to operate upon a stone is not to *know* it. True, to throw a stone is not usually described as a cognitive operation. But it presupposes one. For to throw it, we must *know* that it is a stone we throw, and to some extent what sort of a stone it is. Throwing a pumice stone, e.g., requires a different muscular adjustment from throwing a lump of lead. Thus to use and to be used includes to know and to be known. That it should seem a paradox to insist on the knowledge involved even in the simplest manipulations of objects merely shows how narrow is the intellectualistic notion of knowledge into which we have fallen.

§ 12. "But is not this sheer hylozoism?" somebody will cry. What if it is, so long as it really brings out a genuine analogy? The notion that "matter" must be denounced as "dead" in order that "spirit" may live no longer commends itself to modern science. And it ought to commend itself as little to philosophy. For the analogy is helpful so long as it really renders the operations of things more comprehensible to us, and interprets facts which had seemed mysterious. We need not shrink from words like "hylozoism," or (better) "panpsychism," provided that they stand for interpretations of the lower in terms of the higher. For at bottom they are merely forms of Humanism—attempts, that is, to make the human and the cosmic more akin, and to bring them closer to us, that we may act upon them more successfully.

And there is something in such attempts. They can translate into the humanly intelligible facts which have long been known. For example, we have seen (§ 11) that in a very real sense a stone may be said to know us and to respond to our manipulation, nay, that this sense is truer than that which represents knowing as unrelated to doing. Again, there is a common phenomenon in chemistry called "catalytic action." It has seemed mysterious and hard to understand that although two bodies, A and B, may have a strong affinity for each other, they should yet refuse to combine until a mere trace of an "impurity," C, is introduced, and sets up an interaction between A and B, which yet leaves C unaltered. But is not this strangely suggestive of the idea that A and B did not know each other until they were introduced by C, and then liked each other so well that poor C was left out in the cold? More such analogies and possibilities will probably be found if they are looked for, and in any case we should remember that *all* our physical conceptions rest ultimately on human analogies suggested by our immediate experience.

It is hardly true, then, that inanimate "things" take no notice of our "knowing," and are unaltered by it. They respond to our cognitive operations on the level on which they apprehend them. That they do not respond more intelligently, and so are condemned by us as "inanimate," is due to their immense spiritual remoteness from us, or perhaps to our inability to understand them, and the clumsiness and lack of insight of our manipulations, which afford them no opportunity to display their spiritual nature.

§ 13. Even, however, on the purely physical plane on which our transactions with other bodies are conducted, there is response to our cognitive manipulation *which varies with our operation,* and therefore *there is real making of reality by us.*

Even physically, therefore, "facts" are not rigid and immutable. Indeed, they are never quite the same for any two experiments. The facts we accept and act on are continually transformed by our very action, and so the results of our efforts can slowly be embodied in the world we mould. The key to the puzzle is found in principle, once we abandon intellectualism and grasp the true function of knowledge. For the alien world which seemed so remote and so rigid to an inert contemplation, the reality which seemed so intractable to an aimless and fruitless speculation, grows plastic in this way to our intelligent manipulations.

§ 14. The extent of this plasticity it is, of course, most important for us to appreciate. Practically, for most people at most times, it falls far short of our wishes. Nay, we often feel that if reality is to be remade, it must first be unmade, that if we could only grasp the sorry scheme of things we should shatter it to bits before remoulding it nearer to the heart's desire. Still, this is not the normal attitude of man. There is usually an enormous mass of accepted fact which we do not desire to have remade, and which so has the sanction of our will. Other facts it has never occurred to us to desire to remake. In other cases, we do, indeed, regard an alteration as desirable in the abstract, but for some reason or other, perhaps merely because we are too lazy, or too faintly interested, or too much engrossed by more pressing needs, we do not actually attempt to effect an alteration. The amount of "fact," therefore, which it is ordinarily felt to be imperatively necessary to alter is comparatively small, and this is why most people find (or "make"?) life tolerable.

But whatever our actual desire and power to alter our experience, it is an obvious methodological principle that we must regard the plasticity of fact as adequate for every purpose, i.e., as sufficient for the attainment of the harmonious experience to which we should ascribe ultimate reality. For (a) if we do not assume it, we may by that very act, and by that act alone, as William James has so eloquently shown, shut ourselves out from countless goods which faith in their possibility might realize. (b) Some facts, at least, are plastic, and others look plastic, at least to common sense. And even though some "facts" do not look as if they would speedily yield to human treatment, there is (c) no reason in this for abandoning our methodological principle of complete plasticity. For a *partial* plasticity would be nugatory and unworkable. If we had assumed it, it might always be declared to be inapplicable to the case to which it was applied. And conversely, even if we could somehow know, nonempirically and a priori, that on *some* points the world was quite inflexible, we could not use this knowledge, because we should not know *what* these points were. Nor should we be entitled to infer that we had found them out, even from our failures. For a failure, if it does not discourage us, warrants nothing but the inference that we cannot get what we want in just the way we tried. Hence for the purposes of any particular experiment it would still be necessary to assume that the world was plastic. Whatever "theoretic" views, therefore, we may privately cherish as to the unalterable rigidity of facts, we must *act as if* "fact" were as flexible as ever is needed, if we would act effectively. And as the principle is methodological, it would *not* affect or undermine the *stability* of fact, wherever *that* was needed for our action.

§ 15. Our position, then, as genuine makers of reality seems to be pretty well established. We do not make reality out of nothing, of course, i.e., we are not "creators," and our powers are limited. But as yet we are only beginning to realize them, and hardly know their full extent; we are only beginning cautiously to try to remake reality, and so far (with the exception of some improvement in domesticated plants and animals) our activities have been mainly destructive; in every direction, however, there seems to extend a wide field of experiments which might be tried with a fair prospect of success. Nor do we yet know the full extent of the *cooperation* which our aims might find, or obtain, from other agents in the universe.

For it seems clear that we are *not* the *sole* agents in the world, and that herein lies the best explanation of those aspects of the world which we, the present agents, i.e, our empirical selves, cannot claim to have made. There is no reason to conceive these features as original and rigid. Why should we not conceive them as having been made by processes analogous to those whereby we ourselves make reality and watch its making? For, as we have seen, all the agents in the universe are in continuous interaction, adjusting and readjusting themselves according to the influences brought to bear upon them. The precise nature of these influences varies according to the character and capacity which the various agents have acquired. There is no need to assume *any* character to be original. All the "laws of nature," in so far as they are really objective and not merely conveniences of calculation, may be regarded as the habits of things, and these habits as behaviours which have grown determinate, and more or less stable, by persistent action, but as still capable of further determinations under the proper manipulation.[9]

And lest we should be thought to limit our outlook too narrowly to the agents which our science at present consents to recognize, it ought also definitely to be realized that among the agencies which we have not yet found, because we have not yet looked, or looked only in a halfhearted and distrustful

[9] Chapter 4, § 11. *Formal Logic*, ch. XXI, §§ 9–10.

manner, there may be a being (or perhaps more than one) so vastly more potent than ourselves that his part in the shaping of reality may have been so preponderant as almost to warrant our hailing him as a "creator." And again, it is possible that our own careers, and so our own agency, may extend much farther back into the past than now we are aware.

But these suggestions will seem wild to many, and need not be emphasized or enlarged on. They do not affect the conceivability of the making of reality, nor the conceptual unity of a cosmic process in which there may always be distinguished an aspect of what may be called "cognition," and another of "action," but in which the thought should be conceived as subsidiary, as included, tested and completed by the act.

§ 16. What may, however, more plausibly be thought to affect the conception of the making of reality are two closely connected metaphysical assumptions which we have implied throughout. They may be called (1) the reality of freedom or the determinable indetermination of reality, and (2) the incompleteness of reality. Both of these conceptions we discovered, and to some extent justified, towards the end of the last essay (§§ 10–12). But it may not be amiss to add a few words in justification and confirmation of our choice.

It is evident, in the first place, that if *we* have no freedom, and cannot choose between alternative manipulations and reactions, we are not *agents*, and, therefore, cannot "make reality." Freedom, therefore, is a postulate of the humanist making of reality. Strictly speaking, however, *human* freedom would suffice to validate the notion. For if we can operate alternatively, we can initiate alternative courses of reality.

But there are no stringent reasons for confining freedom, and the plastic indetermination of habit on which it rests, to man alone.[10] It may well be a feature which really pervades the universe. All beings in the world may be essentially determinable, but still partly indeterminate, in their habits and actions. That such is the nature of the universe may indeed be argued from the fact that it responds variously to various modes of handling. And once it is admitted to be partly undetermined, it is not a question of principle how far the inde-

10 Cp. Chapter 4, § 9.

termination goes. Many or all of the other agents beside ourselves may be capable of more or less varying their responses to stimulation, of acquiring and modifying their habits. Thus the whole universe will appear to us as literally the creature of habit, but not its slave. And the more of this "freedom" we can attribute to the universe, the more plastic to good purposes we may expect to find it. For we shall expect to find habit more rigid where intelligence is lacking to suggest readjustment and amendment, more plastic where there is more striving towards a better state; and yet, on the other hand, more stable where there is less impediment to perfect functioning; but everywhere, let us hope, latently plastic enough to render the notion of a perfect, and therefore universal, harmony that of an attainable ideal.

§ 17. If there is freedom in the world, and reality is really being made, it is clear that reality is not fixed and finished, but that the world process is real and is still proceeding. And so we come once more upon the metaphysical objection to the growing, incomplete reality which seems to be demanded by a philosophy of evolution. We have already challenged or defied this prejudice,[11] and may this time try to vanquish it by explaining how it comes about.

This objection springs, we may frankly admit, from a sound methodological principle which has great pragmatic value. When we can allege no reason why a thing should change, we may assume that it remains the same. Applying this maxim to the *quantum* of existence, we conclude that *the amount of being is constant.* Applying it to the *totality* of existence, we conclude that *the universe as a whole cannot change* in any real way, but must be complete and rigid.

These two applications, however, are neither on the same footing nor of equal value. The first yields the sound working assumptions of the indestructibility of "matter" and the conservation of "energy," which are of the utmost pragmatic value in physics. They are, in the first place, the easiest assumptions to work with. For it is far easier to make calculations with constant factors than with variable. They are, in the second place, applicable; for although these principles, like all postulates, are not susceptible of complete experimental proof,

11 Cp. Chapter 4, § 12.

experience does not confute them by discrepancies so great or so inexplicable as seriously to impair their usefulness.[12] In the third place, they are applied only to those abstract aspects of physics which have shown themselves amenable to quantitative treatment, and in regard to which, therefore, such treatment seems valid. The scientific use, therefore, of the principle of constancy is pragmatically justified by the peculiar nature of the subject matter to which it is applied.

But can as much be claimed for its metaphysical double? It is not self-evident that the quantitative aspect of reality is of paramount authority. It is not easy to apply the quantitative notion to the spiritual aspects of existence. It is very difficult to conceive a "conservation" of spiritual values. It is still more difficult to obtain empirical confirmation of this notion. It is almost absurd to deny the reality of our continual experience of change, out of deference to a metaphysical postulate. And, lastly, every human motive urges us to deny the completeness of reality.

For, humanly speaking, this atrocious dogma reduces us and our whole experience to illusion. If we think out its demands, we must concede that nothing is really happening; there is no world process, no history, no time; motion and change are impossible; all our struggles and strivings are vain. They can accomplish nothing, because everything that truly *is* is *already* accomplished. The sum total of reality has been reckoned up, and there is lacking not a single cipher. So all our hopes and our fears, our aspirations and our desperations, *do not count.* For we ourselves are illusions, we, and all our acts and thoughts and troubles—all, save only, I suppose, the thought of the rigid, timeless, motionless, changeless One, which we have weakly postulated to redeem our experience, and which rewards us and resolves our problems by annihilating us! It is a pity only that it does not make a clean job of its deadly work, that it does not *wholly* absorb us in its all-embracing unity. For, after all, ought it not to annihilate the illusion as well as its claim to reality? If we, and the time

[12] Of course, however, it should be remembered that the leakage of energy, which takes place *de facto* in its transformations, is only *theoretically* stopped by the notion of its "degradation" or "dissipation." Moreover, to conceive the universe as "infinite" is really to render the postulate of conservation inapplicable to it. For by what test can it be known whether an infinite quantity of matter or energy is, or is not, "conserved"?

process, and the making of reality, are all fundamentally unreal, we ought not to be able to seem real even to ourselves.
And still less should we be able to devise such blasphemous
objections against the One! Somehow, not even the One knows
how, the "illusion" falls outside the "reality"![13]

And for us, at all events, it *is* reality. For us reality is really
incomplete; and that it is so is our fondest hope. For what
this means is that reality can still be remade, *and made perfect!*

It is this genuine possibility—no assured promise, it is true,
nor a prophecy of smooth things, but still less a proffer of
false coin—which our humanist metaphysic secures to us. It
does not profess to know how the making of reality will end.
For in a world which contains real efforts, real choices, real
conflicts, and real evils, to the extent our world appears to do,
there must be grounds for a real doubt about the issue. We
hardly know as yet how the battle of the Giants and the Gods
is going; we hardly know under what leader, and with what
strategy, we are contending; we do not even know that we
shall not be sacrificed to win the day. But is this a reason for
refusing to carry on the fight, or for denying that Truth is
great and must prevail, because it has the making of Reality?

[13] Monism always ends thus. It begins by professing to include everything,
but ends by excluding everything. It can make nothing of any part of human
experience. Change, time, becoming, imperfection, plurality, personality, all turn
out to be for it surds incompatible with the One; but in reducing them to nought
it disembowels itself of its whole content, and reduces itself to nothing. The
logical source of the paradox that in metaphysics $1 = 0$ is that all significant
predication proceeds by *analysing* a given, and that so any "real" it extracts is
always a selection, and never the whole. A "One," therefore, which is not
thus contrasted with an "other" cannot be thought as real.

PART TWO

Truth and Meaning in Logic and Psychology

Editor's Introduction

THE ASPECT of Pragmatism most susceptible to ridicule is its definition of truth. Thus Russell once wrote:[1]

> Dr. Schiller is fond of attacking the view that truth must correspond with reality; we may conciliate him by agreeing that *his* truth, at any rate, need not correspond with reality. But we shall have to add that reality is to us more interesting than such truth.

MANY THEORIES of truth have been propounded through the centuries; none has been entirely satisfactory. Schiller points out the shortcomings of some of them, particularly the correspondence theory and the coherence theory. The pragmatists believe that no statement wears its truth or falsity like a badge; on the contrary, that can only be determined by what follows from it in the course of experience. Thus "truth" is only a potential. It is a valuation applied as the result of a procedure called "verifying": making true.

James thus expressed it: "The true is the name of whatever proves itself to be good in the way of belief."[2] Schiller declared that the true is the useful. He did *not* say that the useful is the true. Methodological fictions, for example, and fairy tales, are useful; but there is no really useless knowledge. Truth is a matter of degree. In his *Logic For Use*, he mapped out the entire area of "truth claim," ranging from axioms at one end to jokes and lies at the other.

But "useful" is undeniably a vague term. G. E. Moore

---

1 "Transatlantic Truth," *Albany Review*, II (1908), p. 404.
2 *Pragmatism* (New York, 1907), p. 76.

asked[3] whether it meant "having good results" or "causing the race . . . to survive." And Peirce caustically inquired,[4]

> Schiller informs us that he and James have made up their minds that the true is simply the satisfactory. No doubt; but to say "satisfactory" is not to complete any predicate whatever. Satisfactory to what end?

Dewey, however, wrote[5] to James,

> Schiller in his later writings seems to emphasize that the good consequence which is the test of an idea, is *good* not so much in its own nature as in meeting the claims of the idea, whatever the idea is. And here I seem to be nearer him than you.

Since the true is what is true for us as seekers for it, Schiller deplores the divorce of the study of our thinking procedures (psychology) from our evaluating procedures (logic). Any such depersonalization of logic, he says, would be a vicious abstraction. Logic for him should be systematic reflection on actual knowing, a study continuous with the sciences.

It is here perhaps that Schiller faces his greatest opposition. For psychology is now generally regarded as an empirical science which studies the act of thinking, whereas logic is a formal analysis of the result of thought. The precise relation between logic and the sciences is a problem. Why, for example, does the scientist habitually but harmlessly fall into the formal fallacy of "affirming the consequent"? And it is true that there exist psychological components in determining what we shall take for granted in logic, and how we shall proceed therefrom. The concept of "rigor" in mathematics is being steadily revised. At certain critical points, the logician steps outside his realm of pure forms (e.g., the "self-evidence" of the syllogism, or the "necessity" of implication, or the "intuitive apprehension" of what constitutes system or order). But basically logic is a normative activity, and psychology is a

3 "Philosophy of the United Kingdom for 1902," *Archiv für Systematische Philosophie*, X (1904), p. 259.
4 *Collected Papers*, V, par. 552.
5 Quoted in Perry, *Thought and Character of William James*, II, pp. 528–29.

descriptive activity; and Schiller, in scumbling the line between them, did not clarify it. Morris Cohen wrote:[6]

> To me the greatest absurdity of all is the fundamental premise which Mr. Schiller shares with thinkers as diverse as Mill and (at times) Bradley, viz. that logic should be a description of the way we actually think.

Schiller regarded ideas or concepts as instruments of human knowledge, revealing or acquiring their meaning only as they are used. This insight anticipates the demand of the logical empiricists that possible human experience be the criterion of meaningfulness. It is also on this topic that Schiller releases some of his most memorable thunder:[7]

> Wherever there is hypostasisation and idolatry of concepts, and wherever these interpose between the mind and things, wherever they lead to disparagement of immediate experience, wherever the stubborn rigidity of prejudice refuses to adapt itself to the changes of reality, wherever the delusive answers of an *a priori* dialectic leave unanswered questions of inductive research, wherever words lure and delude, stupefy and paralyse, there Truth is sacrificed to Plato.

[6] *Reason and Nature* (New York, 1931), p. 11.
[7] "From Plato to Protagoras," *Studies in Humanism*, p. 43.

Chapter 6

Truth

Argument

Importance of the question *What is truth?* when not asked rhetorically.

I. Answers logical. (1) *Truth as agreement with reality.* Breaks down over the question of the knowledge of this agreement. (2) *Truth as systematic coherence.* Open to objections on the ground (*a*) that not all systems are true; (*b*) no system is true; (*c*) *many* systems are true; (*d*) truth, even if system, is more than system. (1) How about systematic falsehood? (2) How about the imperfection of all actual systems? (3) How about the possibility of alternative systems? (4) How about systems not accepted as true because distasteful, and agreeable truth accepted without being systematic? Is this last argument an invalid appeal to psychology? No, for there is no "pure" thought, and without psychological interest, etc., thought could neither progress nor be described. The psychological side of "system" and "coherence." The necessity of immediate apprehension. Coherence feelings. The infinite regress in inference, if its immediacy be denied. Nonlogical "coherence." Interest as the cement of coherence.

II. Answers psychological. Question as to (1) the psychical nature of the recognition of truth; (2) the objects to which this recognition is referred. Truth as a form of value. Valuation at first random and individual. The ultimateness of the truth valuation. Meaning of "simple" and "complex" for a pragmatist psychology. Truth valuation "simple" for logic.

III. Objectivity of truth. "Truth" and "fact"; "formal" as a means to "material" truth. Subjective truth valuations gradually organized (1) into subordination to individual, (2) into conformity with social ends.

Usefulness as the principle of selection and criterion of truth. Need for the social recognition of truth. Special cases explained.

OF ALL philosophic questions, that of truth is perhaps the most hackneyed and unanswerable, when treated in the usual fashion. Now the usual fashion is to indulge either in ecstatic rhapsodies about the sacredness of truth or in satirical derision of pretensions to have actually attained it. Both these procedures are assured beforehand of popular applause, but both render the question *What is truth?* one thoroughly rhetorical, and so perhaps the one is the proper answer to the other, and "jesting Pilate" has a right to smile at the enthusiast. Nor have the philosophers done much to improve the situation. Ever since one of the noblest of Plato's "noble lies" proclaimed the doctrine that philosophers are lovers of truth, they have been quite willing to believe this, and have often found a people willing to be deceived politely willing to admit it. But perhaps because their passion, even when most genuine, was too distantly "platonic," this philosophic love of truth has hardly influenced perceptibly the course of things, and it might remain in doubt whether the pragmatist philosopher also would care and dare to obtain some more substantial token of Truth's favours, were it not that the cheapest condemnation of his enterprise is to accuse him of a malicious joy in the destruction of Truth's very notion. It becomes incumbent on him therefore to refute such slanders, and to make clear how exactly he proposes to approach, and in what sense to derive, the notion of truth.

This essay, therefore, must examine: I. the chief current definitions of truth, which lay claim to logical validity, and to show that they are neither tenable, nor even intelligible, without reference to its psychological character; II. to describe that psychological character; and III. to explain how Pragmatism extends and alters the traditional conceptions on the subject.

I

Under the head of unpsychological, logical, or "metaphysical" definitions may be instanced (1) the well-known dictum that truth consists in an "agreement" or "correspondence" of thought with its object, viz., reality. This, however, speedily leads to a hopeless impasse, once the question is raised: How are we to *know* whether or not our "truth" "corresponds" or "agrees" with its real object? For to decide this question must we not be able to compare "thought" and "reality," and to contemplate each as it is apart from the other? This, however, seems impossible. "Thought" and "reality" cannot be got apart, and consequently the doctrine of their "correspondence" has in the end no meaning. We are not aware of any reality except by its representation in our "thought," and per contra, the whole meaning of "thought" resides ultimately in its reference to "reality." Again, even if it were assumed that somehow the independent reality mirrored itself in our thought, how should we discover whether or not this image was "true," i.e., agreed with the inaccessible reality it claimed to represent? This whole theory of truth therefore would seem futile. Having started from the radically untrue and unworkable assumption that "truth" and "fact," "thought" and "reality," are two things which have to be brought into relation, it is inevitably driven to the admission that no such relation can validly be established.

(2) A second logical definition looks at first more promising. It conceives truth as essentially systematic coherence, the "true" being that which "fits" into a "system," the "false" that which is discrepant with it. This has the immense advantage of not creating the chasm between "truth" and "reality" in which the former definition was engulfed. Both these conceptions remain immanent in the process of knowledge, which is the construction of a system of "reality" known to be "true" by the coherence of its parts.

This account undoubtedly brings out important features in the nature of truth, but as it stands, it is so incomplete and misleading that we can hardly follow the fashionable logic of the day in accepting it as all we can reasonably want to know about truth. In fact, when we discount the air of mystery, the obscure phraseology, and the pompous magniloquence with which this doctrine is propounded, we shall find that all it comes to is that consistency is a mark of truth, and that when we find that we can maintain our conceptual interpretations of our experiences, we come to treat them as realities. But to take the pronouncement that *truth is what fits in a system* as therefore final would be ludicrously rash, and to detect the limitations of the formula, it suffices to consider what may be said in favour of a string of counterpropositions, such as, e.g., (*a*) that not all systems are true, (*b*) that no system is true, (*c*) that *many* systems are true, and (*d*) that even if all truth be systematic, it is not thereby adequately defined.

(1) To define truth as systematic is at once to raise the question of systematic falsehood. For false assumptions also manifestly tend to complete themselves in a system of inferences, to cohere together, to assimilate fresh facts, and to interpret them into conformity with themselves; in short, to assume all the logical features that are claimed for "truth." Does it not follow, therefore, that something more than systematic coherence is needed to determine truth? As *not all systems are true*, must we not suggest a further criterion to distinguish true from false?

The reply to this objection would have to take the form largely of an acceptance thereof. It would have to be admitted that in proportion as a falsehood or a lie became more systematic, its prospects of being accepted as true grew greater, that coherent lies did often win acceptance, and that a perfectly coherent lie (or error) would be tantamount to absolute truth. Lies can be called false only when they have been found out, and they are found out just because sooner or later they do not fit into our system of "truth." These systematic falsehoods are never quite systematic enough, and so the mimicry of truth by false systems, so far from subverting, rather confirms the doctrine that truth is systematic.

(2) This defence paves the way for a new assault. It would be adequate if we really had an indefeasible system of absolute truth by whose aid we might detect the inconsistencies of the pseudosystems. But where shall we find such truth? The bodies of "truth" which *de facto* we acknowledge in our sciences are all partial systems, incomplete in themselves and discrepant with each other. If nothing short of absolute truth is perfectly systematic, and if all our systems are imperfect, is not all our

"truth" tainted with falsehood, and must it not be admitted that *no* (actual) *"systems"* are *"true"*? To talk of the mimicry of true by false systems is misleading; we should remember that in addition to the protective mimicry of Bates, there exists another form ("Müllerian") in which the mimics cooperate to advertize the undesirable character they have in common. And so our systems may all be mimicking each other and may *all* be false.

Again, I think, the contention must in substance be admitted. The actual systems of our sciences are continually being convicted of error, and cannot seriously sustain their claim to the deference due only to the perfect system. Still, in extenuation one might urge (*a*) that ignorance is not necessarily error, nor incompleteness falsehood; (*b*) that experience would seem to show that even when coherent systems of interpretation have to be recast, what occurs is a transformation rather than a revolution, reinterpreting rather than destroying the "truths" of the older order. Though, therefore, our "systems" may not be wholly "true," we may conceive them as progressively approximating to the truth. And so (*c*) we must conceive them as in the end converging in one absolute and all-embracing system which alone would be strictly and indubitably "true."

(3) This last defence, however, still contains a hazardous assumption. Is the ideal of a complete system absolutely true really the straightforward, unambiguous notion which it seems? Are we entitled to argue from the unity of a concept to a similar unity of the concrete ways of exemplifying that concept, and so to assume that there is *one* system *and no more*, into which all truth must finally be fitted? The assumption is a seductive one, and underlies all monistic argument. But still it is an assumption, and begs some very puzzling questions. It assumes the absolute determination of the universe, and it is only on this assumption that the inference is cogent, that "truth" and "reality" can only be completely construed in one single way. If we doubt, or deny, or demand proof of this assumption, it may well be that *many* alternative systems may be "true," that "reality" can be constructed in various ways by our varying efforts. The poet may have exaggerated in suggesting

> There are nine-and-sixty ways
> Of composing tribal lays,
> And every single one of them is right;

but still, the more sincerely and completely we recognize the presence of human activity in the construction of "truth" and "reality," the more clearly is their contingence suggested, and the less plausible does it seem that all these apparently arbitrary procedures are foredoomed to issue in the unveiling of one single, inevitable, and pre-existing "system." And if we doubt the legitimacy of this assumption, it follows at once that we cannot decide the measure of truth possessed by our actual bodies of knowledge by the mere test of systematic coherence. System A may need reinterpretation into A' to fit in with system B in the final system X; but we might as well or better reinterpret B into B', so that it would fit with A into the final system Y. In such a case are we to consider A + B' or A' + B as ultimately true?

In short, our logic as well as our metaphysic will have to concern itself more scrupulously and less perfunctorily with pluralistic possibilities.

(4) The last objection has brought out the fact that in assuming truth to be univocally determined by the conception of a "system," we went too far, and uncritically settled an important issue; we have now to face a criticism urging that the conception of a system in another direction does not go far enough to determine the nature of "truth." To win from us recognition as "truth," it is not enough to have a number of coherent judgments connected in a system. The "system" to be true must also have *value* in our eyes; the demand for "system" is but part of a larger demand for a "harmony" (actual or at least ideal) in our experience; it is not merely a matter of formal logical consistency, but also of emotional satisfaction. Hence no system is judged intellectually "true" unless it is also a good deal more than this, and embraces and satisfies other than the abstractly intellectual aspects of experience. Thus no completely pessimistic system is ever judged completely "true"; because it leaves unremoved and unresolved a sense of final discord in existence, it must ever stimulate anew to fresh efforts to overcome the discrepancy.

And conversely, it is by no means rare that what impresses us as conducive to harmony should be declared "true" with little or no inquiry into its systematic coherence; indeed, it is probably such perception of their aesthetic self-evidence that often accounts for the adoption of the "axiomatic" postulates that form first principles for knowledge.[1]

Thus the notion of "system" proves doubly insufficient to define "truth." There is "system" which is not valued as "true," and there is "truth" which is so valuable that it need not be "system." We need "system" only as a means to the higher notion of "harmony," and where we can get the latter without the former, we can readily dispense with it.

The bulk, however, of logicians would in all probability strenuously object to this last argument. They would protest against the contamination of the question of "truth" with questions of "harmony" and "valuation." To refer to these is to overpass the bounds of logic, it is to trespass on the lower ground of psychology in which thought soon gets bogged in the reedy marshes of psychical fact. No good can come of such an intermixture of psychology with logic; our criterion of truth must be logical, our thought "pure." To talk of desire, interest, and feeling in a logical context is sheer madness, and to require logical theory to take account of their existence is to require it to adjust itself to the alogical.

If the defence of logical conventions is imprudent enough to take this ground, it can meet with nothing but disaster. For we shall at once have to defy the logician (a) to produce his "pure" thought; (b) to account for the *movement* of thought by anything but an appeal to psychological motives, desire, feeling, interest, attention, will, etc.; (c) even to describe what he conceives to happen in strictly logical terms and without constant recourse to psychology.

The first two of these points will probably be conceded by all except belated Hegelians, but the third may need some illustration, the more so as we may draw from it also an independent (fifth) reason for denying the adequacy of the conception of truth as a system. I may point out therefore (5) that the ultimate terms of this (as of every other) definition of truth are primarily psychological. If we take it that

1 Cp. *Axioms as Postulates*, § 48.

a "system" means a body of coherent judgments, it needs but a little reflection to see that the logical evaluation of the "system" presupposes its psychical existence, and the previous discussion of a number of psychological questions. (1) How, e.g., is the system recognized? (2) What is the nature, and what (3) the cause of its "coherence"?

As to (1) it must surely be admitted that the logical system, to be a system for us, must be apprehended as such by us. Before, that is, an alleged "truth" can be subjected to logical reflection, it has to be actually judged "true"; its truth has to be *felt* before it is *understood*. Even, therefore, if logic could find and reserve for itself among our conscious processes such a thing as a process of "pure" thought, a distinct mental act would yet be necessary for its apprehension, and this act would be psychological. In other words, no truth actually occurs without, in the first place, a psychic process; hence every truth as such is conditioned by a variety of psychological influences of the kind just mentioned.

The attempt, therefore, to represent "thought" and a fortiori "truth" as wholly an affair of mediation between self-subsistent relations fails; at every step in its progress the mediate inference has to be immediately recognized, and the mediate "knowledge about" rests upon and returns into an immediate "acquaintance-with."[2] If, therefore, we call them respectively "thought" and "feeling," we shall have to say that an "element" of "feeling" is bound up with and accompanies every act of "thought," and that no actual thought either is or can be conceived as "pure." Moreover, the *movement* of thought would have in any case to be pronounced psychological. For the *selection* of the points in the self-subsistent system, between which the thought mediated, could not be ascribed to the intrinsic nature of the system, but only to the human interest which effects the selection.

Now if such be the state of the case, why on earth should it not be recognized in logic? Logic, I presume, in the very act of constituting norms for thought, presupposes the facts of thought, and if all actual thinking, good, bad, or indifferent, is impelled by interest, then interest *ipso facto* must become a factor in the logical analysis of thought. Why, then, should

2 James, *Principles of Psychology*, I, 221.

we insist on tortuous and complicated misdescriptions in terms of "pure thought" of processes which are quite simple and intelligible when we consent to regard their full psychic nature?[3]

(2) *Mutatis mutandis*, what has been said of the logical system applies also to its "coherence." The coherence of judgments is a psychical fact which justifies, nay demands, psychological treatment. We find accordingly that it is (*a*) a matter of immediate apprehension. However we refine upon the logical concept of coherence, we can do nothing without observing that *de facto* judgments stick together. (*b*) We observe also certain coherence "feelings," whose strength is best measured by that of the feeling of (logical) necessity[4] which supervenes when we try to part the "coherent" judgments. Truths "cohere" when they afford us the peculiar satisfaction of feeling that they "belong together," and that it is "impossible" to separate them.[5]

And (*c*) if the cohesion of our thoughts, the belonging together, e.g., of A — B, were not immediately felt, but had to be established by mediate reasoning, it would follow that for any two truths to cohere a reason would have to be alleged why they should do so. But this would have to be another truth, and the attempt to "understand" the immediate psychical cohesion would have to be renewed upon this, until it became obvious that an infinite process was implicit in the simplest inference.[6] Is it not much more reasonable to suppose that the cohesiveness is a psychical feature of the thinking itself? Finally (*d*) it would seem that not every sort of co-

---

[3] All the squabbles about the "activity" or "movement" of thought are due to perversities of this sort. Abstract thought is not active, or even alive; it does not exist. What is active is the thinking being with a certain psychical idiosyncrasy in consequence whereof he pursues his ends by various means, among which thinking is one. The nature of his thought everywhere refers to the purpose of his thinking.

[4] See *Personal Idealism*, p. 70 *n.*

[5] It is never strictly impossible to reject a "truth," only in some cases the cost is excessive. To accept, e.g., a formal contradiction stultifies the assumption that definite meanings exist, and should consequently debar us from the further use of thinking. This is too much, and as we have an alternative, we usually prefer to reconsider the thought that has ended in a contradiction. Moreover, if we desire to entertain contradictory beliefs, there is a much easier way; we have merely to refuse to think them together. This indeed is what the great majority of men have always done.

[6] For an amusing illustration of this existence of an immediate apprehension in all mediate cogency see "Lewis Carroll's" dialogue between Achilles and the Tortoise in *Mind*, N.S. No. 14, p. 278.

herence in thought was regarded as logically important. The sort of coherences, e.g., which proceed from associations and lead to puns and plays upon words are relegated to that undignified limbo in which "fallacies" are huddled together. But if not all coherence is logical, then the logician plainly needs a preliminary psychology to distinguish for him the kind of coherence which is his concern.

(3) If logic is to make the attempt to exclude psychology, the real cause of logical coherence must be pronounced to be extralogical. For it is nothing that can plausibly be represented[7] as inherent in the nature of thought *qua* thought, i.e., of thought as logicians abstractly conceive it. The cause of logical coherence may be summed up in the one word *interest,* and "thought" which is not set in motion by interest does not issue in thinking at all. If, therefore, interest is to be tabooed, the whole theory of thought becomes a mere mass of useless machinery. For it is interest which starts, propels, sustains, and guides the "movement" of our thought. It effects the necessary *selection* among the objects of our attention, accepting what is consonant, and rejecting what is discrepant, with our aim in thinking. If, then, the *purposiveness* of our thought is its central feature, psychologically, how can a logic set it aside without the grossest travesty? How fundamental is the fact of purposive interest in mental life is apparent from the cases where the normal control of consciousness is weakened or suspended. In sleepiness, reverie, dream, delirium, madness, etc., the purposive guidance of our thought grows lax—with the result that anarchy speedily overtakes the soul. Thoughts "cross" the mind in the most "illogical" way, and though our mental images may still continue to mimic meaning, they have ceased to mean anything coherent, and *pro tanto* logical thinking ceases to exist.

Thus in trying to understand the doctrine that truth is system we have been driven to the conclusion that in psychology, if anywhere, the clue to the mystery of truth must lie. For not only the definitions we have examined, but all others of

[7] I am willing to suppose it just possible to translate all the features of our thinking into a completely and consistently intellectualist phraseology. Philosophers have made endless attempts to do so, but none have succeeded, though it is I suppose a merit of Hegel's to have tried more elaborately, and to have failed more obscurely, than the rest. But the philosophers' insistence on reducing everything to pure thought is merely one of their professional prejudices.

the sort, must presuppose a psychological treatment of the psychical facts.[8]

II

Let us turn, therefore, to psychology. And to begin with let us formulate our psychological questions more precisely, as (1) *what is the psychical nature of the "recognition" of "truth"?* and (2) *to what part of our experiences is this recognition attached?*

To the first question the summary answer would appear to be that *Truth is a form of value,* and for this reason related to, and largely interchangeable with, our other modes of valuation. Now such evaluation of our experience is a natural, and in the normal consciousness an almost uninterrupted, process. We are forever judging things as "true" and "false," "good" and "bad," "beautiful" and "ugly," "pleasant" and "unpleasant." So continuous is this habit that existence without "appreciation," "fact" without "value," is rather a figment of abstraction than a possible psychical experience. Now it is the *de facto* existence of this habit of valuation that gives rise to the normative sciences, and the function of logic as a normative science is to regulate and systematize our spontaneous valuations of "true" and "false." For of course these logical valuations also will need regulation. At first they are bestowed by individuals pretty much at random. Anything may commend itself to anybody as "true," nay, even as *the* truth,[9] and there are no guarantees that any man's valuations will be consistent with any other man's, or even with his own at other times. It is only as the needs of social intercourse and of consistent living grow more urgent that *de facto* "truth" grows systematic and "objective," i.e., that there come to be truths which are (roughly) "the same for all." And finally, when most of the hard work has actually been done, the logician arises and "reflects" on the genesis of "truth," which, in the end, he mostly misrepresents.

It is fairly plain, therefore, that the psychical fact of the

---

8 The definition, e.g., that *truth is what we are forced to believe* obviously implies psychological presuppositions as to the nature of "belief" and "necessity." Other inadequate formulas are discussed in *Riddles of the Sphinx* (new ed.), pp. 83–9.

9 Cp. the inexhaustible variety of the "systems" of religion and philosophy.

existence of truth valuation must be the starting point for the psychological account of truth. Whether it should be called the foundation of the whole structure, or whether it should not be likened to the intrinsic nature of the bricks of which the structure is built up, seems to be a matter of the choice of metaphors. At any rate, without this valuation there would be no "truth" at all.

Of course, however, further psychological questions may be raised about it. We may ask, for instance, whether the fact that we judge things true and false is psychologically simple and ultimate, or whether we could not analyse out a common element of value from our various valuations. The answer to such questions might grow long and somewhat intricate, but we are hardly bound to go into them very deeply. It will suffice to point out that the "simple" in psychology can only mean *what it is no use to analyse further.*[10] In other words, the distinction of "simple" and "complex" is always relative to the purpose of the inquiry. The "elements" out of which the "complex" states of mind are put together do not exist as psychic facts. In the actual experiencing, most states of consciousness form peculiar and recognizable wholes of experience, which feel "simple." Thus the taste of lemonade is emphatically *not* the taste of sugar plus the taste of lemon; though of course it is by squeezing the lemon and dissolving the sugar that we compose the lemonade and procure ourselves the taste. The experiences which really are "complex" to feeling are comparatively rare, as e.g., when we feel the struggle of incompatible desires. On the other hand, when we reflect upon our experience, it is easy enough to represent it all as "complex," and to break it up into factors, which, we say, were present unobserved in the experience. But the justification of this procedure is that it enables us *to control the original experience,* and the factors which the "analysis" arrives at are whatever aids this purpose. It is in no wise incumbent on us to go on making distinctions for their own sake and from inconsistent points of view, without aim and without end. Indeed, the practice of aimless analysis, though it seems to form the chief

10 I owe this definition to Prof. A. W. Moore's excellent account of the functional theory of knowledge in Locke in the *Chicago University Contributions to Philosophy,* III, 23.

delight of some philosophers, must be pronounced to be as such trivial, irrelevant, and invalid. We have a right, therefore, to declare "simple" and ultimate what it is useless to treat as "complex" for the purpose in hand, and in this instance we shall do well to avail ourselves of this right. For an analysis of the valuation "true" and "false," whether or not it is possible for other purposes, would hardly be germane to logic.

III

We are, however, still sufficiently remote from what is ordinarily meant by "truth." For truth is conceived as something "objective" and "coherent," while the truth valuations we have recognized are individual claims, and so far seem chaotic. We may have found, indeed, the bricks out of which the temple of Truth is to be built, but as yet we have but a heap of bricks and nothing like a temple. Before, moreover, we can venture to erect the actual structure of objective Truth, we must consider (1) the nature of the ground over which the truth valuation is used, (2) the way in which our bricks cohere, i.e., the "formal" nature of truth.

As to (1), the use of "truth" lies in the valuation of "fact": "truth" is value in the apprehension of "fact." The objects of our contemplation when valued as "true" become "facts," and "facts" (or what we take to be as such) become available for knowledge when valued as "true." The system of truth therefore is constructed by an interpretation of "fact." But this interpretation conforms to certain building laws, as it were. It consists in the use of concepts, and postulates the fundamental principles of thought.

Hence (2) these result in a certain formal character of truth. Every assertion formally claims to be "true," and causes endless confusion if this formal claim is identified with real, and even "absolute," truth. Again, whatever is harmonious ("consistent") with the fundamental assumptions of our conceptual interpretation of reality is in one sense "true." Any noncontradictory collocation of words has formal truth. But it is truth in a narrower sense than that required for "material" truth. In its fullest sense our truth must harmonize not only with its own formal postulates but with our whole experience, and it may well be that the merely formal truth of consistency is never able to attain results sufficient for our wider purpose, and so is not fully "true." In point of fact it is useful within limits; to show that a "truth" follows formally is not enough to prove it *de facto* true, but tests our premisses; to show that it involves a formal flaw is not enough to invalidate it, but requires us to reword it. For we would rather renounce our conclusion than the use of our formal principles.

After premising which, we may return to our problem of constructing an objective truth out of subjective truth valuations, of, as we saw, the most varied nature. Every one of these subjective valuations is the product of a psychological interest, and aims at the satisfaction of such an interest. But even in the individual there is much regulation of his subjective valuations, and some consolidation and subordination of interests under the main purposes of his life. Hence many of his initial interests will be suppressed, and the valuations which ministered to them will tend to be withdrawn, to be judged *useless* and, ultimately, *false*. In other words, there begins to operate among our subjective truth valuations *the great pragmatist principle of selection,* viz., that the "useless" is not to be valued as "true." The "use" appealed to and the "truth" extracted by this criterion are wholly psychological and, at first, only individual. But not even of the individual is it true to say that his *feeling* a thing "true" and *calling* it so *makes* it so. His "intuitions," guesses, and demands have to be *verified,* and are sifted by the manner of their working. Thus the question of the *sustaining* of the valuation after it is made is a distinct one; and is perhaps the one we mostly want to raise when we inquire: What is truth?

This question becomes more intricate, but also more interesting, when we take into account the social environment. For man is a social being, and truth indubitably is to a large extent a social product. For even though every truth may start in a minority of one, its hold upon existence is exceedingly precarious, unless it can contrive to get itself more extensively appreciated. Truth is one of the few things of which no one desires a monopoly. Those unfortunate enough to have acquired and retained an exclusive view of truth are usually secluded in prisons or asylums, unless their "truth" is so harmlessly abstruse as not to lead to action, when they are sometimes styled philosophers! Truth, then, to be really safe, has to be more than an individual valuation; it has to win social recognition, to transform itself into a common property.

But how? It is by answering this question that Pragmatism claims to have made a real advance in our comprehension of truth. It contends that once more, only more signally and clearly than in the individual's case, it is the usefulness and efficiency of the propositions for which "truth" is claimed that determines their social recognition. The use criterion selects the individual truth valuations, and constitutes thereby the objective truth which obtains social recognition. Hence in the fullest sense of truth its definition must be pragmatic. Truth is the useful, efficient, workable, to which our practical experience tends to restrict our truth valuations; if anything the reverse of this professes to be true, it is (sooner or later) detected and rejected.

As an account of truth this is not so much a speculative theory as a description of plain fact. Whenever we observe a struggle between two rival theories of events, we find that it is ultimately the greater conduciveness of the victor to our use and convenience that determines our preference and its consequent acceptance as true. Illustrations of this fact might be multiplied without limit, because in every advance of knowledge there is always something of a struggle between the old values which seemed true, and the new, which are better. The shocking cases occur when the convenience of a science is sacrificed to that of its practitioners, and doctrines continue to be taught, like formal logic, though they are known to be false. These exemplify an illegitimate use of the pragmatic principle. As a legitimate case we may allude to the well-known fact that what decided the rejection of the Ptolemaic epicycles in favour of the Copernican astronomy was not any sheer failure to represent celestial motions, but the growing cumbrousness of the assumptions and the growing difficulty of the calculations which its "truth" involved. Similarly when I affirm (as I have now been doing for a good many years) that the metaphysical theory of the Absolute is *false,* I only mean that it is *useless,* that it simplifies nothing and complicates everything, and that its supposed advantages are one and all illusory. And I hope that as the pragmatist way of looking at things grows to be more familiar, more of my philosophic confreres will allow themselves to perceive these simple facts.

Of course, there still remain complications of detail about the doctrine that social usefulness is an ultimate determinant of "truth." It is obvious, for example, that delicate questions may arise out of the fact that not only does what works receive social recognition, but also that what receives social recognition for this very reason largely works. Effete superstitions always try to sustain their "truth" in this way. Again, there may be old-established mental industries which have outlived their usefulness, but have not yet been condemned as false. Other truths again are intrinsically of so individual a character that society accepts, e.g., Smith's statement that he has a headache, or that he dreamt a dream, on his *ipse dixit*. And while new truths are struggling for recognition, it may come about that much that is useful is thought to be useless and vice versa, and that the discrepancy between truth as it is supposed, and as it turns out to be, grows great. Then, again, few societies are so severely organized with a sole view to efficiency as not to tolerate a considerable number of useless persons pursuing "useless" knowledge, or useful knowledge in a useless way. Of course, there is a certain amount of social pressure brought to bear upon such persons, but it is not enough to produce complete social agreement, and the elimination of all discrepant truth. Indeed, the toleration of socially useless, and even pernicious, "truths," which are individually entertained, seems on the whole to be increasing. This only shows that we can afford the luxury. In earlier times, the thinkers of divergent views had short shrift granted them, and so, partly as the result of much past brutality, we now enjoy considerable bodies of "objective" truth. And considering how much use philosophers have always made of this indulgence to differ from their fellows, it would be gracious if they at least gave honour where honour was due, and appreciated the labours of their ancestors, instead of attributing the whole credit of the conformity which exists to the initial constitution of the Absolute. Or if they insist on it, they might at least, in common fairness, attempt to tell us to whom the *discredit* should attach for the discrepancy and nonconformity, which exist no less and are by far more troublesome, even if they are too indolent to help in the practical work of science, which enlarges the limits of practical agreement and constitutes objective truth.

To sum up: the answer to the question *What is truth?* to which our Pragmatism has conducted us is this. As regards the psychical fact of the truth valuation, truth may be called an ultimate attitude and specific function of our intellectual activity. As regards the objects valued as "true," truth is that manipulation of them which has after trial been adopted as useful, primarily for any human end, but ultimately for that perfect harmony of our whole life which forms our final aspiration.

Chapter 7

The Ambiguity of Truth[1]

Argument

> The great antithesis between Pragmatism and Intellectualism as to the nature of truth. I. The predication of truth a specifically human habit. The existence of *false* claims to truth. How then are *false* claims to be discriminated from *true?* Intellectualism fails to answer this, and succumbs to the *ambiguity of truth* ("claim" and "validity"). Illustrations from Plato and others. II. Universality and importance of the ambiguity. The refusal of Intellectualism to consider it. III. The pragmatic answer. Relevance and value relative to purpose. Hence "truth" a valuation. The convergence of values. IV. The evaluation of claims proceeds pragmatically. "Truth" implies relevance and usually reference to proximate ends. V. The pragmatic definition of "truth"; its value for refuting naturalism and simplifying the classification of the sciences. VI. A challenge to Intellectualism to refute Pragmatism by evaluating any truth nonpragmatically

THE PURPOSE of this essay is to bring to a clear issue, and so possibly to the prospect of a settlement, the conflict of opinion now raging in the philosophic world as to the nature of the conception of "truth." This issue is an essential part of the greater conflict between the old intellectualist and the new "pragmatist" schools of thought, which extends over the whole field of philosophy. For, in consequence of the difference between the aims and methods of the two schools, there is probably no intellectualist treatment of any problem which does not need, and will not bear, restatement in voluntarist terms. But the clash of these two great antithetical attitudes towards life is certainly more dramatic at some points than at others. The influence of belief upon thought, its value and

[1] A revised form of a paper which appeared in *Mind* for April, 1906 (N.S. No. 58).

function in knowledge, the relation of theory to practice, the possibility of abstracting from emotional interest, and of ignoring in logic the psychological conditions of all judgment, the connexion between knowing and being, truth and fact, origin and validity, the question of how and how far the real which is said to be discovered is really made, the plasticity and determinable indetermination of reality, the contribution of voluntary acceptance to the constitution of fact, the nature of purpose and of mechanism, the value of teleology, the all-controlling presence of value judgments and the interrelations of their various forms, the proper meaning of "reason," "faith," "thought," "will," "freedom," "necessity"—all these are critical points at which burning questions have arisen or may arise, and at all of them the new philosophy seems able to provide a distinctive and consistent treatment. Thus there is throughout the field every promise of interesting discoveries and of a successful campaign for a thoroughgoing Voluntarism that unsparingly impugns the Intellectualist tradition.

But the aim of the present essay must be restricted. It will be confined to one small corner of the battlefield, viz., to the single question of the making of "truth" and the meaning of a term which is more often mouthed in a passion of unreasoning loyalty than subjected to calm and logical analysis. I propose to show (1) that such analysis is necessary and possible; (2) that it results in a problem which the current intellectualist logic can neither dismiss nor solve; (3) that to discard the abstractions of this formal logic at once renders this problem simple and soluble; (4) that to solve it is to establish the pragmatist criterion of truth; (5) that the resulting definition of truth unifies experience and rationalizes a well-established classification of the sciences; and (6) I shall conclude with a twofold challenge to intellectualist logicians, failure to meet which will, I think, bring out with all desirable clearness that their system at present is as devoid of intellectual completeness as it is of practical fecundity.

This design, it will be seen, deliberately rules out the references to questions of belief, desire, and will, and their ineradicable influence upon cognition, with which Voluntarism has made so much effective play, and this although I am keenly conscious both that their presence as psychical facts in all knowing is hardly open to denial,[2] and that their recognition is essential to the full appreciation of our case. But I am desirous of meeting our adversaries on their own ground, that of abstract logic, and of giving them every advantage of position. And so, even at the risk of reducing the real interest in my subject, I will discuss it on the ground of as "pure," i.e., as *formal*, a logic as is compatible with the continuance of actual thinking.

I

Let us begin then with the problem of analysing the conception of truth, and, to clear up our ideas, let us first observe the extension of the term. We may safely lay it down that the use of truth is ἴδιον ἀνθρώπῳ, a habit peculiar to man. Animals, that is, do not attain to or use the conception. They do not effect discriminations within their experience by means of the predicates "true" and "false." Again, even the philosophers who have been most prodigal of dogmas concerning the nature of an "infinite" intelligence (whatever that may mean!) have evinced much hesitation about attributing to it the discursive procedures of our own, and have usually hinted that it would transcend the predication of truth and falsehood. As being then a specific peculiarity of the human mind, the conception of "truth" seems closely analogous to that of "good" and of "beautiful," which seem as naturally to possess antithetical predicates in the "bad" and the "ugly," as the "true" does in the "false." And it may be anticipated that when our psychology has quite outgrown the materialistic prejudices of its adolescence, it will probably regard all these habits of judging experiences as just as distinctive and ultimate features of mental process as are the ultimate facts of our perception. In a sense, therefore, the predications of "good" and "bad," "true" and "false," etc., may take rank with the experiences of "sweet," "red," "loud," "hard," etc., as ultimate facts which need be analysed no further.[3]

2 In point of fact such denial has never been attempted; inquiries as to how logic can validly consider a "pure" thought, abstracted from the psychological conditions of actual thinking, have merely been ignored. My *Formal Logic* may now, however, be said to have established that such "logic" is meaningless.
3 The purport of this very elementary remark, which is still very remote from the real problem of truth, is to confute the notion, which seems dimly to underlie some intellectualist criticisms, that the specific character of the truth predication is ignored in pragmatist quarters.

We may next infer that by *a truth* we mean a proposition to which this attribute "true" has somehow been attached, and which, consequently, is envisaged *sub specie veri*. *The truth,* therefore, is the totality of things to which this mode of treatment is applied or applicable, whether or not this extends over the whole of our experience.

If now all propositions which involve this predication of truth really deserved it, if all that professes and seems to be "true" were really true, no difficulty would arise. Things would be "true" or "false" as simply and unambiguously as they are "sweet" or "sour," "red" or "blue," and nothing could disturb our judgments or convict them of illusion. But in the sphere of knowledge such, notoriously, is not the case. Our anticipations are often falsified, our claims prove frequently untenable. Our truths may turn out to be false, our goods to be bad; falsehood and error are as rampant as evil in the world of our experience.

This fact compels us (1) to an enlargement, and (2) to a distinction, in the realm of truth. For the logician, "truth" becomes a problem, enlarged so as to include "falsity" as well, and so, strictly, our problem is the contemplation of experience *sub specie veri et falsi*. Secondly, if not all that claims truth is true, must we not distinguish this initial claim from whatever procedure subsequently justifies or validates it? *Truth, therefore, will become ambiguous.* It will mean primarily a claim which may or may not turn out to be valid. It will mean, secondarily, such a claim *after* it has been tested and ratified, by processes which it behooves us to examine. In the first sense, as a claim, it will always have to be regarded with suspicion. For we shall not know whether it is really and fully true, and we shall tend to reserve this honourable predicate for what has victoriously sustained its claim. And once we realize that *a claim to truth is involved in every assertion as such,* our vigilance will be sharpened. A claim to truth, being inherent in assertion as such, will come to seem a formal and trivial thing, worth noting once for all, but possessing little real interest for knowledge. A formal logic, therefore, which restricts itself to the registration of such formal claims, we shall regard as solemn trifling; but it will seem a matter of vital importance and of agonized inquiry what it is that validates such claims and makes them really true. And with regard to any "truth" that has been asserted, our first demand will be to know what is *de facto* its condition, whether what it sets forth has been fully validated, or whether it is still a mere, and possibly a random, claim. For this evidently will make all the difference to its meaning and logical value. That "$2 + 2 = 4$" and that "truth is indefinable" stand, e.g., logically on a very different footing: the one is part of a tried and tested system of arithmetical truth, the other the desperate refuge of a bankrupt or indolent theory.

Under such conditions, far-reaching confusions could be avoided only by the unobtrusive operation of a beneficent providence. But that such miraculous intervention should guard logicians against the consequences of their negligence was hardly to be hoped for. Accordingly we find a whole cloud of witnesses to this confusion, from Plato, the great originator of the intellectualistic interpretation of life, down to the latest "critics" of Pragmatism with all their pathetic inability to do more than reiterate the confusions of the *Theaetetus*. For example, this is how Plato conducts his refutation of Protagoras in a critical stage of polemic:[4]

"*Socrates*. And how about Protagoras himself? If neither he nor the multitude thought, as indeed they do not think, that man is the measure of all things, must it not follow that the truth [*validity*] of which Protagoras wrote would be true [*claim*] to no one? But if you suppose that he himself thought this, and that the multitude does not agree with him, you must begin by allowing that in whatever proportion the many are more than one, his truth [*validity*] is more untrue [*claim*] than true? [Not necessarily, for all truths start their career in a minority of one, as an individual's claims, and obtain recognition only after a long struggle.]

"*Theodorus*. That would follow if the truth [*validity*] is supposed to vary with individual opinion.

"*Socrates*. And the best of the joke is that he acknowledges the truth [*as claim*, Protagoras; *as validity*, Plato] of their opinion who believe his own opinion to be false; for he admits that the opinions of all men are true [*as claims*]."

For a more compact expression of the same ambiguity we

4 *Theaetetus*, 170 E–171 B, Jowett's translation. Italics mine.

may have recourse to Mr. Bradley. "About the *truth* of this Law [of Contradiction] so far as it applies, there is in my opinion no question. The question will be rather as to how far the Law applies and how far *therefore* it is *true*."[5] The first proposition is either a truism or false. It is a truism if "truth" is taken in the sense of "claim"; for it then only states that a claim is good if the question of its application is waived. In any other sense of "truth" it is false (or rather self-contradictory), since it admits that there *is* a question about the application of the "Law," and it is not until the application is attempted that validity can be tested. In the second proposition it is implied that "truth" depends not on the mere claim, but on the possibility of application.

Or, again, let us note how Professor A. E. Taylor betters his master's instruction in an interesting article on "Truth and Practice" in the *Philosophical Review* for May, 1905. He first lays it down that "true propositions are those which have an unconditional *claim* on our recognition" (of their *validity,* or merely of their *claim*?), and then pronounces that "truth is just the system of propositions which have an unconditional *claim* to be recognized as *valid*."[6] And lest he should not have made the paradox of this confusion evident enough, he repeats (p. 273) that "the truth of a statement means not the actual fact of its recognition (i.e., of its *de facto* validity), "but its *rightful claim* on our recognition" (p. 274).[7] In short, as he does not distinguish between "claim" and "right," he cannot see that the question of truth is as to when and how a "claim" is to be recognized as "rightful." And though he wisely refrains from even attempting to tell us how the clamorousness of a claim is going to establish its validity, it is clear that his failure to observe the distinction demolishes his definition of truth.

Mr. Joachim's *Nature of Truth* does not exemplify this confusion so clearly merely because it does not get to the point at which it is revealed. His theory of truth breaks down before this point is reached. He conceives the nature of truth to concern only the question of what "the ideal" should be,

5 *Mind*, N.S. No. 20, V, 470. Italics mine.
6 Pp. 271, 288. Italics mine.
7 Cp. also pp. 276 and 278.

even though it should be unattainable by man, as indeed it turns out to be. Thus the problem of how *we* validate claims to truth is treated as irrelevant.[8] Hence it is only casually that phrases like "entitled to claim" occur (p. 109), or that the substantiating of a claim to truth is said to consist in its recognition and adoption "by all intelligent people" (p. 27). Still, on p. 118 it seems to be implied that a "thought which claims truth as affirming universal meaning" need not undergo any further verification. It is evident, in short, that not much can be expected from theories which have overlooked so vital a distinction. Their unawareness of it will vitiate all their discussions of the nature of "truth," by which they will mean now the one sense, now the other, and now both, in inextricable fallacy.

II

Our provisional analysis, therefore, has resulted in our detecting an important ambiguity in the conception of truth which, unless it can be cleared up, must hopelessly vitiate all discussion. In view of this distressing situation, it becomes our bounden duty to inquire *how an accepted truth may be distinguished from a mere claim, and how a claim to truth may be validated*. For any logic which aims at dealing with actual thinking, the urgency of this inquiry can hardly be exaggerated. But even the most "purely" intellectual and futilely formal theory of knowledge can hardly refuse to undertake it. For the ambiguity which raises the problem is absolutely all-pervading. As we saw, a formal claim to truth is coextensive with the sphere of logical judgment. No judgment proclaims its own fallibility; its formal claim is always to be true. We are always liable, therefore, to misinterpret every judgment. We may take as a validated truth what in point of fact is really an unsupported claim. But inasmuch as such a claim may always be erroneous, we are constantly in danger of accepting as validly true what, if tested, would be utterly untenable. Every assertion is ambiguous, and as it shows no outward indication of what it really means, we can hardly be said to know the meaning of any assertion whatsoever. On any view of logic,

8 As it is by Mr. Bradley, who, as Prof. Hoernle remarks, "deals with the question how *we* correct our errors in a footnote!" (*Mind*, XIV, 321.)

the disastrous and demoralizing consequences of such a situation may be imagined. It is imperative, therefore, to distinguish sharply between the formal inclusion of a statement in the sphere of *truth or falsity,* and its incorporation into a system of tested truth. For unless we do so, we simply court deception.

This possibility of deception, moreover, becomes the more serious when we realize how impotent our formal logic is to conceive this indispensable distinction and to guard us against so fatal a confusion. Instead of proving a help to the logician, it here becomes a snare, by reason of the fundamental abstraction of its standpoint. For if, following Mr. Alfred Sidgwick's brilliant lead, we regard as formal logic every treatment of our cognitive processes which abstracts from the concrete application of our logical functions to actual cases of knowing, it is easy to see that no such logic can help us, because the meaning of an assertion can never be determined apart from the actual application.[9] From the mere verbal form, that is, we cannot tell whether we are dealing with a valid judgment or a sheer claim. To settle this, we must go behind the statement: we must go into the rights of the case. Meaning depends upon purpose, and purpose is a question of psychical fact, of the context and use of the form of words in actual knowing. But all this is just what the abstract standpoint of formal logic forbids us to examine. It conceives the meaning of a proposition to be somehow inherent in it as a form of words, apart from its use. So when it finds that the same words may be used to convey a variety of meanings in various contexts, it supposes itself to have the same form, not of words, but of judgment, and solemnly declares it to be as such ambiguous, even though in each actual case of use the meaning intended may be perfectly clear to the meanest understanding! It seems more than doubtful, therefore, whether a genuine admission of the validity of our distinction could be extracted from any formal logician. For even if he could be induced to admit it in words, he would yet insist on treating it too as purely formal, and rule out on principle attempts to determine how *de facto* the distinction was established and employed.

Although, therefore, our distinction appears to be as clear

9 Cp. Chapters 2, § 2, and 8, § 10.

as it is important, it does not seem at all certain that it would be admitted by the logicians who are so enamoured of truth in the abstract that they have ceased to recognize it in the concrete. More probably they would protest that logic was being conducted back to the old puzzle of a general criterion of truth and error, and would adduce the failures of their predecessors as a valid excuse for their present apathy. Or at most they might concede that a distinction between a truth and a claim to truth must indeed be made, but allege that it could not take any but a negative form. The sole criterion of truth, that is, which can be given is that truth is not self-contradictory or incoherent.

This statement, in the first place, means a refusal to go into the actual question how truth is made; it is an attempt to avoid the test of application, and to conceive truth as inherent in the logical terms in the abstract. But this is really to render "truth" wholly *verbal*. For the inherent meanings are merely the established meanings of the words employed. It is, secondly, merely dogmatic assertion; it can hardly inspire confidence so long as it precedes and precludes examination of the positive solutions of the problem, and assumes the conceptions of "self-contradiction" or "incoherence" as the simplest things in the world. In point of fact neither of them has been adequately analysed by intellectualist logicians, nor is either of them naturally so translucent as to shed a flood of light on any subject. As, however, we cannot now enter upon their obscurities, and examine what (if anything) either "coherence" or "consistency" really means, it must suffice to remark that Captain H. V. Knox's masterly article in the April, 1905, number of *Mind*[10] contains ample justification for what I have said about the principle of contradiction. If on the other hand the "negative criterion" be stated in the form of incoherence, I would inquire merely how intellectualist logic proposes to distinguish the logical coherence, to which it appeals, from the psychological coherence, which it despises. Until this difficult (or impossible?) feat has been achieved, we may safely move on.[11]

10 N.S. No. 54; cp. *Formal Logic,* ch. X.
11 Cf. also Chapter 6.

III

Let us proceed therefore to discard old prejudices and to consider how in point of fact we sift claims and discriminate between "claims" and "truths," how the raw material of a science is elaborated into its final structure, how, in short, truth is made. Now this question is not intrinsically a hopeless one. It is not even particularly difficult in theory. For it concerns essentially facts which may be observed, and with care and attention it should be possible to determine whether the procedures of the various sciences have anything in common, and if so what. By such an inductive appeal to the facts, therefore, we greatly simplify our problem, and may possibly discover its solution. Any obstacle which we may encounter will come merely from the difficulty of intelligently observing the special procedures of so many sciences and of seizing their salient points and general import; we shall not be foredoomed to failure by any intrinsic absurdity of our enterprise.

Now it would be possible to arrive at our solution by a critical examination of every known science in detail, but it is evident that this procedure would be very long and laborious. It seems better, therefore, merely to state the condensed results of such investigations. They will in this shape stand out more clearly and better exhibit the trend of an argument which runs as follows:

It being taken as established that the sphere of logic is that of the antithetical valuations "true" and "false," we observe, in the first place, that in every science the effective truth or falsity of an answer depends on its relevance to the question raised in that science. It does not matter that a physicist's language should reek of "crude realism" or an engineer's calculations lack "exactness," if both are right enough for their immediate purpose. Whereas, when an irrelevant answer is given, it is justly treated as nonexistent for that science; no question is raised whether it is "true" or "false." We observe, secondly, that every science has a definitely circumscribed subject matter, a definite method of treating it, and a definitely articulated body of interpretations. Every science, in other words, forms a system of truths about some subject. But inasmuch as every science is concerned with some aspect of our total experience, and no science deals with that whole under every aspect, it is clear that sciences arise by the limitation of subjects, the selection of standpoints, and the specialization of methods. All these operations, however, are artificial, and in a sense arbitrary, and none of them can be conceived to come about except by the action of a purposing intelligence. It follows that the nature of the *purpose* which is pursued in a science will yield the deepest insight into its nature; for what we want to know in the science will determine the questions we put, and their bearing on the questions will determine the standing of the answers we attain, If we can take the answers as relevant to our questions and conducive to our ends, they will yield "truth"; if we cannot, "falsity."[12]

Seeing thus that everywhere truth and falsity depend on the purpose which constitutes the science and are bestowed accordingly, we begin to perceive, what we ought never to have forgotten, that the predicates "true" and "false" are not unrelated to "good" and "bad." For good and bad also (in their wider and primary sense) have reference to purpose. "Good" is what conduces to, "bad" what thwarts, a purpose. And so it would seem that "true" and "false" were valuations, forms of the "good"-or-"bad" which indicates a reference to an end. Or, as Aristotle said long ago, "in the case of the intelligence which is theoretical, and neither practical nor productive, its 'good' and 'bad' is 'truth' and 'falsehood.' "[13]

Truth, then, being a valuation, has reference to a purpose. What precisely that reference is will depend on the purpose, which may extend over the whole range of human interest. But it is only in its primary aspect, as valued by individuals, that the predication of "truth" will refer thus widely to any purpose anyone may entertain in a cognitive operation. For it stands to reason that the power of constituting "objective" truth is not granted so easily. Society exercises almost as severe a control over the intellectual as over the moral eccentricities and nonconformities of its members; indeed, it often so organizes itself as to render the recognition of *new* truth nearly impossible. Whatever, therefore, individuals may recognize and

---

[12] But cp. note on p. 183.
[13] *Eth. Nic.* VI, 2, 3. Cp. *De Anim.* III, 7, 431 b 10, where it is stated that "the true and false are in the same class with the good and bad," i.e., are valuations.

value as "true," the "truths" which *de facto* prevail and are recognized as objective will only be a *selection* from those we are subjectively tempted to propound. There is, therefore, no real danger lest this analysis should destroy the "objectivity" of truth and enthrone subjective license in its place.

A further convergence in our truth valuations is produced by the natural tendency to subordinate all ends or purposes to the ultimate end or final purpose, the Good. For in theory, at least, the "goods," and therefore the "truths," of all the sciences are unified and validated by their relation to the Supreme Good. In practice no doubt this ideal is far from being realized, and there arise at various points conflicts between the various sorts of values or goods, which doubtless will continue until a perfect harmony of all our purposes, scientific, moral, aesthetic, and emotional has been achieved. Such conflicts may, of course, be made occasions for theatrically opposing "truth" to (moral) "goodness," "virtue" to "happiness," "science" to "art," etc., and afford much scope for dithyrambic declamation. But a sober and clear headed thought will not be intolerant nor disposed to treat such oppositions as final and absolute; even where under the circumstances their reality must provisionally be admitted, it will essay rather to evaluate each claim with reference to the highest conception of ultimate good which for the time being seems attainable. It will be very chary, therefore, of sacrificing either side beyond recall; it will neither allow the claims of truth to oppress those of moral virtue nor those of moral virtue to suppress art. But it will still more decidedly hold aloof from the quixotic attempt to conceive the sphere of each valuation as independent and as wholly severed from the rest.

IV

We have seen so far that truth is a form of value, and the logical judgment a valuation; but we have not yet raised the question as to what prompts us in bestowing or withholding this value, what are our guiding principles in thus evaluating our experience. The answer to this question takes us straight into the heart of Pragmatism. Nay, the answer to this question *is* Pragmatism, and gives the sense in which Pragmatism professes to have a criterion of truth. For the pragmatist contends that he has an answer which is simple, and open to inspection and easily tested. He simply bids us go to the facts and observe the actual operations of our knowing. If we will but do this, we shall "discover" that in all actual knowing, the question whether an assertion is "true" or "false" is decided uniformly and very simply. It is decided, that is, by its consequences, by its bearing on the interest which prompted to the assertion, by its relation to the purpose which put the question. To add to this that the consequences must be *good* is superfluous. For if and so far as an assertion satisfies or forwards the purpose of the inquiry to which it owes its being, it is so far "true"; if and so far as it thwarts or baffles it, it is unworkable, unserviceable, "false." And "true" and "false," we have seen, are the intellectual forms of "good" and "bad." Or in other words, a "truth" is what is useful in building up a science; a "falsehood" what is useless or noxious for this same purpose.[14] A "science," similarly, is "good" if it can be used to harmonize our life; if it cannot, it is a pseudoscience or a game. To determine, therefore, whether any answer to any question is "true" or "false," we have merely to note its effect upon the inquiry in which we are interested, and in relation to which it has arisen. And if these effects are favourable, the answer is "true" and "good" for our purpose, and "useful" as a means to the end we pursue.[15] Here, then, we have exposed to view the whole rationale of Pragmatism, the source of the famous paradoxes that "truth" depends on its consequences, that the "true" must be "good" and "useful" and "practical." I confess that to me they have never seemed more than truisms so simple that I used to fear lest too elaborate an insistence on them should be taken as an insult to the intelligence of my readers. But experience has shown that I was too sanguine,

[14] After allowance has been made for methodological assumptions, which may turn out to be "fictions." "Lies" exist as such only after they have been detected; but then they have usually ceased to be useful.
[15] Strictly both the "true" and the "false" answers are, as Mr. Sidgwick says, subdivisions of the "relevant," and the irrelevant is really unmeaning. But the unmeaning often seems to be relevant until it is detected; it is as baffling to our purpose as the "false"; while the "false" answer grows more and more "irrelevant" as we realize its "falsity"; it does not mean what we meant to get, viz., something we can work with. Hence it is so far unmeaning, and in a sense all that *fails* us may be treated as "false."

and now I even feel impelled to guard still further against two possible misapprehensions into which an unthinking philosopher might fall.

I will point out, in the first place, that when we said that truth was estimated by its consequences for some purpose, we were speaking subject to the social character of truth, and quite generally. What consequences are relevant to what purposes depends, of course, on the subject matter of each science, and may sometimes be in doubt, when the question may be interpreted in several contexts. But as a rule the character of the question sufficiently defines the answer which can be treated as relevantly true. It is not necessary, therefore, seriously to contemplate absurdities such as, e.g., the intrusion of ethical or aesthetical motives into the estimation of mathematical truths, or to refute claims that the isosceles triangle is more virtuous than the scalene, or an integer nobler than a vulgar fraction, or that heavenly bodies must move not in ellipses but in circles, because the circle is the most perfect figure. Pragmatism is far less likely to countenance such confusions than the intellectualist theories from which I drew my last illustration. In some cases, doubtless, as in many problems of history and religion, there will be found deep-seated and enduring differences of opinion as to what consequences and what tests may be adduced as relevant; but these differences already exist, and are in no wise created by being recognized and explained. Pragmatism, however, by enlarging our notions of what constitutes relevant evidence, and insisting on *some* testing, is far more likely to conduce to their amicable settlement than the intellectualisms which condemn all faith as inherently irrational and irrelevant to knowledge. And, ideally and in principle, such disagreements as to the ends which are relevant to the estimation of any evidence are always capable of being composed by an appeal to the supreme purpose which unifies and harmonizes all our ends. In practice, no doubt, we are hardly aware of this, nor agreed as to what it is; but the blame, surely, attaches to the distracted state of our thoughts and not to the pragmatic analysis of truth. For it would surely be preposterous to expect a mere theory of knowledge to adjudicate upon and settle offhand, by sheer dint of logic, all the disputed questions in all the sciences.

My second caution refers to the fact that I have made the predication of truth dependent on relevance to a proximate rather than an ultimate scientific purpose. This represents, I believe, our actual procedure. The ordinary "truths" we predicate have but little concern with ultimate ends and realities. They are true (at least pro tem) if they serve their immediate purpose. If anyone hereafter chooses to question them he is at liberty to do so, and if he can make out his case, to reject them for their inadequacy for his ulterior purposes. But even when the venue and the context of the question have thus been changed, and so its meaning, the truth of the original answer is not thereby abolished. It may have been degraded and reduced to a methodological status, but this is merely to affirm that what is true and serviceable for one purpose is not necessarily so for another. And in any case it is time perhaps to cease complaining that a truth capable of being improved on, i.e., capable of *growing,* is so far not absolutely true, and therefore somewhat false and worthy of contempt. For such complaints spring from an *arbitrary* interpretation of a situation that might more sensibly be envisaged as meaning that none of the falsehoods out of which our knowledge struggles in its growth is ever wholly false. But in actual knowing we are not concerned with such arbitrary phrases, but with the bearing of an answer on a question actually propounded. And whatever really answers is really "true," even though it may at once be turned into a steppingstone to higher truth.

If therefore we realize that we are concerned with human "truth" alone, and that truth is ambiguous, there is no paradox in affirmatively answering Professor A. E. Taylor's question (*Philosophical Review,* XIV, 268) as to whether "the truth of a newly discovered theorem is created" (it should be "made," i.e., out of earlier "truth") "by the fact of its discovery." He asks "did the doctrine of the earth's motion become true when enunciated by the Pythagoreans, false again when men forgot the Pythagorean astronomy, and true a second time on the publication of the book of Copernicus?" The ambiguity in this question may be revealed by asking: "Do you mean 'true' to refer to the valuation of the *new* 'truth' by us, or to the *re-valuation* of the old?" For the "discovery" involves *both,* and both are products of human activity. If then we grant (what is,

I suppose, the case) that the Pythagorean, Ptolemaic, and Copernican systems represent stages in the progress of a successful calculation of celestial motions, it is clear that each of them was valued as "true" while it seemed adequate, and revalued as "false" when it was improved on. And "true" in Professor Taylor's question does not, for science, mean "absolutely true." The relativity of motion renders the demand for absolute answers scientifically unmeaning. As well might one ask, "What exactly *is* *the* distance of the earth from the sun?" Moving bodies, measured by human instruments, have *no* fixed distance, no absolute place. The successive scientific truths about them are only *better* recalculations. Hence a very slight improvement will occasion a change in their valuation. Professor Taylor has failed to observe that he has conceived the scientific problem too loosely in grouping together the Pythagorean and the Copernican theory as alike cases of the earth's motion. No doubt they may both be so denominated, but the scientific value of the two theories was very different, and the Ptolemaic system is intermediate in value as well as in time. He might as well have taken a more modern instance and argued that the emission theory of light was true "all along" because the discovery of radioactivity has forced its undulatory rival to admit that light is sometimes produced by the impact of "corpuscles."

The reason, then, why it seems paradoxical to make the very existence of truth depend on its "discovery" by us is that in *some* cases there ensues upon the discovery a transvaluation of our former values, which are now revalued as "false," while the new "truth" is *antedated* as having been true all along. This, however, is conditioned by the special character of the case, and would have been impossible but for the human attempt to verify the claim. When what is "discovered" is gold in a rock, it is supposed to have been there "all along"; when it is a burglar in a house, our common sense rejects such antedating. So the whole distinction remains *within* the human evaluation of truth, and affords no occasion for attributing to "truth" any real independence of human cognition; the attempt to do so really misrepresents our procedure. It is a mere error of abstraction to think that because a "truth" may be judged "independent" *after* human manipulation, it is so per se, irrespectively of the procedure to which it owes its "independent" existence. And to infer further that therefore logic should wholly abstract from the human side in knowing is exactly like arguing that because children grow "independent" of their parents, they must be conceived as essentially independent, and must have been so "all along."

V

We now find ourselves in a position to lay down some humanist definitions. Truth we may define as logical value, and a claim to truth as a claim to possess such value. The validation of such claims proceeds, we hold, by the pragmatic test, i.e., by experience of their effect upon the bodies of established truth which they affect. It is evident that in this sense truth will admit of degrees, extending from the humble truth which satisfies *some* purpose, even though it only be the lowly purpose of some subordinate end, to that ineffable ideal which would satisfy *every* purpose and unify all endeavours. But the main emphasis will clearly fall on the former, for to perfect truth we do not yet attain, and after all, even the humblest truth may hold its ground without suffering rejection. No truth, moreover, can do more than do its duty and fulfil its function.

These definitions should have sufficiently borne out the claim made at the beginning (p. 172), that the pragmatic view of truth unifies experience and rationalizes the classification of the normative sciences; but it may not be amiss to add a few words on both these topics. That, in the first place, the conception of the logical judgment as a form of valuation connects it with our other valuations, and represents it as an integral part of the ἔφεσις τοῦ ἀγαθοῦ, of the purposive reaction upon the universe which bestows dignity and grandeur upon the struggle of human life is, I take it, evident. The theoretic importance of this conception is capital. It is easily and absolutely fatal to every form of naturalism. For if every "fact" upon which any naturalistic system relies is at bottom a valuation, arrived at by selection from a larger whole, by rejection of what seemed irrelevant, and by purposive manipulation of what seemed important, there is a manifest absurdity in eliminating the human reference from results which have implied it at every step. The humanist doctrine, therefore, affords a protection against naturalism which ought to be the more appreciated by those interested in taking a "spiritual" view of life now that it has become pretty clear that the protection afforded by idealistic absolutism is quite illusory. For the "spiritual nature of the Absolute" does nothing to succour the human aspirations strangled in the coils of materialism; "absolute spirit" need merely be conceived naturalistically to become as impotent to aid the theologian and the moralist as it has long been seen to be to help the scientist.[16]

The unification of logic with the other normative sciences is even more valuable practically than theoretically. For it vindicates man's right to present his claims upon the universe in their integrity, as a demand not for truth alone, but for goodness, beauty, and happiness as well, commingled with each other in a fusion one and indiscerptible; and what perhaps is for the moment more important still, it justifies our efforts to bring about such a union as we desire. Whether this ideal can be attained cannot, of course, be certainly predicted; but a philosophy which gives us the right to aspire, and inspires us with the daring to attempt, is surely a great improvement on monisms which, like Spinoza's, essay to crush us with blank and illogical denials of the relevance of human valuations to the truth of things.

In technical philosophy, however, it is good form to profess more interest in the formal relations of the sciences than in the cosmic claims and destinies of man, and so we may hasten to point out the signal aid which Humanism affords to a symmetrical classification of the sciences. If truth also is a valuation, we can understand why logic should attempt normative judgments, like ethics and aesthetics; if all the natural sciences make use of logical judgments and lay claim to logical values, we can understand also how and why the normative sciences should have dominion over them. And lastly, we find that the antithetical valuations and the distinction between claims and their selection into norms run through all the normative sciences in a perfectly analogous way. Just as not everything is true which claims truth, so not everything is good or right or beautiful which claims to be so, while ultimately all

[16] Chapter 3, § 5.

these claims are judged by their relation to the perfect harmony which forms our final aspiration.

VI

This essay was pledged at the outset to conclude with a twofold challenge, and now that it has set forth some of the advantages proffered by the pragmatic view of truth, we must revert to this challenge, in a spirit not of contentiousness so much as of anxious inquiry. For it is to be feared that a really resolute adherent of the intellectualist tradition would be unmoved and unconvinced by anything we, or anyone, could say. He would simply close his eyes and seal his ears, and recite his creed. And perhaps no man yet was ever convinced of philosophic truth against his will. But there are beginning to be signs (and even wonders) that our Intellectualism is growing less resolute. So perhaps even those who are not yet willing to face the new solutions can be brought to see the gaps in the old. If, therefore, we bring these to their notice very humbly, but very persistently, we may enable them to see that the old Intellectualism has left its victims unprovided with answers to two momentous questions. Let us ask, therefore, how, upon its assumptions, they propose (1) to evaluate a claim to truth, and (2) to discriminate between such a claim and an established truth? These two questions constitute the first part of my challenge. They are, clearly, good questions, and such that from any theory of knowledge with pretensions to completeness an answer may fairly be demanded. And if such an answer exists, it is so vital to the whole case of Intellectualism that we may fairly require it to be produced. If it is not produced, we will be patient, and hope that someday we may be vouchsafed a revelation of esoteric truth; but human nature is weak, and the longer the delay, the stronger will grow the suspicion that there is nothing to produce.

The second part of our challenge refers to the intellectualist's rejection of our solution. If we are so very wrong in our very plain and positive assertion that the truth (validity) of a truth (claim) is tested and established by the value of its consequences, there ought surely to be no difficulty about producing abundant cases in which the truth (validity) of a doubtful assertion is established in some *other* way. I would ask, therefore, for the favour of *one clear case of this kind*.[17] And I make only one stipulation. It should be a case in which there really was a question, so that the *true* answer might have, before examination, turned out *false*. For without this proviso we should get no illustration of actual knowing, such as was contemplated by the pragmatist, whose theory professes to discriminate cases in which there is a real chance of acquiring truth and a real risk of falling into falsity. If on the other hand specimens merely of indubitable or verbal truths were adduced, and it were asserted that these were true not because they were useful, but simply because they were true, we should end merely in a wrangle about the historical pedigree of the truth. We should contend that it was at one time doubtful, and accepted as true because of its tested utility; our opponent would dispute our derivation and assert that it had always been true. We should agree that it was *now* indisputable, we should disagree about the origin of this feature; and the past history would usually be too little known to establish either view. And so we should get no nearer to a settlement.

By observing on the other hand *truth in the making*, inferences may be drawn to the nature of truth *already made*. And whether truth is by nature pragmatic, or whether this is a foul aspersion on her character, it is surely most desirable that this point should be settled. Hitherto the chief obstacle to such a decision has been the fact that while in public (and still more in private) there has been much misconception, misrepresentation, and abuse of our views, there have been no serious attempts to contest directly, unequivocally, and outright, *any of our cardinal assertions*.[18] And what perhaps is still more singular, our critics have been completely reticent as to what alternative solutions to the issues raised they felt themselves in a position to propound. They have not put forward either any account of truth which can be said ul-

---

[17] Prof. Taylor attempted to answer an earlier form of this challenge in *Mind*, N.S. No. 57. My reply in N.S. No. 59, entitled "Pragmatism and Pseudo-Pragmatism," showed that he had misunderstood even the elementary "principle of Peirce."

[18] Prof. Taylor has now supplied this desideratum, by denying that psychology has any relevance to logic (*Phil. Rev.* XIV, 267, 287). Yet immediately after (p. 287), he feels constrained to argue that the efficient cause of his accepting any belief as true is a specific form of emotion! Surely the fact that no truth can be accepted without this feeling constitutes a pretty substantial connexion between psychology and logic. Cp. Chapter 8.

timately to have a meaning, or one that renders it possible to discriminate between the "true" and the "false." The whole situation is so strange, and so discreditable to the *prestige* of philosophy, that it is earnestly to be hoped that of the many renowned logicians who so vehemently differ from us, some should at length see (and show us!) their way to refute these "heresies," as clearly and articulately as their θυμοειδές[19] permits their φιλόσοφον,[19] and as boldly as their φιλόσοφον permits their θυμοειδές, to express itself.

[19] The "spirited" and "philosophic" parts of the soul, according to Plato.

Chapter 8

The Relations of Logic and Psychology[1]

Argument

§ 1. Humanism as logical "psychologism." § 2. It is beneficial to a logic which has lapsed into scepticism, because it has abstracted from actual knowing. § 3. Definition of psychology as a descriptive science of concrete mental process. It can recognize cognitive values and claims, though, § 4, Logic must evaluate them, and thus arises out of psychology. Impossibility of forbidding it to describe cognitive processes. § 5. Definition of logic, a normative science arising out of the existence of *false* claims. § 6. Interdependence of the two sciences. The risks of abstracting from any psychical fact. § 7. (1) Thinking depends essentially on psychological processes, such as interest, purpose, emotion, and satisfaction. § 8. (2) The fundamental "logical" conceptions, "necessity," "certainty," "self-evidence," "truth," are primarily psychical facts. "Logical" certainty due to the extension of potential beyond actual purpose in thinking. § 9. (3) The fundamental "logical" operations have psychological aspects. E.g., the postulate of "identity." *Meaning* dependent on context and purpose. The actual meaning

[1] The necessity of treating this subject from a humanist point of view is evident. It was borne in upon me with peculiar force by two circumstances. The first was that the excellent articles on "Pragmatism *versus* Absolutism," by Prof. R. F. A. Hoernle in *Mind* (N.S. Nos. 55 and 56, XIV) seemed to imply a serious misapprehension of the conception of psychology which we are bound to entertain. Such misapprehension, however, is so natural, so long as no formal treatment of the interrelations of logic and psychology is in print, that it seemed imperative to attempt its removal.

Secondly, being called upon to start a discussion before the Aristotelian Society, in which Prof. Bosanquet and Dr. Hastings Rashdall also participated, I selected the question whether logic can abstract from the psychological conditions of thinking. The discussion which ensued will be found in the Society's *Proceedings* for 1905–6, and though it was rather at cross purposes, and on the whole illustrates only the difficulty philosophers have in understanding one another, it enabled me to realize what a radical difference exists between the humanist and the intellectualist conceptions of these sciences. It seemed helpful, therefore, to discuss these conceptions, and so this essay is based in part on the "symposium" of the Aristotelian Society.

vs. the meaning per se. The problem of understanding. The "logical" abstractions as to meaning dangerous and false. *Judgment* an intimately personal affair, which cannot be depersonalized, and is naturally related to questions and postulates. § 10. Can even desire be abstracted from? A case of postulatory reasoning examined. § 11. As meaning always depends on context, and context on personality, is logic entitled to abstract from the knower's personality? § 12. The antipsychological standpoint of intellectualist logic. Its assumptions. (1) "Pure," and (2) "independent" thought. (3) "Depersonalization." (4) The separation of thinking from "willing" and "feeling." § 13. Is its standpoint descriptive or normative? or both and either? § 14. Incompetence of logic for psychological description: its unjust encroachment on psychology and result, § 15, the stultification of psychology and the suicide of logic, teste Prof. Bosanquet. § 16. The great abstraction which ruins logic. § 17. "Depersonalization" involves abstraction from error, which must yet be acknowledged to exist. Mr. Joachim's confessions. Hence, § 18, the complete breakdown of intellectualist logic, owing to a separation of the ideal and the human which renders both meaningless. This is Plato's old error, in the *Theaetetus.* § 19. The remedy is to refrain from *dehumanizing* knowledge, by (1) *etherealizing* it, i.e, abstracting from its *application,* and (2) *depersonalizing* it, i.e., abstracting from the knower's purpose.

§ 1. It will, probably, be conceded by all philosophers that the sciences are all (in some sense) connected with one another, and that the precise way in which their connexion is conceived will depend on the way we conceive the sciences themselves. Nor will it be disputed that since the definitions of a growing science must to some extent change with the growth of our knowledge of the data of that science, the relations of such sciences to each other cannot be immutable. Consequently it may be inferred with some confidence that the humanist movement must have introduced some modifications and novelties into our conceptions of logic and psychology, and of their relations to each other. This has, indeed, been pretty widely recognized. In Germany, for example, the analogous tendencies are commonly described as "Psychologism," and if "Psychologism" means a demand that the psychical facts of our cognitive functioning shall no longer be treated as irrelevant to logic, it is clear both that Humanism is Psychologism, and that the demand itself is thoroughly legitimate, and not to be dismissed with a mere *non possumus*. For when Humanism demands that philosophy shall start from, and satisfy, the whole man in his full concreteness, and not exclusively concern itself with a sort of elegant extract, a highly perfumed and sophisticated "essence" of man, dubbed "the rational intelligence," there is certainly included in its demand a much greater respect for the actual procedures of human cognition and a much less easygoing acceptance of petrified conventions than the traditional logic will find at all convenient.

§ 2. Yet a sincere attempt to comply with the demands made upon it, whether in the name of psychology or of humanity, would do logic no harm. Nay, it might even prove its salvation. For its present condition is anything but prosperous. It has lapsed into an impotent scepticism, which is irremediable so long as it cannot, or will not, emancipate itself from intellectualistic presuppositions which render actual knowing inherently "irrational." So it has been forced practically to abandon the attempt to account for knowing. It has been driven to represent the processes by which *de facto* knowledge is increased as logically invalid. Predication has become for it a puzzle, inference a paradox, proof an impossibility,[2] discovery a wonder, change a contradiction, temporal succession incompatible with science (which all the while is busily engaged with predicting the future!), individuality an irrelevance, experience an impertinence, sensation a piece of unmeaning nonsense, thinking "extralogical," and so forth and so on. After delivering itself of these valuable "criticisms" of our ordinary cognitive procedures, it has retired into an "ideal" world of its own invention, out of space, out of time, out of

2 See Prof. Case's article on "Logic" in the *Encyclopaedia Britannica* (10th ed., XX, 338) for a lucid exposition of this situation, with some excellent comments.

sight (and almost out of mind!), where it employs its ample leisure with studying "types" that never lived on land or sea, and constructing a *hortus siccus* of "forms," and compiling unworkable "systems," and concocting unrealizable "ideals," of "thought," all of which have about as much relation to actual knowing and to human truth as the man in the moon! But even in its suprasensible asylum, the Erinyes of the reality it has abandoned and betrayed pursue it; it cannot manipulate to its satisfaction even the figments and phantoms of the imaginary world which haunt it. Its "forms" do not afford it aesthetic satisfaction; its "types" are broken before ever they are used; its "systems" will not hold together; its "ideals" decline to be harmonious. In vain does it cry out to metaphysics to save it from imminent collapse into the abyss of scepticism; its cognate metaphysics have abundant troubles of their own, and are even more hopelessly involved in morasses that border the brink of the pit; they find, moreover, *all* the sciences beset by similar distresses, and can vouchsafe no answer save that the real, at all events, does not appear, nor can what appears be real.

In such a desperate plight it is surely not unbecoming to approach the logician with the suggestion that his troubles may be largely of his own making, that possibly his conception of logic is at fault and capable of amendment, and gently to point out to him that after all, what he originally undertook to do, but has now apparently quite forgotten, was to provide a reasoned theory of actual knowing, that the existence of such actual knowing is an empirical fact which is not abolished by his failure to understand it, that this fact constitutes his datum and his *raison d'être,* that he may as well accept it as the touchstone of his theories, and that it is the "ideals of thought" which must be accounted wrong if they cannot be rendered compatible with the facts which formed their basis. He may at least be called upon to consider the possibility that, if he consents to start from actual knowing, and refrains from welcoming "ideals" until they have been authenticated by their connexion with the facts and verified by their working *when applied,* he may reach an altogether more profitable and effective conception of logic than that which is falling to pieces.

§ 3. Let us make bold, then, to redefine our sciences and to reconceive their relations.

And first of all let us consider the wider and lower of these sciences, to wit, psychology. Without concerning ourselves with the questions as to how far psychology is, or may be, experimental or explanatory, and even as to how far its descriptions should be "functional" rather than "structural," as not affecting our present purpose, we may most conveniently conceive it at present as a *descriptive* science, whose aim is the description of mental process as such. It is implied in this, and hardly in need of explicit statement, that the mental processes of individual minds are intended. For we cannot experience or observe mental processes in any other way. Still, it is worth noting that, in this implication, psychology gives us a certain guarantee that it will do justice to the concreteness of the actual human soul; so far, at least, as the necessary abstraction of its standpoint consequent on the limitation of its purpose permits it to do.

The definition we have adopted clearly assigns to psychology a very extensive field of operations—practically the whole realm of direct experience. It recognizes *a psychological side also to everything that can be known,* inasmuch as everything known to exist must be connected with our experience, and known by a psychical process. In so far as any real is known, a process of experiencing is involved in it, and this process appertains to the science of psychology. Thus all physical objects and questions become psychological, so soon as we ask how they can be experienced, and whether the psychical process of experiencing them warrants our claiming for them an "objective reality." In some cases, as e.g., with regard to the existence of sea serpents, N rays, and ghosts, the question about the "reality" of these objects is really one as to whether the psychological treatment does not exhaust their significance, or whether the psychical processes are such as to justify our interpreting them as indicative of "objective reality."

Now among mental processes those which may be called "cognitive" are very common and predominant, and therefore the description of cognitive process will properly fall into the province of psychology. It stands to reason, moreover, that it must be described as it occurs, and without arbitrary attempts at reserving some of its aspects for the exclusive consideration of another science. Now, as cognitive process is naturally productive of "knowledge," and valuable as such, it follows that cognitive values are properly subject to psychological description. Mental life is, naturally and in point of fact, packed with values ethical, aesthetical, and cognitive ("logical"), of which it is the vehicle. It is the plain duty, therefore, of psychology to record this fact, and to describe these values. Cognitive values, as psychical occurrences, are facts for psychology. It is their specific character which subsequently renders them subjects for logic. Their specific character is that they are *claims to truth,* and employ the predicates "true" and "false"; precisely as, e.g., ethical judgments use the predicates "right" and "wrong."

The special value, however, of these specific valuations and their functions in the organization of life form no part of the purpose of psychology. Having a merely descriptive purpose, it is content to record all values merely as made, and as facts. Thus it is psychologically relevant to recognize that the predication of "true" and "false" occurs, and that what A judges "true," B may judge to be "false." But it is psychologically indifferent that A is a much *better* judge than B. Psychology, that is, does not seek to *evaluate* these claims, to decide which is really "right," or what is really "true"; still less to frame generalizations as to how in general claims are to be sustained, and humanly valid judgments to be attained. All processes of immanently and reciprocally criticizing, systematizing, harmonizing, and utilizing the claims actually made fall as such without its purpose; they are the business of logic.

§ 4. The relation of the two sciences to cognitive process, and to each other, is thus quite simple. Yet it has been woefully misunderstood. Thus it is commonly asserted that psychology does not recognize values, nor logic care about psychical existence. Yet if so, how could values enter human minds, and how could truths ever become facts?[3]

---

[3] No one, probably, has given greater currency to this fallacious notion than Mr. Bradley, by the sharp contrast he drew in his *Logic* (ch. I, e.g., pp. 7, 8, and 526) between the validity of the "idea" (=concept) and the psychical existence of the "idea" (=mental image). It has, unfortunately, not been as extensively recognized that his remark in *Appearance and Reality* (p. 51) that "It is not wholly true that 'ideas are not what they mean,' for if their mean-

Still more extraordinary is the assumption that psychology is not to describe values. Yet this assumption is made without the least consciousness of its monstrosity, and without the slightest attempt to defend it, as if it were self-evident, by writers of repute. Dr. Hastings Rashdall gravely assures us that "the Psychologist . . . knows nothing of the truth or falsity of judgments."[4] And even Professor Hoernle takes it for granted[5] that "truth, in fact, is not an object of inquiry to Psychology at all. That certain of the mental processes which it studies have the further character of being[6] true or false, is, for Psychology, an accident," and infers that "this inability to deal with validity seems to beset all psychologies alike." This arbitrary restriction on the functions of psychology is no doubt in the interest of an impracticable conception of logic, which instinctively seeks to reduce psychology to an equal or greater futility; but we, assuredly, can have no reason to accept it.

For us the function of logic develops continuously, rationally, and without antagonism out of that of psychology. Cognitive values and claims to truth exist as empirical facts. If they were all indefeasible, congruous, and compatible with each other, as e.g., my having a toothache is compatible with your not having one, there would be no ground for a further science. But in point of fact *false* claims to truth are commoner than valid ones, and they not only conflict with the

---

ing is not psychical fact, I should like to know how and where it exists" is, *inter alia*, a scornful self-correction.

Prof. Bosanquet (*Logic*, ch. I, p. 5) declares that "in considering an idea as a psychical occurrence we abstract from its meaning"; but *ibid.*, ch. II, p. 16 *n.*, he advocates the remarkable doctrine that "when psychical images come to be employed for the sake of a meaning which they convey, they *ex hypothesi* are not treated as fact. And their meaning is not itself a psychical fact, but is an intellectual activity which can only enter into fact by being used to qualify reality." This is sufficiently oracular, and it would be interesting to hear the reasons *why* psychology should be debarred from recognizing "intellectual activities" as psychical facts.

[4] *Arist. Soc. Proc.* 1905–6, p. 249.
[5] *Mind*, XIV, 473.
[6] This should be "claiming to be"; for no one supposes that psychology is concerned with the *decision* between conflicting claims to truth. Whether what claims to be true really *is* true is admittedly left to logic. Here, however, it seems to be argued that because psychology cannot *decide* between claims, it may not even *register* them, nor describe cognitive values. I fear that Prof. Hoernle throughout has not steered quite clear of the confusion between *claim* (psychological fact) and *validation* (logical fact), which so effectively vitiates the intellectualistic theories of truth. For the distinction see Chapter 7, especially § 1.

"truth," but also with each other, so that the problem of error cries out for further treatment.

§ 5. There is need, therefore, for a discipline which will evaluate these claims, and try to determine the various degrees of validity and trustworthiness which may be assigned to them. Logic is the traditional name for the science which undertakes this function. It may be defined as *the systematic evaluation of actual knowing*. It is, a normative science, because it not only records defects, but prescribes remedies; it reflects on the claims actually made, and prescribes methods for their evaluation. But its normative function arises quite naturally out of our actual procedures, when we observe that some cognitive processes are in fact more valuable than others, and select the more valuable among conflicting claims. Thus the need for logic, its genesis, and its procedures all seem to be essentially empirical, and it is quite conceivable that no special science of logic should ever have arisen. If all claims were *ipso facto* true and valid, if we had never been confronted with conflicting claims or driven by our "errors" to rescind our first assertions, what need were there for logic? Our attention would never be called to the problem of values, our primary attributions would stand, and no superior science would be devised to adjudicate between conflicting judgments.

As it is, the natural process has to be regulated and controlled, and so falls a prey to *two* sciences. The same cognitive values occur twice over, first in psychology as so many facts, then in logic, as subjects for critical evaluation. Nor is it difficult to understand how two sciences can work over the same ground: they cultivate it, with a different purpose, and so raise different crops.

§ 6. It is manifest, moreover, that the two sciences must work together hand in glove. Logic requires trustworthy descriptions of cognitive happenings before it can evaluate them with safety; for these it should be able to rely on the cooperation of psychology. In other words, the collection and preparation of the material which the logician proposes to use is essentially a psychological function, alike whether it is performed by a psychologist who bears in mind the needs of logic, or whether the logician is enough of a psychologist to do it for himself. In the latter case he resembles a painter who, like those of old, makes and mixes his own colours; the logician, on the other hand, who proposes to dispense with the aid of psychology is like a painter who will not use anything so gross as colours wherewithal to paint his "ideal" pictures.

Thus logic and psychology, though perfectly distinct, are perfectly inseparable. It is, moreover, because they are so intimately related that they must be so sharply distinguished, and because they have been so clearly distinguished that they can be so closely connected. It is hardly possible to exaggerate the intimacy of their relations. Nothing psychological can be affirmed a priori to be irrelevant to logic. The logician, no doubt, from motives of practical convenience or necessity, often abstracts provisionally from trivial characteristics of the actual psychic process; but, except in cases where he has learnt from experience what features are unessential and may safely be neglected, he always takes a certain risk in so doing. Now this risk may be fatal to the validity of his argument, and in any case impairs its theoretical exactness. The formal logician, therefore, can never, as such, claim to be the *final* judge of the value of any argument. He can never by his "rules" preclude the examination of its "material" worth; however formally perfect the syllogism which expresses it, a fatal flaw may lurk in its actual application; however grotesque its formal fallacy, a road to the truth may be barred by its rejection. If he is wise, therefore, he will not magnify his office of reminding reasoners of what they are about, and of how far their reasonings are attaining the ends they aim at. Thus the burden of proof, at any rate, lies on those who affirm that the logician may assume the irrelevance of any psychic fact.

Nay, more. One never can tell whether the proper answer to a "logical" claim does not lie in the psychological domain, and take the form of a psychological explanation. Thus a claim to have discovered the secret of the universe is not usually met by a "logical" refutation, but by an inquiry into the assertor's "state of mind," and the revelations of mystic ecstasies are treated as exhibitions of mental pathology. We know, in short, that it is folly to reason with the mentally deranged, and that, even in dealing with the sane, it is usually more effective to *persuade* than to *convince*.

We may take it, therefore, that the logician's ignoring of psychology, and abstracting from the psychical concomitants of actual thinking, can only be very hazardous affairs, which must be understood to be strictly conditioned and limited by the requirements of his temporary purpose. When the logician really knows what he is about, he does not intend them to be more than provisional, nor dream of transcending human experience by their aid. Unfortunately, however, this simple situation has been misapprehended so long, and so profoundly, that it is imperative to set forth in greater detail the thoroughgoing dependence of logic on psychological assistance. We shall do well, therefore, to show (1) that without processes which are admittedly psychological, the occurrence of cognition, and even of thinking, is impossible; (2) that all the processes which are regarded as essentially and peculiarly "logical" have a well-marked psychological side to them, and that their logical treatment develops continuously out of their psychological nature.

§ 7. (1) All actual thinking appears to be inherently conditioned throughout by processes which even the most grasping logician must conceive as specifically psychological. It is difficult to see, therefore, on what principle logic has any business to ignore them, and to claim to be "independent" of what must influence its own structures in every fiber. At any rate the *onus probandi* would seem to lie on those who affirm that these correlated and interpenetrating processes do not influence each other, and that, therefore, their psychical nature may be treated as logically irrelevant. Without, however, standing on ceremony, let us show by actual examples that our thinking depends for its very existence on the presence in it of (*a*) interest, (*b*) purpose, (*c*) emotion, (*d*) satisfaction, and that the word "thought" would cease to convey any meaning if these were really and rigidly abstracted from.

(*a*) Where can we discover anything deserving of the name of thought which is not actuated by psychological interest? To affirm this, moreover, seems merely a truism. It is merely to deny that thinking is a mechanical process like, e.g., gravitation. It is to assert that the processes during which the course of consciousness comes nearest to being a purposeless flux of mental images are most remote from cognition. It is to deny that thinking proceeds without a motive and without an aim, and to assert that, in proportion as interest grows more disciplined and concentrated, thought becomes more vigorous and more definitely purposive.

The only way of contesting our inference would seem to be to affirm that the specifically logical interest is *sui generis,* and not to be confounded with the common herd of its psychological congeners.[7] This contention, however, we must regard as merely an arbitrary fiat. It is merely a refusal to let psychology describe all interests as such. And this refusal can only be prompted by ulterior motives. Moreover, even if the allegiance this special interest owes to logic exempted it from psychological description, it could do so only *qua* its *specific* nature. *As an interest* it would still fall into the province of the science which describes the *generic* nature of interests. Lastly, a humanist logic can recognize no reasons for relegating the cognitive interest to a world apart, as if it were unconcerned with life and dissociated from personality. On all these grounds, then, we must repudiate the claim that a thought which depends on interest can be independent of psychology.

(*b*) Purpose may be conceived as a concentration of interest, and thinking must be conceived as essentially purposive, and as the more consciously so, the more efficient it grows. Whenever logic, therefore, seeks to represent the actual nature of thinking, it can never treat of "the meaning" of propositions in the abstract. It must note that the meaning depends on the use, and the use on the user's purpose. Now this purpose is primarily a question of psychical fact, which admits of being psychologically determined, and which no theory can safely ignore. If we attribute to logical rules a sort of inherent validity, a sort of discarnate existence apart from their application to cases of actual thinking, we reduce them to phantoms as futile as they are unintelligible.

7 This I take to be the meaning of Prof. Bosanquet's remarks in *Arist. Soc. Proc.,* 1905–6, p. 238. He insists that it can either be "adequately investigated within the bounds of logic proper," so as to leave nothing for "a further scrutiny of these phenomena as purely psychical disturbances," or that the common psychological element can make no specific difference in the logical interest. But how, as a logician, is he to know all this? And how if the psychologists dispute this claim? He is setting up as a judge in a case to which he is a party.

(c) Emotion accompanies actual cognition as a shadow does light. Even so unexciting an operation as counting has an emotional tone. The effect of this emotional tone seems to be various, but may be salutary; we can often observe how love and hate inspire men with an insight to which the fishlike eye of cold indifference could never penetrate. It need not be denied, however, that in some people and in some forms it may have a hurtful effect on the value of the cognitive results. But this must be shown, and cannot be assumed, in any given case. Nor is its alleged hurtfulness a reason for denying the existence of this emotional bias, except to those who are very far gone in that application of "Christian Science" to philosophy which declares all evil to be "appearance." Our only chance of counteracting emotional bias, moreover, lies in admitting its existence.

(d) If a feeling of satisfaction did not occur in cognitive processes, the attainment of truth would not be felt to have value. In point of fact such satisfactions supervene on every step in reasoning. Without them, logical "necessity," "cogency," and "insight" would become meaningless words.

It seems clear, therefore, that without these psychological conditions which have been mentioned, thinking disappears, and with it, presumably, logic.[8] They cannot, therefore, be dispensed with. Purpose, interest, desire, emotion, satisfaction are more essential to thinking than steam is to a steam engine.

§ 8. (2) The most fundamental conceptions of logic, like "necessity," "certainty," "self-evidence," "truth," "meaning," are primarily descriptions of processes which are psychical facts. They are inseparably accompanied by specific psychical feelings. What is called their "strictly logical" sense is *continuous with* their psychological senses, and whenever this connexion is really broken off, its meaning simply disappears. This need not here be set forth at length. The logician's embarrassments in discriminating "logical" from "psychological" necessity[9] and self-evidence are well known. It is also beginning to be clear that he had not, until the pragmatic controversy arose,

[8] Some symbolic logicians, however, seem to regard thinking, i.e., judging and inferring, as so inherently psychological as to be extralogical. Cp. *Formal Logic*, p. 377.
[9] Cp. *Personal Idealism*, p. 70 *n.*

ever seriously considered what was the nature of truth predication as a psychic process.

But the conception of "certainty" is often considered the essential differentia of logical thought, and, therefore, may deserve a brief discussion. Everyone, of course, would have to admit that all "certainty" in its actual occurrence was accompanied by a psychical feeling of certainty in various degrees of intensity. An appeal might, however, be made to the distinction of "logical" and "psychological" certainty. Psychological certainty, we commonly say, is "subjective," and exists for individuals; logical certainty is "objective," and imposed on intelligence as such. Again, psychological certainty may set in long before logical proof is complete, often long before it ought; and conversely our psychological stupidity may rebel against mathematically demonstrated truths. From these current distinctions the logician is apt to infer that psychological and logical certainty have really nothing to do with each other and ought not to be confused. But if this be true, why are they both called by the same name? Surely, if logicians wished to keep them apart and could afford to do so, they could label them differently. That they have not done so is a strong presumption that it is impracticable.

Indeed, the truth would seem to be (a) that if the *feeling* of certainty is eliminated the word becomes unmeaning, and (b) that "logical" is quite continuous with psychological certainty. The notion of "logical" certainty arises from the extension of potential beyond actual purpose in thinking. We actually stop at the point at which we psychologically are satisfied and willing to accept a claim to truth as good; but we can sometimes conceive ulterior purposes which would require further confirmation, and other minds that would be satisfied less easily. This engenders the ideal of a complete "logical" proof transcending that which is good enough for us, and capable of compelling the assent of all intelligences. But even if it could be attained, its certainty would still be psychological, as certainly psychological as is our capacity to project the ideal. Both are dependent on the actual powers of individual minds. Thus for the moment mathematical demonstration seems to satisfy the logical ideal of most intellectualist logicians, and is praised as absolutely certain. But that they think it so is merely psychical fact. For the reason simply is that so far they do not seem to have psychologically conceived the thought of varying the postulates on which such demonstration rests. If they had recognized the hypothetical basis of mathematical certainty, they could conceive something more "certain."

§ 9. The fundamental logical operations, like meaning, conceiving, discriminating, identifying, judging, inferring, all have psychological aspects, and could not come about by "pure" thought. I have suggested elsewhere[10] that logical identity is always a postulate. It should be stated as that *"what I will shall mean the same, is (so far) the same."* And by "the same" I do not mean *indistinguishable* (though this criterion too rests on a psychological property) as Mr. Bradley does in what he considers "the indisputable basis of all reasoning," the axiom that *"what seems the same is the same,"* which he himself calls "a monstrous assumption."[11] Logical identity emphatically does not rest on an easy acquiescence in appearances or psychical carelessness about noticing differences. It is a conscious act of purposive thinking, performed *in spite of observed differences.* "The same" means a *claim* that for our purposes these differences may be ignored, and the two terms treated alike.

The principle, therefore, is not mere psychological fact, carrying no logical consequences. Nor certainly is it a mere tautology, "A is A." It is ultimately one of the devices which we have hit upon for dealing with our experience. As such it may be supposed to have passed through an experimental stage as a mere postulate; and even now a certain risk remains inherent in its use. That there shall be identity we have good grounds for insisting, but our claim that any A is A may often be frustrated. That therefore every attempted "identification" should come true would be the experience only of an omnipotent being, whose volitions the course of events could never contravene. Only to such a being (if such can be conceived) would it be self-evidently, invariably, and "necessarily" true that "A is A"; in our human thinking, the identities we select may prove to be mistaken. Thus the validity of the principle in

10 *Personal Idealism,* pp. 94–104; *Formal Logic,* ch. X, §§ 8, 10.
11 *Principles of Logic,* p. 264.

the abstract in no wise guarantees its validity in its actual use, or its application to any particular case. But on the whole the principle is valuable enough for us to ascribe our failures not to its inapplicability to our world, but to our own stupidity in selecting the "wrong" identities.

Meaning is a psychical fact which should have great interest for psychology. It is also a fundamental function for logic. But unfortunately intellectualist logicians, by abstracting too easily from its concrete nature as a psychical process, have involved the whole subject in confusion and completely obscured the problem of understanding.

As we saw in Chapter 2, § 2, meaning depends upon purpose, i.e., upon *context,* as the purpose lies in the context. Now that context is of logical importance is, in a manner, recognized. But this reçognition takes the form of asserting that the meaning (and truth) of an assertion depends on the totality of knowledge; and this at once rules out *human* knowledge. For as we cannot know this totality, if meaning depends on this, it is impossible. This interpretation of context, however, is quite false. Meaning is not in the first instance logical at all, but psychological. It is primarily a question of what the person who made the assertion *actually meant.* And as, of course, *the whole of his concrete personality* went to the making of the assertion, and contributed to his actual meaning, a case must be made out for its mutilation by "logic." The next question is the problem of the "understanding" or transference of the meaning. We have to discover not merely what the assertor meant, but also how he was understood. The inherent difficulty of this problem, to which since the days of Gorgias "logic" has paid little heed, lies in this, that practically meaning must be transferred by verbal symbols, and conveyed in "propositions." But such propositions must always be ambiguous. They *may* mean whatever they can be used to mean. They are blank forms to be filled up with concrete meanings according to requirements. They afford, therefore, no security that the meaning which they are *taken* as conveying is identical with that which they were *intended* to convey. Until we have assured ourselves of this, it is vain to discuss "the meaning" of the assertion, or to attempt its logical evaluation. Consequently the logical treatment of meaning is *meaningless,* until these psychological preliminaries have been settled.

What now is the way in which these matters have been treated by "logic"? It has made a series of monstrous abstractions, which break down as soon as they are applied to the facts of actual knowing.

(1) It has abstracted from context, i.e., from the *actual* context in which the assertion was made and tried to convey its meaning, as being psychological and irrelevant. This is a gigantic blunder, after which it is vain to seek to provide for the "logical" relevance of context. For the "logical" context never recovers its full concreteness, and so can never guarantee to "logic" a knowledge of the actual meaning. (2) It has framed the abstraction of "the logical meaning" of the assertion, which it has usually conceived also as existing per se and independently of human assertors, and taken it for granted that it could be used as the standard to which to refer the meanings meant and understood. But in actual knowing, "the meaning" is *the* problem. It is not what we may presume, but what we must discover. It is an ideal to be reached, and not a presupposition to be started from. It does not exist; it has to be made—by mutual understanding. Moreover, for the reasons given above, the abstract "meaning per se" of the assertion reduces itself in practice to the *average meaning* of a form of words which will *probably* be used in a certain sense, but may be used in any sense in which anyone can convey (or try to convey) *his* meaning. "The meaning," therefore, *is infinitely ambiguous.*[12] And hence to operate with it is always hazardous and often false. (3) In abstracting from the assertor's actual meaning, "logic" always runs the risk of excluding the real point. For this may lie in some of the "irrelevant" psychical details of the actual meaning, whose essence may not lie in its plain surface meaning, but in some subtle innuendo. Moreover, even where "the logical meaning" does not miss the real point, it nearly always fails to convey the *whole* meaning. For the actual meaning is fully concrete, and contains much more than it conveys, and infinitely more than "the logical

[12] Thus the assertion "Smith is red-haired" has as many "meanings" as there are past, actual, and potential Smiths, of whom it can be (truly or falsely) predicated, and occasions on which it can be made.

meaning" of the form of words. The latter, therefore, is always something *less* than what was actually meant, and fails to express it fully. For the appropriateness of an assertion always depends in some degree on the personality of the assertor and the particularity of the occasion. (4) "Logic," in abstracting from the psychological problem, has burked the whole question of the communication of meaning. It has assumed that there is *only one* meaning with which it need concern itself, and that everyone must understand it. In point of fact, there are usually two or more meanings concerned in every question. For the assertor commonly fails to convey his meaning, or his whole meaning, and his assertion is taken in a meaning different from that in which it was meant. There are, in consequence, at least as many "meanings" as parties to the discussion, and the "logic" which is concerned only about "the meaning" is troubling about the nonexistent. Whereas if it were recognized that what is called "the meaning" is an indication, but not a guarantee, of the real meaning, and that the meaning understood may not be that intended, we should take more care to secure a real identity of meaning before beginning to dispute, and so the chances are that many "logical questions" would never arise.

(5) Lastly, "logic" has assumed not only that "the meaning" of an assertion can be ascertained without regard to the psychological facts, but also that it can be quite dissociated from the personality of its assertor. It becomes, consequently, a matter of indifference whether it was made by A or by B, nay, even whether or not it was (or could be) made by anyone. Whoever made it, "it" is equally true, even though A was a fool or a crank asserting it at random, and B a great authority who knows the subject. Our common sense accordingly protests against this paradox, and urges that the status of the assertor must make a difference to the assertion. And the practice of science would seem to bear this out. The logical value of an assertion is constantly treated as conditioned by the qualifications of its author. If these are adequate, it is received with respect; if they are nil, it is treated as scientifically null and disregarded. Thus dozens of sailors have sighted sea serpents, but the testimony of the two competent naturalists on the *Valhalla* is far more likely to shake the incredulity of

zoologists.[13] On the other hand, when Professor Curie reported the extraordinary and unparalleled properties of radium, his assertions were at once accepted. The solution of the paradox lies of course in the falsity of the assertion that when two persons "say the same thing" (i.e., *use the same form of words*) they make the same assertion. They really make *two* assertions, which may (or may not) subsequently be made to coincide and identified with the (usual) meaning of the proposition they use. But they *need not mean* the same thing, nor understand alike. They will probably make the assertion on different grounds, and will certainly have different motives and aims. What *their* assertion means will vary accordingly. And so will its logical value, which here plainly shows itself as dependent on psychological circumstances. Why then should "logic" stubbornly blind itself to these facts, and insist on cutting meaning loose from its psychological roots, and on confounding in its abstract "forms" cases which all actual knowing must discriminate? The practical convenience and rough adequacy of the easygoing convention that "the meaning" may be taken as identical with the meanings meant and understood is surely no defence *an intellectualistic logical theory* can plead against the charge of false abstraction and inadequate analysis.

As regards judging, it may suffice to suggest that "the judgment" is as dangerous an abstraction as "the meaning" which is ascribed to it. For what is called *one* is usually *many*. It follows, moreover, from our last discussion both that every judgment, in its actual use, is an intimately personal affair, and that its personal aspects often have (and always may have) important bearings on its logical value. No judgment could come into being, even in the world of thought, if some individual mind were not impelled by its total psychical contents and history to affirm it upon some suitable occasion, and to stake its fortunes on this personal affirmation. And even after it has come into being, its logical status is still vitally dependent on its relations to the minds which entertain it. The judgment, therefore, essentially presupposes a mind, a motive, and a purpose. To "depersonalize" it is to do violence to its concrete nature. Similarly, its "objective validity" is not

13 Cp. *Nature,* No. 1914, p. 202.

a question of the interrelation of absolute static truths in a supercelestial sphere. It depends on its adaptation to our world and its congruousness with the opinions and aims of others. Hence every recognition of a judgment by others is a social problem, often of a very complicated character.

To bring out the unreality of the logician's conception of judgment, we may note also that "logic" is always held to exclude the evaluation of questions and commands. And yet are not postulates often the basis of our reasonings, and are not all real judgments the implicit or explicit answers to a question? Does any sane person knowingly argue about what is universally admitted? Ought it not to be truly "illogical," then, to sever the connexion between things which belong so closely together? To confine logic to categorical statements in the indicative mood is to abstract at one blow from the sense and actual use of judgments. Contrast with this an intellectualist view of the question's function. Professor Bosanquet, e.g., is "disposed to doubt whether we can interrogate ourselves" otherwise than rhetorically, and urges that questions which we cannot answer and know that we cannot answer cannot be "genuine questions." He concludes that "thus a question cannot be an act of thought as such, just as a lie is not, and for the same reason, that it is not an attitude that the intellect can maintain within itself. . . . It is a demand for information; its essence is to be addressed to a moral agent, not ourselves, in whom it may produce action" (*Logic,* ch. I, p. 36).

Clearly, however, this whole paradox rests on the abstraction of truth from its consequences, on the divorce of "thought" from its psychical context. The question is taken as unrelated to anything that precedes and follows. If this is done, only two cases remain; we ask ourselves a question to which we either do, or do not, know the answer. And of course the question is in both cases futile. In actual knowing, however, we only ask ourselves questions where, though we do not yet know the answers, *we want to know them and are willing to take steps to find them out.* A question, therefore, is logically futile only if we decline to *act* on it, and this would be equally true of a question addressed to others, if they, similarly, did not react upon it. Really, therefore, the putting of questions is, as the Greeks well knew, a natural and necessary process as a preliminary to the satisfaction of a cognitive need, and one which may be of the greatest value, if the right questions are clearly formulated.

§ 10. Lastly, not so much because further illustration should be needed, as in order to force a clear issue, let us consider one more case, that which has been most disputed, viz., that of reasoning openly inspired by desire, i.e., of a conclusion affirmed because we should like it to be true. Is it always true that we attain truth only by suppressing desire? Take the familiar argument: *The world is bad, therefore there must be a better.* It all rests on the desire for good and the postulate of perfection. Now if postulation is as such invalid, and desire a mere obstacle to truth, it clearly follows that this argument is hopelessly illogical; which is accordingly what intellectualist logicians have everywhere maintained.[14] A bad world is logically evidence *against*, not *for*, the existence of a better.

Now, against such abstract and a priori notions of what is good reasoning, we may lay it down that good reasoning is that which leads us right and enables us to discover what we are willing to acclaim as truth. And so tested, the desire-inspired reasoning may clearly often be the better. It may prompt to more active inquiry, to keener observation, to more persevering experiment. The logician who declares *de non apparentibus et non existentibus eadem est ratio,* who declines to look for what he wants but does not see, who does not seek to penetrate beyond the veil of appearances, is, frankly, an ass. He frustrates his avowed purpose, the discovery of truth, by debarring himself from whatever truth lies beneath the surface. His self-approbation, therefore, of the heroic self-sacrifice of his volitional preferences to "objective truth," which he "feels himself bound" to commit, is simply silly. What right, indeed, has he even to "feel bound"? Does not the phrase betray the emotional origin also of *his* attitude to truth? He accomplishes the sacrifice of "personal preference" to "objective truth" by dint of an emotional desire to mortify himself (or, more often, others), the satisfaction of which

14 *Qua* human they have, of course, not infrequently relapsed into the postulatory way of reasoning. Thus it is a favourite inference from the fact that all the parts of the world are imperfect, that the whole must be perfect. But if in this case it is legitimate to argue to the ideal from the defects of the actual, why not in others?

appears to him as a good. How then is he other or better than the voluntarist who makes bold to postulate, and verifies his anticipations?

Moreover, if we supply the missing premiss in the contention of the intellectualist, we find that it must take a form something like this, that it is *wrong* to anticipate nature, to go beyond what you can see, wicked to try whether the apparent "facts" cannot be moulded or remoulded into conformity with our desires. He must say "it is *wrong*." He cannot say "it is impossible." For it is constantly done, and with the happiest effects.

If now we ask, *Why wrong?* we force the intellectualist to reveal the full measure of his prejudice. To defend his assumption he must do one of two things: (1) He may fall back upon his own feeling of the aesthetical or ethical impropriety of the voluntarist's procedure. But if so, his objection ceases to be purely logical. It may be declared to be only his idiosyncrasy, and be met by the retort: "But it does not seem improper to me. I do not, will not, and cannot share your devil worship of disagreeable fact and unwelcome truth. I do not, cannot, and will not call a universe good which does not satisfy my desires, and I feel strongly that it *ought* to do so. Whether it does, or can be made to do so, I do not know as yet; it is one of the chief things I am staying in the universe to find out. If (*a*) it does, or can, then my desires are to be regarded as a sound, logical indication of the nature of reality and a valid method of penetrating to its core. If (*b*) it does not, I may have, no doubt, to admit unwelcome truths and unpalatable facts. But I shall do so provisionally, and with a clear intention of abolishing them as soon and as far as I am able. If (*c*) it sometimes does, and sometimes not, why then I am entitled, nay, bound, to try *both* methods. I have a right both to treat my wishes as clues to reality, and to subordinate them on occasion to facts which are too strong for me. And I observe that (whether you approve or blame) this is what, in fact, men have always done."

If (2) the intellectualist tries to find something more objective than his instinctive feeling on the wrongness of the voluntarist's procedure, what resource has he? Must he not appeal to the consequences of the two methods? Must he not try to show that the consequences of submission are always, or mostly, good—those of postulation always, or mostly, bad? But can he show this? Notoriously he cannot. And in either case has he not used the pragmatic test of logical value?

It is vain, therefore, to seek an escape from the conclusion that actual thinking is pervaded and conditioned through and through by psychological processes, and that logic gains nothing, and loses all vitality and interest, all touch with reality, by trying to ignore them. To emphasize this is not, of course, to deny that for logical purposes some psychological conditions may sometimes be irrelevant. Thus in using concepts it is generally possible to abstract from the particular nature of the psychological imagery. The reason is that identity of meaning overpowers diversity of imagery; if this were otherwise, the use of concepts would be impossible. Again an error, say of counting, may be psychologically a very complex fact; it may, nevertheless, be logically a very simple error. By my counting 2 and 3 as 6, there may hang a lengthy tale; but for the logician it may be enough to say that the result ought to have been 5. It should be observed, however, even here, that the logical description of this process as an "error" involves an appeal to psychology; the error could not be recognized as such but for my capacity to correct it, or at least to admit the validity of processes which enable others to correct it. If I were psychologically incapable of counting $2 + 3$ as other than 6, I could not recognize my "error," a "common" arithmetic would disappear, and there would remain no way of deciding which process was counting and which miscounting but the experience of the respective consequences and the slow test of survival.

§ 11. Whenever, then, the logician abstracts from the concrete facts of reasoning, he should do so with a consciousness of the nature and dangers of his procedure. He should feel that he may have left out what is essential, that he may have failed to notice the actual meaning of the thought he examined, and have substituted for it some wholly different imagination of his own. The proposition which he solemnly writes down an "error" or a "fallacy" may not have been a prosaic affirmation at all; it may have beeen poetical hyperbole or an hypothesis, a jest or a sarcasm, a trap or a lie. He will, therefore, get a very little way into the analysis of actual thinking if he declines to recognize that in its actual use the same form of words may serve all these purposes, and cannot be treated logically until he has found out what its actual meaning is. A lie is, I presume, a proposition which claims truth like any other. But the claim is for export only; the liar himself knows it to be "false," and has rejected the claim, even though he has persuaded all the world. There is no "lie" unless there is deception, and no deception unless there are deceivers and deceived. The difference of the persons concerned, therefore, is essential. How then can "the meaning" of such a proposition be represented as single and simple? How can its logical status even be discussed without going into these facts? Does it not follow that formal logicians have no right to their habit of speaking of "the meaning" of a proposition as if it were a logical fixture? *The actual* meaning is always a psychical fact, which in the case of an ambiguity intended, implied, or understood may be many. The "logical" meaning is potential; it is at best the *average* meaning with which the proposition is most commonly used. It is only more or less probable, therefore, as the interpretation of an actual judgment. And to build a system of apodictic doctrine on foundations such as these —what is it but to build a house of cards?

It would be possible to show in this manner, and with the utmost fullness and unlimited examples, that vastly more than the textbooks recognize is really relevant to logic, that every logical process, conception, method, and criterion springs naturally and continuously out of psychological soil, and is essentially a *selection from,* and *valuation of,* a more extensive psychical material. But enough has probably been said to suggest that logic can take nothing for granted, and itself least of all. In view of the complete dependence and reliance of every logical process on the psychical nature of man in general and of men in particular, in view of the manifest adjustment of every logical principle to the needs of human life, is it not high time that *a systematic doubt were cast on the assumption that the theory of knowledge must abstract from the personality of the knower?*

§ 12. It should now be clear what is the meaning, the ground and the aim of our humanist "Psychologism," but we may clinch the argument by supplementing it negatively by a proof that the antagonistic conception of an "independent" logic (1) involves unintelligible and self-contradictory mis-descriptions; (2) assumes a standpoint which it cannot justify, and (3) is so unable to deal with actual knowing, that (4) it ends in scepticism and intellectual collapse. It will be seen, in short, that the intellectualistic treatment of logic "necessarily conducts to a complete debacle of the intellect."[15]

It has already been implied that it is usual to formulate the conception, and to expound the claims, of logic in an anti-psychological way radically opposed to ours. One still hears of logic as the science of "pure" thought, endowed with a standpoint and nature of its own, which is "free" and "inde-pendent" of man and human psychology, and anything it may do or say about such merely human processes as "willing" and "feeling," as a science which by "depersonalizing" itself has risen to communion with the eternal and immutable Ideal, and of course cares not one jot about our personal interests or attitude towards truth.

These epithets, however, are chiefly ornamental, and merely serve to curry favour for the assumptions on which it is at-tempted to rest the science.

(1) The notion of "pure thought," for example, must not be pressed. It is not a fact of actual knowing, but a barefaced fiction, which can at most be defended as a methodological necessity for the purposes of intellectualist logicians. Its fic-titious nature has nowadays to be avowed, whenever it is directly challenged. Even Mr. Bradley "agrees" with Professor Dewey, that "there is no such existing thing as pure thought," it is true only just before proceeding to declare that "if there is to be no such thing as *independent* thought, thought that is which in its actual exercise *takes no account of the psycho-logical situation,* I am, myself, in the end, led inevitably to scepticism. The doctrine that *every judgment essentially de-pends on the entire psychical state* of the individual, and de-rives from this its falsehood or truth, is, I presume, usually

15 Capt. H. V. Knox in *Mind,* XIV, 210. Cp. *Formal Logic.*

taken to amount to complete scepticism."[16] "Pure thought," then, is not to be the same as "independent." But what is "pure" thought *pure from?* Psychological contamination? If so, will it not coincide with "independent" thought? For that too "takes no account of the psychological situation." But if so, has not an imperious need of logic been equated with a nonexistent? The puzzle grows more perplexing when we recall the pronounced emotionalism which is somehow combined with Mr. Bradley's Intellectualism, and to which Mr. Sturt has lately drawn attention.[17] How can an intellect so emotionally conditioned be either "pure" or "independent"?

The truth, however, seems to be that the sacrifice of "pure thought" goes greatly against the grain of Intellectualism. Only constant vigilance can prevent it from wriggling itself back into the claim to be an actual fact, and whether Intellectualism can afford wholly to dispense with it, especially in its arguments about "useless" knowledge, seems more than doubtful.

(2) The "independence" of logic and its standpoint is in every way a most difficult notion. It is hard to understand, harder to derive, hardest to justify. Nay, in the end it will turn out so anarchical as to be fatal to the theory that entertained it. For the present, however, it may suffice to point out the difficulty of ascertaining the meaning of a word which is constantly employed in current discussions, and never defined. Its meaning appears to vary with the work it has to do. In its most rigorous sense it describes the iniquity of pluralism in claiming "independence" for its reals, the impossibility of which provides an a priori refutation of this metaphysical "heresy."[18] In this sense it means apparently "totally unconnected with." A more lenient sense is in vogue when Intellectualism has to defend its abstractions against humanist attacks. For in that case we learn, e.g., that every logic is "inde-

---

[16] *Mind,* XIII, 309 *n.* Italics mine. We learn from this amazing passage that it is complete scepticism to take complete account of the facts in a cognitive procedure, and that if we will not deliberately falsify them, we are doomed to end as sceptics! It is surely strange that such falsification should be a necessary preliminary to the search for truth, and one is tempted to reply that if Logic demands this falsification, then the sooner the conception of Logic is amended the better. But it is evidently Mr. Bradley who is predestined to scepticism; every theory of Logic he touches turns to scepticism in his hands, and even when he flees to metaphysics he fares no better. Probably the peculiarity is, in his case, psychological.

[17] *Idola Theatri,* ch. V, §§ 4–7.

[18] *Appearance and Reality,* ch. X.

pendent" of psychology, nay, that every well-conducted theoretic truth preserves a virtuous independence. Similarly we are told by "realists," that in the act of knowing, the object of knowledge is quite "independent" of the knowing act. And, finally, Mr. Bradley sometimes equates it with "relative freedom"![19] It is clear that if these ambiguities were done away with, either the argument about the impossibility of pluralism, or that about the independence of pure thought and logic, would have to disappear from the armoury of our intellectualists.

(3) The "depersonalization" which is regarded as characteristic of an "independent" logic is usually defended by the example of science, which is said to ignore all human interest as irrelevant. But this assertion is hardly true. The abstraction practised by science is *not* analogous to that advocated for logic. It is *not* true that science as such abstracts from *all* human interest. It does *not* abstract from the scientist's interest in his particular science. And this is still a human interest. For it is what generates the science, and incites men to its study.[20] Psychologically it represents not an *absence,* but a *concentration* of interest, such as is demanded, more or less, for the attainment of every purpose, and for the satisfaction of every interest. And it can occur *only in a highly developed personality.* The "depersonalization," therefore, which is postulated for logic obtains no support whatever from scientific procedure. And we shall soon see how ill it serves the ends of "logic."

(4) The analysis of psychic process into "thinking," "willing," and "feeling," in order to justify the restriction of "logic" to the first and the exclusion of the two latter, appears to be an unwarranted piece of amateur psychologizing. For the analysis in question is valuable only as a rough reference for popular purposes, and is really a survival from the old "faculty" psychology. Scientifically its descriptive, like its explanatory, value is nil. No one nowadays seriously supposes that a soul can actually be put together out of thought, will, and feeling, or that this "analysis" represent its actual genesis. For

19 *Mind,* XIII, 322.
20 This remark, of course, is not inconsistent with the pragmatic doctrine that all science is ultimately useful. For it refers only to the immediate psychological motive.

in actual knowing all three always cooperate. There is no thought process which is not purposively initiated and directed (i.e., more or less "willed"), or which is not coloured by feelings and emotions. It is false, therefore, to conceive "thought" in abstraction from "will" and "feeling," if we intend to examine actual knowing. But it is just this intention which Intellectualism leaves in doubt. It is hard to see, therefore, why a "thought" which has abstracted from purpose, interest, emotion, and satisfaction should any longer be called thought at all; at any rate, it is no longer human thought, and can have no relation to human life.

But the unfortunate fact remains that all these phrases have long been taken for granted, with little or no warrant or criticism. They are traditionally part and parcel of an "independent" logic *which has begged its "standpoint."*

§ 13. Formally this standpoint is bafflingly indeterminate. It is neither consistently descriptive nor consistently normative, but either, or both, as suits the occasion. Sometimes it appeals to what logical procedure actually is, sometimes to what it ideally ought to be; i.e., what *by us* would be called psychological and logical considerations alternate in the most confusing way. In its own phraseology this confusion is cloaked by its conception of "the logical Ideal," which can be represented either as what human thought naturally aspires to, or as what controls its wayward vagaries.

Let us consider a few representative examples. Mr. Bradley prefaces his *Principles of Logic* with the confession that he is not sure where logic begins or ends; but no attentive reader can fail to see that his "logic" begins in psychology and ends in scepticism. It is, moreover, just because the standpoints of fact and of validity are so inextricably mingled that nothing can save his "logic" from surrender to scepticism, except a desperate appeal to metaphysics, the aid of which *Appearance and Reality* was subsequently to prove illusory.[21]

21 It need not, of course, be denied that nevertheless Mr. Bradley's *Logic* is a great work, which has exercised a well-deserved influence on English thought. But its defects are so glaring that its influence has been very mixed. The sort of thing complained of may be illustrated, e.g., by comparing Mr. Bradley's criticism of Mill's conception of induction with his criticism of the syllogism. When he objects to the former that induction is not proof, his standpoint is clearly that of validity. But when he protests that the syllogism is not the universal form of (*de facto*) valid reasoning, and gives "specimens

Professor Bosanquet seems to incline more distinctly to the descriptive standpoint. He declines to call logic normative; but calls its object "self-normative."[22] The preface of his *Logic* tells us that "the conception of Logical Science which has been my guide is that of an unprejudiced study of the forms of knowledge in their development, their interconnexion, and their comparative value as embodiments of truth." In his discussion with me he calls it "the science which considers the nature of thought as manifested in a fully self-consistent form."[23]

Still, even here, both sides are observable. A "study of the forms of knowledge," and of "the nature of thought," sounds like a purely descriptive undertaking. But the notion of "comparative value" is as distinctly normative; so is that of a fixed ideal or "system" which claims to regulate and control the natural development of cognitive procedures, quite irrespective of their use as the means to the ends of human knowing.

§ 14. This whole conception of the logical standpoint is, however, open to the gravest objection. *Qua* descriptive, it either instigates logic to poach on the preserves of psychology, and to interfere with its functions, or, if you please, to become itself psychology. In the latter case it must become bad or ignorant psychology. In the former case it must either *prohibit* psychology from describing cognitive processes, or *duplicate* the psychological descriptions. We should get, that is, a two-fold description of the same events, the one dubbed "logic" and the other "psychology." One or the other of these would surely be superfluous or mistaken. Or if both of them could

---

of inference" which are not syllogistic as they stand and rest on relations evident to us on empirical and psychological grounds, has he not plainly passed over to the standpoint of description of the actual?

[22] *Arist. Soc. Proc.*, 1905–6, p. 263. This looks suspiciously like an attempt to run with the hares and to hunt with the hounds. At any rate, it involves the "depersonalization" we have objected to, and ignores the fact that logical norms are values *for man,* and the offspring of our interests.

[23] *Ibid.*, p. 237. He gives as an alternative to this, "as manifest in the endeavor to apprehend truth." But it would appear that, even in these definitions, logic has not succeeded in manifesting herself in a fully consistent form. For even if we make explicit what is presumably intended, viz., that they take "truth" as = "the fully self-consistent form" of thought (an essentially formal view which seems to render it a wholly intrinsic affair of thought, and to rule out all testing of our predications on the touchstone of reality), the two definitions cannot be made to coincide. For "the *endeavor* to apprehend truth" adds a consideration wholly extraneous and alien to the formal self-consistency of thought, and one, moreover, which is plainly psychological.

somehow (e.g., by a reference to the different purposes of the two sciences?) be maintained, it would become necessary to consider their relation to each other. This would be just as necessary, and much more difficult, when both sciences are conceived as descriptive, as when one is conceived as normative. For the attempt to adjust their relations would have to start from an open conflict about the ground each was to cover.

Moreover, even as descriptive psychology, this logic would be defective. It would either have to ignore the "willing" and "feeling" indubitably present in cognition, or to insist on describing them, as far as its purposes required. In the former case it would be certain, in the latter it would be probable, that the description would be incomplete. For the descriptive interest would be restricted by the logical purpose, and in any case, would not extend to the whole psychical context.

But surely, when we describe, we should try to describe completely, without obliterating psychical values and without any *arrière-pensée*. The omission of any feature which *de facto* accompanies knowing demands caution and an explicit justification. For how can it be taken for granted that anything is unessential? The context of any reasoning extends indefinitely into the psychological; the actual meaning always depends upon the context, and when we abstract from any of it, we take a risk. Before any train of thought is capable of logical analysis, it must somehow be determined what features in it are important and vital, and what unimportant and unessential. But how can the logician determine this, without the aid either of psychology or of experience? There is no prospect then that his descriptions will be adequate, either logically or psychologically.

Even though, therefore, someone should suggest as a compromise that logic and psychology should both describe the actual psychic process, but that logic should have a monopoly of the cognitive features, the compromise would be equally futile and intolerable. For if so, who or what is to decide which is which, and how much of the whole is logically relevant? What if the parties disagree, and the subjects decline to be separated?

Finally, in assigning to logic a descriptive function, a serious concealment has been practised. Its study of cognitive process assuredly was *not* "unprejudiced." It has made *de facto,* but secretly and unconsciously, very definite and peculiar assumptions as to the nature of the logical standpoint. A big encroachment has been made on the domain of psychology, which has been robbed of the most valuable portion of its territory. It has been assumed (as we saw in § 4) that psychology has no right to treat cognitive values, and must perforce content itself with what is left over after logic has claimed all it has a mind to for its province. And this despoliation has been committed by sheer importunity, without the least pretence of a rational delimitation of scientific frontiers, and with no attempt at an equitable arbitration of the dispute!

§ 15. The results of this monstrous injustice are not slow to show themselves. First of all, psychology is reduced to absurdity, to the care of the shreds and dregs of a disrupted soul. And then, by a thoroughly deserved Nemesis, the unjust abstraction made by logic ends in her own paralysis!

The first stage of this process, the arbitrary stultification of psychology, may best be studied in Professor Bosanquet's Aristotelian Society papers;[24] the second, the suicide of "independent" logic, in Mr. H. H. Joachim's book *The Nature of Truth.*

"Psychological process," says Professor Bosanquet, "when it differs from the process which is the object-matter of logic, differs by being inarticulate, circuitous, fragmentary. It is the logical process broken up and disguised," "a Glaucus," whose divine original, however, is "never found typically perfect in actual psychological process."[25] Thus "logical process is the psychological process in its explicit and self-consistent form," freed from the "interruptions" and "irrelevance" of "purely psychical disturbances."

And so the "self-normative," "independent" logic, "dropping out abstract psychical processes," haughtily "goes forward on the path of concrete fulfilment or individuality"[26]—to what end will presently appear.

Now the division of territories propounded in these words should certainly secure to logic the most brilliantly prosperous

24 *Op. cit.*, pp. 237–47, 262–65.
25 *Ibid.*, pp. 239, 240.
26 *Ibid.*, p. 265.

career. It appears to give logic every advantage. It reduces psychology to such pulp that its voice can scarce be heard in the Council of the Sciences. One hardly dares to point out in remonstrance that Professor Bosanquet's "psychological process" with "pure" and "mere" conditions differs radically from the concrete psychical process of humanist psychology, and is obviously incapable of performing the functions of the latter. It is conceived as a miserable abstraction, not (as is legitimate in a special science) as regards limitation of standpoint, but as regards the content it is permitted to treat, and is almost deserving of the contempt poured upon it. For what is it but a mere rubbishy residuum, all that is left behind when its values have been extracted from the actual psychic process, and its life has been extinguished?

Compared with this "misshapen Glaucus" postulated by logical theory, almost anything may claim to be concrete. Even Professor Bosanquet's "logic process," which has been allowed to select all that seemed to be of value, and to abstract only from the merest and most worthless dross. So at least it seems, in the triumphant self-assertion of an "independent" logic. It seems almost fantastic to suggest a doubt whether after all psychology has been despoiled enough, whether after assigning to the "logical" the whole purposiveness of psychic process and leaving the psychological a purposeless chaos, Professor Bosanquet has not abstracted from something which was needed to make thought truly purposive.

§ 16. Meanwhile, what can we reply? Nothing, it is to be feared, our intellectualist logicians will deign to listen to.

We shall protest in vain that the "mere" or "pure" psychological conditions, which Professor Bosanquet flung aside as worthless on the rubbish heap, are pure fictions which bear no resemblance to the psychical processes of actual knowing, that we never meant to relate *them* to logic, that what we meant was not this fantastic abstraction, but the most concrete thing imaginable, viz., the actual psychic process in its all-inclusive activity, and with nothing at all, however worthless it might seem, abstracted from. We shall observe in vain that however "concrete" the logic process may appear by comparison with the artificial abstraction of the "merely psychological," it is admitted to be an ideal never realized in actual thinking, that therefore it *has* abstracted from something, and that it remains to be seen whether that was really as unessential as was asserted, or whether an immense abstraction has unwittingly been made, which in the end proves ruinous to logic. We shall ask in vain how logic has arrived at a standpoint which gives it such crushing superiority over psychology, and entitles it to take and leave whatsoever it likes, without condescending to give reasons for its procedure.

We shall ask all these questions vainly, because logic is "independent," nay autocratic. It gives an account of its self-normative procedure to no man or science. "It can only be judged by itself at a further stage," its friends haughtily declare.[27] We must therefore perforce let it go its own way. It cannot be refuted; it can only be developed.

§ 17. Let us therefore follow the developments of logic. Having successfully maintained her right to "depersonalize" herself, having got rid of the "merely psychological" encumbrances of her "Glaucus," her "old man of the sea," she should be able to soar to the illimitable heights of an infinite "ideal" of a "timelessly self-fulfilled . . . all-inclusive, significant whole . . . whose coherence is perfect truth."[28] She proceeds to do so, until only our deep-seated British respect for what we cannot understand hinders us from declaring that in her Hegelian disguise she has become wholly unintelligible, and that clouds of German metaphysics have rendered her invisible in her ascension.

But just as we had despaired of ever seeing her again, to our amazement there ensues a catastrophe which brings her back to earth with more than Icarian suddenness, and in as completely shattered a condition.

There was an error in her calculations which has brought about her fall. Or rather, error was *not* taken into her calculations, when she assumed her standpoint, discarded the merely human as "merely psychological," and constructed her ideal. "The Ideal" does not admit of error; and yet on earth error impudently takes the liberty to exist. It is, of course, a mere illusion, but its persistent phantom yields not to the exorcisms of logic.

27 Prof. Bosanquet (*op. cit.*, p. 265).
28 H. H. Joachim, *The Nature of Truth*, pp. 169–70 and *passim*.

The situation must be set forth in the words of one who has seen the vision, and suffered its denouement: our own would be suspect and inadequate.[29] "The confused mass of idiosyncrasies," we are told, which are "my and your thinking, my and your 'self,' the particular temporal processes, and the extreme self-substantiation of the finite 'modes,' which is error in its full discordance: these are incidents *somehow* connected with the known truth, *but they themselves, and the manner of their connexion, are excluded from the theory of knowledge,*"[30] which "*must* rule out as irrelevant *some*—perhaps *most*, but certainly not *all*—of the temporal and finite conditions under which truth is known." "Truth, beauty, and goodness" (for all the ideals as conceived by Intellectualism must break down in the same way when they try to transcend their reference to man) "are timeless, universal, independent structures; and yet it is also essential to them to be manifested in the thinking of finite subjects, in the actions and volitions of perishing agents."[31] Hence error is "unthinkable," a "declaration of independence, where that which declares is nothing real, and nothing real is declared."[31]

But why should not "Logic" free herself from these embarrassments by cutting the last thin thread that attaches her to an earthly existence and a human function which are infested with "merely psychological" accidents and idiosyncrasies, and vitiated by the errors of human beings of which she ought surely to have divested herself when she proceeded to "depersonalize" herself? Why do these human trappings cling, like a shirt of Nessus, to the naked Truth? Can it be that "Logic" could not "depersonalize" herself completely, nay, that her effort was a sheer delusion?

Mr. Joachim makes answer.[32] Logic "must *render intelligible* the dual nature of human experience. . . . It must show how the complete coherence, which is perfect truth, involves as a necessary 'moment' in its self-maintenance the self-assertion of the finite modal minds: a self-assertion which in its extreme form is Error. It must reconcile this self-assertive independence with the modal dependence of the self-asserting

---

29 *Ibid.,* pp. 167–68.
30 Italics mine. Cp. p. 168 *n.* 2.
31 *Op. cit.,* p. 163.
32 *Ibid.,* pp. 170–71.

minds. . . . Otherwise human knowledge remains, for all we can tell, unrelated to ideal experience."[33]

In other words, when "Logic" commenced her nuptial flight towards "the Ideal," she quite forgot that after all, human forces raised her, that all her beauteous visions were conceived by the eye of human minds, and that she has repaid our devotion by disavowing her creators.

The natural result is sheer, unmitigated, inevitable, and irreparable contradiction, as Mr. Joachim most honourably recognizes. Logic is met by "demands which both *must be* and *cannot be* completely satisfied."[34] To satisfy them completely, complete truth would have to be manifest to itself. Whereas what we can conceive ourselves as attaining is only complete truth *manifest to us*. And as manifested in human truth, the opposition of subject and object persists; our knowledge is always thought *about* an Other: "the opposition of the thought and its Other is apparently vital." It cannot attain to union with its Other; and so the significant Whole cleft by a self-diremption, falls into halves.[35] The whole theory, therefore, "falls short of the absolute truth manifest to itself."[36] The "theory of truth, based on the coherence-notion, is not itself true *qua* coherent."[37] It is "not only *de facto* unaccomplished, but is impossible by the very nature of the case."[37]

And so Mr. Joachim, though he tries to soften the effect of his idol-breaking blows for the benefit of his friends by protesting that their common theory is *"as true as a theory can be,"*[38] finishes up as a sceptic *malgré lui* amid the ruins of *all* the intellectualistic conceptions of logic, and of his own "Hegelian" metaphysic.

§ 18. Of a surety we did well to allow logic to go on her way, and to be "judged by herself at a further stage," by her "approach to completeness and comprehensiveness."[39] Her debacle has certainly approached completeness, and is quite comprehensible to us.

---

[33] *Ibid.*, p. 172.
[34] *Ibid.*, p. 171. The italics are Mr. Joachim's.
[35] *Ibid.*, pp. 171–72 (in substance).
[36] *Ibid.*, p. 178.
[37] *Ibid.*, p. 176.
[38] *Ibid.*, p. 178.
[39] *Arist. Soc. Proc.* 1906, p. 265.

For there is nothing either new in her overthrow or obscure in its causes.

The Hegelian theory of knowledge and reality—for Mr. Joachim, taught perhaps by the negative outcome of *Appearance and Reality,* has rightly renounced the pretence of salving logic by metaphysics—has broken down completely. It has broken down precisely as it was predicted that it must break down so soon as it was thought out consistently and to the end.[40] It has broken down precisely as every intellectualistic conception of logic has always broken down, at precisely the same point and for precisely the same reasons. It has not failed, assuredly, for any lack of ingenuity or perseverance in its advocates, who have left no stone unturned to save a hopeless situation, and could no doubt with ease have lifted the burden of Sisyphus to the summit of any hill of hell. But their labour was more than Sisyphean: they had, unfortunately, committed "logic" to a fundamental blunder. It has wilfully, wantonly, and of malice prepense abstracted from humanity. Instead of conceiving God as incarnating himself in man, it has sought God by disavowing and belittling man. And as a reward it has itself been terrified to death by an incredible monster—the creature of its own unhealthy nightmare!

In other words, it has fallen into a χωρισμός a fatal separation between the human and the ideal which renders *both* unmeaning, but was rendered inevitable and irretrievable by its presuppositions as to the value of human psychology. Once our psychic processes are denied logical value and excluded from the nature of truth, we are playing with abstractions, even though we may not realize this until at the end our "Ideal" is required to find room for our errors. Once we exalt the limited and relative, and merely "pragmatic," "independence" of truth, which remains safely immanent *within the sphere of human valuations* and can always be withdrawn and modified as our needs and purposes require, into an absolute and infinite "independence" which entirely transcends our human experience, we have ascribed to truth the "dual nature" which so perplexes Mr. Joachim, and can by no device be unified. For a dualistic chasm has been constructed between the human and "psychological," and the ideal and

40 Cp. Chapter 6.

"logical." No real relation can be established between them; all attempts at connecting them break down so soon as they are tested. Nor can any real theoretic progress be made. The utmost ingenuity only brings "logicians" to the brink of the chasm. And that is "nearer" to the other side only in an illusory fashion. It remains only to *postulate* a reconciliation of the discrepant halves of a knowledge which is rent asunder from top to bottom, by a supreme and mystic act of faith. But as the jejune rationalism of the theory in question had previously prohibited all acts of faith, it has manifestly fallen into a pit of its own digging.

Or shall we rather say, of Plato's? For he it was that first led the way into the pit into which, with a few despised exceptions, the whole company of philosophers has followed him, as patiently and submissively as a flock of sheep follows its bellwether, and out of which no one has been able, and not too many have even tried, to escape.

Throughout the *Theaetetus,* for example, Plato has made the assumptions that "knowledge" is of "universals" and not concerned or connected with the fleeting and variable judgments of individual men about their personal experience, that thought and sense perception are antithetical and hostile, that the logical concept is something wholly superior to and independent of the psychical process (e.g., 152 D), and that the Protagorean suggestion to start the theory of knowing from the actual knowing of the individual's perceptions is a proposal for the abolition of truth. No wonder after this that it becomes for him a serious "contradiction" when A judges to be warm what B judges to be cold, seeing that "it" cannot be both. But "it" does not exist out of relation to the divergent judgments: "it" stands in this case for *the problem of constructing a "common" perception;* if the two "its" are to be brought together into an "objective" scheme of temperature, A and B must set to work to construct a thermometer, as to the readings of which they can agree. Plato, therefore, has merely debarred himself from understanding the *de facto* genesis and development of our common world of subjective intercourse, and by starting with abstraction from the *personal* character of both judgments, he has manufactured a fallacious contradiction. Can we wonder after this that the Platonic theory of knowledge remains plunged in unmitigated dualism, and that in the end it has to be admitted (209) that "knowledge" can never condescend to the particular and personal, and is unable to discriminate between Theaetetus and Socrates? For was it not pledged, *ex vi definitionis,* to leave out whatever part of reality concerns a "this," "here," and "now"? But instead of inferring from this impotence, and from the self-abnegation of an "ideal" of knowledge which is not even ideally adequate, because it renounces the duty of knowing the individual perfectly *in its uniqueness,* that there must be a radical flaw in a conception of knowledge which has led to this absurdity, what does Plato do? He proclaims the sensible unknowable and unintelligible as such, attributes to all "phenomenal" reality an all-pervasive taint of "not being," and retains his Ideal Theory though well aware that it cannot cross the gulf between the truly real and the sensible! How very human are even the greatest of philosophers!

It would never, therefore, occur to us to be surprised that not only should the *Theaetetus* in the end leave the problem of error unsolved and confess to utter inability to say what knowledge is, but that the whole Platonic theory of knowledge should remain immersed in obscurity and contradiction. But one thing is clear, viz., that whoever had learnt the lesson of the *Theaetetus* could have predicted the failure of all intellectualistic epistemologies down to *The Nature of Truth.*

§ 19. And the remedy for this sceptical paralysis of Intellectualism? It is simple—so simple that it will be hard to get philosophers to look at it. But it cuts very deep. It demands a complete reversal of inveterate assumptions, and a re-establishment of logic on very different foundations. We have merely to refrain from the twin abstractions which every intellectualistic logic makes, and which must, if carried through consistently, prove fatal to its very existence. These two assumptions, which have troubled us throughout, may now be called (1) the *etherealizing,* and (2) the *depersonalizing* of truth, and together they effect the complete *dehumanizing* of knowledge.

(1) By the *etherealizing* of truth is meant the abstraction from the actual use and verification of an assertion, which is made in assuming that its truth is independent of its *applica-*

tion. This really destroys its whole significance, although at first it seems to leave its "truth" a matter of self-consistency and intrinsic "coherence." But if we try to take truth in this purely formal way, we identify truth with claim to truth,[41] and render the testing of claims extralogical. And it is then discovered that all reference to reality has been excluded,[42] that "self-consistency" means nothing but a juggle with words whose meanings are presumed to be perfect and stable in their truth, and that the distinction between truth and error has become incomprehensible. Error (as contrasted with self-contradiction, which destroys the meaning wholly) is nothing inherent in the form of the judgment, but lies in a failure of its application. It is a failure of *our* thought to attain *its* object. And as our conception of "truth" is determined by its contrast with error, to abstract from error is really to abstract from "truth." Hence a logic which abstracts from error implicitly despairs also of giving an intelligible account of truth. It ceases at any rate to be a theory of real knowledge, and the formal "truth," the semblance of meaning, which it verbally retains, no longer possesses relevance to human knowing.

(2) But the *depersonalizing* of truth deprives the logic of Intellectualism even of this show of meaning. It makes abstraction from the meaning actually intended, from the purpose of the meaner. Now as every judgment is prompted and kept together by a purpose which forms the uniting bond between its subject and its predicate, *the purpose is logically vital.* It is also a concrete fact of an intensely personal kind, which ramifies indefinitely into human psychology. Hence it is often logically inconvenient, as complicating the situation beyond the powers of formal analysis. But to abstract from it, wholly and systematically, is to disintegrate the judgment. To do this destroys its intrinsic coherence, as well as its reference to real truth. It amounts to *a complete annihilation of meaning.*

It is difficult to suppose, therefore, that when intellectualist

---

41 Cp. Chapter 7.
42 It is characteristic of intellectualist "logic" not to have noticed the discrepancy between its two assertions (1) that "truth" is wholly a matter of the intrinsic "self-consistency" of its "ideal," and independent of all "consequences"; and (2) that all judgment involves a "reference to reality" beyond itself.

logic fully realizes the situation to which its abstractions lead, it will continue to presume without trial that the full concreteness of psychic process is logical irrelevance, and that man is a negligible quantity in the formation of truth.

A reformed and rehumanized logic, on the other hand, will flatly refuse to immolate all human knowledge, all fact, and all reality to intellectualist prejudices. It will conceive and value the old abstractions merely as instruments, as methodological simplifications, which may be freely used, so long as the *limits* of their usefulness are not overlooked, and their authority is not made absolute.

And here will be the rub. For these abstractions have been misconceived so long! It is such a time honoured custom with philosophers to believe that "universals" are loftier and more sacred than "particulars," that their *formation* is not to be inquired into nor tested, that their value is wholly independent of their application, that they would subsist in unsullied excellence and truth, even though they never were, nor could be, used. It will take, therefore, generations for philosophers to convince themselves that the essential function of universals is to *apply to particulars,* that they are *actually true* only because, and when, they are used, that when they become inapplicable they become unmeaning, that their abstraction, therefore, from time, place, and individuality is only superficial and illusory, and that in short they are instruments for the control and improvement of human experience.

"But will not the attempt to build knowledge on so untried and paradoxical a basis be fraught with unsuspected difficulties, and in its turn conduct us back to scepticism? Is it credible that so many generations of thinkers can have been mistaken in acquiescing in the unproved assertion of the good man, Plato, that Protagoreanism necessitates scepticism?"

In view of the outcome of intellectualistic "logic," this menace of scepticism seems a grotesque impertinence, and it might be well to retort that even an untried basis was better than one which had been tried and found to be so self-destructive. But the threat has been used so often that it will hardly be relinquished all at once: so we had better face it. It is a mere bogey—a Chimaera summoned from the House of Hades to scare us back into the Labyrinth of the Minotaur. No proof has ever been vouchsafed of its contention. And seeing that Plato's genius has failed so signally to refute Protagoras, we may await with equanimity the advent of a greater man than Plato to confute the inherent Humanism of man's thought.

Chapter 9

The Making of Truth

Argument

§ 1. The problem of relating "truth" to "fact." Difficulties of conceiving "fact" as "independent" of our knowing: (1) The paradoxes of realism; (2) the additional contradictions of rationalism. The old assumptions to be given up. (1) *Truth is human;* (2) *fact is not "independent,"* but (3) *dependent and relative to our knowing.* § 2. The problem of validating claims to truth, and avoiding error. § 3. Actual knowing our starting point: its seven features dominated by the *pragmatic test of truth.* § 4. The fact of previous knowledge. § 5. The acceptance of a basis of fact. The ambiguity of fact: "real" fact evolved from "primary," by a process of *selection.* Individual variations as to acceptance of fact. Fact never merely objective. § 6. The problem of "objectivity." It does not = unpleasantness. Pragmatic recognition of "unpleasant fact" and its motives. § 7. The place of interest and purpose in our knowing. "Goods" and "ends." § 8. The validation of a claim by its consequences. § 9. (1) Complete success; (2) partial and conditional success leading to methodological or practical "truth"; (3) failure, to be variously explained. § 10. The growth of knowledge a growth of efficiency as well as of "system," but "system" tested by its efficiency. § 11. The making of truth in its application to the future and the past. Antedating and revaluing of truth. Can all the truth be conceived as "made"? Difficulties. No "creation out of nothing." The problems of "previous knowledge" and "acceptance of fact." § 12. The "previous knowledge" to be treated pragmatically. Uselessness of fundamental truths which cannot be known. § 13. The "making of truth" *ipso facto* a "making of reality": (1) beliefs, ideas, and desires, as real forces shaping the world; (2) the efficacy of ideals; (3) the dependence of "discovery" upon endeavour. § 14. The further analysis of the factual basis is really metaphysics, and pragmatic method need not be carried so far. Conflict between the pragmatic value (1) of the real world of common sense, and (2) of the making of truth. But (2) is of superior authority because (1) is a pragmatic construction. Also the real making of reality may be analogous to our own.

§ 1. THE PROBLEM of "the making of truth" issues from the epistemological situation of the day at two points. It arises out of two burning questions: (1) how "truth" is related to "fact"; and (2) how "truth" is discriminated from "error," or how "claims" to truth are "validated."

On both these questions we have already abundantly seen that the intellectualistic theories of knowledge have argued themselves into a complete impasse. They have put the questions in such a way that no answer is possible. Their "doctrines" in the end amount merely to confessions of failure. They cannot understand how error is possible, or how, if it nevertheless exists, it can be discriminated from truth; and the only answer they can give to the question how truth is made is to declare that it is never really *made,* but must pre-exist ready-made as an eternal ideal (whether in a nonhuman mind, or a supercelestial space, or in independent being is a matter of taste), to which our human truths have to approximate. But when it turns out *on their own showing* that the attainment of this ideal by us is eternally impossible, what option have we but to treat this answer as no answer at all?

Again, they involve themselves in insuperable difficulties as to the relation of truth to fact. They start from an uncriticized assumption that truth must be the apprehension of "independent" fact; but they cannot understand how "fact" can be "independent" of our knowing. For how, if it is in any way dependent on us, can it remain "fact," or "truth" remain true? Can we *make* "truth" and "fact"? Away with the monstrous, impious thought! And yet it is too plain that *our human knowing* seems to do these very things. And that in what must seem to them the most dubious ways. For it employs a multitude of arbitrary processes, commended only by the psychological hold they have over our mortal nature, and, when these are abstracted from, it simply ceases to work. But how, Intellectualism must ask, can such processes be more than subjective, how dare we attribute them to an eternal mind, to an independent reality? It would be flat absurdity. But if they are merely subjective, must they not hopelessly vitiate the facts, distort the image of reality, and utterly unfit *our* "truth" to be the passionless mirror of reality which it is assumed it has to be?

Nor does it matter from what side this puzzle is approached. If it is approached from the "realist" side, we come upon the sheer, unmitigated, incredible paradoxes that the "independent fact" is (1) to be known by and in a process which *ex hypothesi* it "transcends"; (2) to be apprehended by a subjective activity which is confessed to be largely, if not wholly, arbitrary; that (3) this is to make *no difference whatsoever* to the fact; and (4) that *we are to know this also,* to know, that is, that the "correspondence" between the "fact" as it is in itself and outside our knowledge, and the fact as it appears in our knowledge, is somehow perfect and complete!

If we come upon it from the absolutist side, we find an "eternal ideal of truth" supervening upon, or perhaps taking the place of, the "independent fact." In the former case we have, evidently, achieved nothing but a complication of the problem. For it will now be a question how "eternal truth" is related to "independent fact," and also how both of them are to be related to "truth" and "fact" for us. But even in the latter case there is no gain, because this ideal also is still supposed to be "independent" of us and our doings. The difficulties, therefore, remain precisely the same. Nay, they are added to by the demand that we are to know that the "correspondence" between the human and the ideal *must be imperfect as well as perfect!* For the ideal has been so constructed that our knowledge *cannot* fully realize it, while yet it *must* fully realize it, in order that we may assure ourselves of its "truth," by observing its "correspondence" with the ideal! Absolute truth, therefore, as conceived by Absolutism, is not merely *useless* as a criterion of *our* truth, because we do not possess it, and cannot compare it with our truth, nor estimate where and to what extent our truth falls short of its "divine" archetype; it is not merely the adding of one more to the multitude of (human) truth conceptions which have to be accommodated to one another, and out of which there has to be compounded the "objective" truth and the "common" world of practical life. It is positively *noxious,* actively disruptive of the whole notion of truth, and pregnant with self-destructive consequences.

Surely this situation should be painful and irrational enough to stagger even the most rationalistic faith in the sufficiency of intellectualistic assumptions, and to impel it at least to investigate the alternative conception of the problem which Pragmatism has had the boldness to propound!

To us, of course, it will be as clear as daylight that *the old assumptions are wrong,* proved to be wrong by the absurdity of their consequences, and must be given up. We shall infer frankly (1) that whether or not we have constructed a wholly unexceptionable theory of knowledge, it is folly any longer to close one's eyes to the importance and all-pervasiveness of subjective activities in the making of truth. It must frankly be admitted that *truth is human truth,* and incapable of coming into being without human effort and agency; that human action is psychologically conditioned; that, therefore, the concrete fullness of human interests, desires, emotions, satisfactions, purposes, hopes, and fears is relevant to the theory of knowledge and must *not* be abstracted from.

(2) We shall perceive that the futile notion of a really "independent" truth and fact, which cannot be known or related to us or to each other, even by the most gratuitous of miracles, must be abandoned. If we insist on preserving the word, it must at any rate be used no longer as a label for the problem of relating the human to a nonhuman which cannot possibly be related to it. It must, at least, be interpreted pragmatically, as a term which discriminates certain behaviours, which distinguishes certain valuations, *within* the cognitive process which evolves *both* "truth" and "fact" for man.[1]

(3) Instead of wasting our ingenuity, therefore, in trying to

[1] Cp. Chapter 5, § 10.

unite conceptions which we have ourselves made contradictory, let us try the alternative adventure of *a thoroughly and consistently dependent truth,* dependent, that is, on human life and ministering to its needs, made by us and referring to our experience, and evolving everything called "real" and "absolute" and "transcendent" *immanently* in the course of its cognitive function. It will have at least this great initial advantage over theories which assume an antithesis between the human and the "ideal" or the "real," that its terms will not have to be laboriously brought into relation with each other and with human life.

§ 2. The second question, as to how claims to have judged "truly" are to be made good, and how "truth" is to be distinguished from "error," raises the problem of the making of truth in a still more direct fashion. Indeed, it may in this form be said to be the pragmatic problem par excellence, and we have already taken some steps towards its solution. We have seen the nature of the distinction between "claim" and "validity" and its importance (Chapter 7). We may also take it for granted that as there is nothing in the claim itself to tell us whether it is valid or not (Chapter 8, § 18), the validation of claims must depend on their consequences (Chapter 2). We have also vindicated the right of our actual human knowledge to be considered by logic in its full concreteness (Chapter 8). We have noted, lastly, that the collapse of the rationalistic theory of truth was to be traced to its inveterate refusal to do this (Chapters 7 and 8), and more particularly to recognize the problem of error, and to help human reasoners to discriminate between it and truth.

But all this is not enough to give us a positive grasp of the making of truth. To do this we must analyse a simple case of actual knowing in greater detail. But this is difficult, not so much because of any intrinsic difficulty of being aware of what we are doing, as because the contemplation of actual human knowledge has fallen into such disuse, and the simplest facts have been translated into the language of such weird fictions, that it is hard to bespeak sufficient attention for what actually occurs. Philosophers have strained their ingenuity to prove that it is impossible, or at least indefensible, to test the simplest truth in the most obvious manner, without dragging in "the a priori Deduction of the Categories," or the "Dialectic of the Notion." And all the while they are oblivious of the very real presuppositions of our knowing, and systematically exclude from their view the fact that all our "truths" occur as personal affirmations in the life of persons practically interested to attain truth and to avoid error. Thus, when I take someone coming towards me from a distance to be my brother, and subsequently perceive that he is not, this correction of a false claim seems an act of cognition well within the powers of any man; it seems gratuitous to regard it as a privilege reserved for the initiates of "the higher logic," the seers of "the Self-development of the Absolute Idea," while totally ignoring such facts as that I was (1) anxiously expecting my brother, but also (2) unfortunately afflicted with shortsightedness.

§ 3. Let us begin, then, quite simply and innocently, with our immediate experience, with the actual knowing, just as we find it, of our own adult minds. This proposal may seem hopelessly "uncritical," until we realize (1) that our actual minds are always the *de facto* starting points, from which, and with the aid of which, we *work back* to whatever starting points we are pleased to call "original" and "elementary"; (2) that we always read our actual minds into these other starting points; (3) that no subtlety of analysis can ever penetrate to any principles really certain and undisputable *to start with*; (4) that such principles are as unnecessary as they are impossible, because we only need principles which will work and grow more certain *in their use,* and that so even initially defective principles, which are improved, will turn out truer than the truest we could have started with; (5) that in all science our actual procedure is "inductive," experimental, postulatory, tentative, and that demonstrative form into which the conclusions may afterwards be put is merely a trophy set up to mark the victory. If we are met with reluctance to accept our contentions, let us not delay in order to argue them out, but proceed with the pragmatic confidence that, if they are provisionally assumed, the usefulness of the resulting view of knowledge will speedily establish them.

By tentatively assuming, then, this "common sense" starting point, we are enabled to observe that even one of the simplest acts of knowing is quite a complicated affair, because in it we are (1) using a mind which has had some prior experience and possesses some knowledge, and so (2) has acquired (what it greatly needs) some basis in reality, which it is *willing to accept as "fact,"* because (3) it needs a "platform" from which *to operate further on a situation* which confronts it, in order (4) to realize some *purpose* or to satisfy some *interest*, which defines for it an "end" and constitutes for it a "good." (5) It consequently *experiments* with the situation by some voluntary interference, which may begin with a tentative predication, and proceeds by reasoned inferences, but always, when completed, comes to a *decision* ("judgment") and issues in an *act.* (6) It is guided by the results ("consequences") of this experiment, which go to verify or to disprove its provisional basis, the initial "facts," predications, conceptions, hypotheses, and assumptions. Hence (7) if the results are satisfactory, the reasoning employed is deemed to have been *pro tanto good*, the results *right,* the operations performed *valid,* while the conceptions used and the predications made are judged *true.* Thus successful predication extends the system of knowledge and enlarges the borders of "fact." Reality is like an ancient oracle, and does not respond until it is questioned. To attain our responses, we make free to use all the devices which our whole nature suggests. But when they are attained, the predications we judge to be "true" afford us fresh revelations of reality. Thus truth and reality grow for us *together,* in a single process, which is *never* one of bringing the mind into relation with a fundamentally alien reality, but always one of improving and extending an already existing system which *we know*.

Now this whole process is clearly dominated by the *pragmatic test of truth.* The claims to truth involved are validated by their consequences when used. Thus Pragmatism as a logical method is merely the *conscious* application of a *natural* procedure of our minds in actual knowing. It merely proposes (1) to realize clearly the nature of these facts, and of the risks and gains which they involve, and (2) to simplify and reform logical theory thereby.

§ 4. We may next consider some of these points in greater detail. First as to the use of an already formed mind [§ 3 (1)]. That empirically knowledge arises out of pre-existing knowl-

edge, that we never operate with a raw and virgin mind, has
been an epistemological commonplace ever since it was au-
thoritatively enunciated by Aristotle, though the paradox it
involves with regard to the first beginning of knowledge has
never quite been solved. For the present, however, we need
only add that the development of a mind is a thoroughly *personal* affair. Potential knowledge becomes actual, because of
the purposive activity of a knower who brings it to bear on
his interests, and uses it to realize his ends. Knowledge does
not grow by a mechanical necessity, nor by the self-development of abstract ideas in a psychological vacuum.

§ 5. Next, as to the acceptance of a basis of fact [§ 3 (2)].
It is extraordinary that even the most blindly hostile critic
should have supposed Pragmatism to have denied this. It has
merely pointed out that the *acceptance* must not be ignored,
and that it is fatal to the chimera of a "fact" for us existing
quite "independently" of our "will."

It is, however, important to note the *ambiguity of "fact."*
(1) In the wider sense everything is "fact," *qua* experienced,
including imaginings, illusions, errors, hallucinations. "Fact"
in this sense is anterior to the distinction of "appearance"
and "reality," and covers *both.* To distinguish it we may call
it "primary reality." For though it is always perceived by us
in ways defined, or "vitiated," by our past interests and acts
(individual and racial), and we are rarely conscious of all we
read into our data, there is undeniably a "given" in experience,
or rather a givenness about it. We never experience it as
purely given, and the nearer it comes to this the less we
value it, but in a sense this "primary reality" is important. For
it is the starting point, and final touchstone, of all our theories
about reality, which have for their aim its transformation. It
may, certainly, in a sense, be called "independent" of us, if
that comforts anyone. For it is certainly not "made" by us,
but "found." But, as it stands, we find it most unsatisfactory
and set to work to remake it and unmake it. It is not what we
mean by "real fact" or "true reality." For, as immediately experienced, it is a meaningless chaos, merely the raw material
of a cosmos, the stuff out of which real fact is made. Thus the
need of operating on it is the real justification of our cognitive
procedures.

These make it into (2) "fact" in the stricter and more familiar sense (with which alone scientific discussion is concerned), by processes of analysis, *selection,* and *valuation,* which *segregate* the "real" from the "apparent" and the "unreal." It is only *after* such processes have worked upon "primary reality" that the distinction of "appearance" and "reality" appears on which Intellectualism seeks to base its metaphysic. But it has failed to observe that the ground it builds on is already hopelessly vitiated for the purpose of erecting a temple to its idol, the "satisfaction of pure intellect." For in this selection of "real reality" our interests, desires, and emotions inevitably play a leading part, and may even exercise an overpowering influence fatal to our ulterior ends.

Individual minds differ as greatly in their acceptance of "facts" as in other respects. Some can never be got to face *unpleasant* "facts," or will accept them only at the point of the sword. Most prefer to contemplate the more agreeable alternative. A few are driven by their fears unduly to accept the worse alternative. The devices for ideally rectifying the harshnesses of actual experience are endless. We console ourselves by postulating ideal realities, or extensions of reality, capable of transfiguring the repugnant character of actual life. We so conceive it, or interpret it, as to transform it into a "good." Or sometimes plain and generally recognized "facts" are disposed of by a sheer assertion of their "unreality," as is, e.g., the existence of pain by "Christian Science," and of evil by absolutist metaphysics. It is clear that psychologically all these attitudes towards "fact" more or less work, and so have a certain value.

It is clear also that the recognition of "fact" is by no means a simple affair. "Facts" which can be excluded from our lives, which do not interest us, which mean nothing to us, which we cannot use, which are ineffective, which have little bearing on practical life, tend to drop into unreality. Our neglect, moreover, really tends to make them unreal, just as, conversely, our preference for the ideals we postulate makes them real, at least as factors in human life.

The common notion, therefore, that "fact" is something independent of our recognition, needs radical revision, in the only sense of "fact" which is worth disputing. It must be admitted that without a process of selection by us, there are no real facts for us, and that this selecting is immensely arbitrary. It would, perhaps, be infinitely so, but for the limitations of human imagination and tenacity of purpose in operating on apparent fact.

§ 6. Through this atmosphere of emotional interest, how shall we penetrate to any "objective" fact at all? Where shall we find the "hard facts" our forefathers believed in, which are so whether we will them or not, which extort recognition even from our sturdiest reluctance, whose unpleasantness *breaks* our will and does not *bend* to it?

Certainly it may not be quite easy to discern the old objective facts in their new dress, but that is a poor reason for denying them the subjective atmosphere in which they have to live.

(1) We may begin, however, by remarking on the curious equating of "objective" with "unpleasant" facts and truths. Its instinctive pessimism seems to imply a mind which is so suspicious of fact that it can be driven to recognize the reality of anything only by pains and penalties, which is so narrowly contented with its existing limitations as to be disposed to regard all novelties as unwelcome intrusions, which has, in short, to be *forced* into the presence of truth, and will not go forth to seek it and embrace it. Such, certainly, is not the frame of mind and temper of the pragmatist, who prefers to conceive "the objective" as that which he aims at and from, and contends that though "facts" may at times coerce, it is yet more essential to them to be "accepted," to be "made," and to be capable of being "*remade*."

(2) At all events, he thinks that the coerciveness of "fact" has been enormously exaggerated by failure to observe that it is never sheer coercion, but always mitigated by his choice and acceptance, by which it ceases to be *de facto* thrust upon him, and becomes *de jure* "willed." Even a forced move, he feels, is better than no power to move at all; and the game of life is not wholly made up of forced moves.

(3) He finds no difficulty, therefore, in the conception of *unpleasant* "fact." It indicates the better of two disagreeable alternatives. And he can give good reasons for accepting unpleasant fact, without on that account conceiving "fact" as such to be unpleasant and coercive. He may (*a*) accept it as

the *less unpleasant* alternative, and to avoid worse consequences, much as man may wear spectacles rather than go blind. He may (*b*) prefer to sacrifice a cherished prejudice rather than to deny, e.g., the evidence of his senses, or to renounce the use of his "reason." He may (*c*) accept it *provisionally*, without regarding it as absolute, merely for the purposes of the act or experiment he is contemplating. For to recognize the *pragmatic reality* of an unpleasant fact means nothing metaphysical, and entails no serious consequences. It only implies willingness to accept it for the time being, and is quite compatible with a disbelief in its ultimate reality, and with its subsequent reduction to unreality or illusion. Hence (*d*) such a pragmatic acceptance of unpleasant fact does not impair our liberty of action; it is no obstacle to subsequent experimentation, which may "discover" the illusoriness of the presumed "fact." But even where it does not lead to this, it may (*e*) be a preliminary to making the unpleasant fact *unreal*, and putting something better in its place; thus proving, in another way, that it never was the absolute hard fact it was supposed to be, but dependent on our inaction for its continued existence.

Thus (4) it turns out that the existence of unpleasant fact, so far from being an objection to the pragmatic view of fact, is an indispensable ingredient in it. For it supplies the motive for that transformation of the existing order, for that unmaking of the real which has been made amiss, which, with the making fact of the ideal and the preservation of the precious, constitutes the essence of our cognitive endeavour. To attain our "objective," the "absolutely objective fact," which would be absolutely satisfactory, we need a "platform" whence to act and aim. "Objective fact" is just such a platform. Only there is no need to conceive it as anchored to the eternal bottom of the flux of time; it *floats,* and so can move with the times, and be adjusted to the occasion.

§ 7. As to § 3 (4), we have already seen that interest and purpose can be eliminated from cognitive process only at the cost of stopping it (Chapter 8, § 7). A being devoid of interests would not *attend* to anything that happened, would not *select* or *value* one thing rather than another, nor would any one thing make more of an impression on its apathy than any other. Its mind and its world would remain in the chaos of primary reality (§ 5), and resemble that of the "Absolute" (if it can be said to have a mind).

The human mind, of course, is wholly different. It is full of interests, all of which are directly or indirectly referable to the functions and purposes of life. Its organization is biological and teleological, and in both cases selective. If we except a few abnormal and morbid processes such as idiocy, insanity, and dream, mental life may be called wholly purposive; that is, its functioning is not intelligible without reference to actual or possible purposes, even when it is not aiming at a definite, clearly envisaged end. Definite purposes are, it is true, of gradual growth. They arise by selection, they crystallize out from a magma of general interestedness and vaguely purposive actions, as we realize our true vocation in life, much as "real" reality was selected out of "primary." Thus we become more and more clearly conscious of our "ends," and more and more definite in referring our "goods" to them. But this reference is rarely or never carried through completely, because our nature is never fully harmonized. And so our "desires" may continue to hanker after "goods" which our "reason" cannot sanction as conducive to our ends, or our intelligence may fail to find the "good" means to our ends, and be deceived by current valuations of goods which are really evils. Thus the "useful" and the "good" tend to fall apart, and "goods" to seem incompatible. But properly and ideally, there are no goods which are not related to the highest good, no values which are not goods, no truths which are not values, and therefore, none which are not useful in the widest sense.

§ 8. As to § 3 (5), experience is experiment, i.e., *active*. We do not learn, we do not live, unless we try. Passivity, mere acceptance, mere observation (could they be conceived) would lead us nowhere, least of all to knowledge.

(1) Every judgment refers sooner or later to a concrete situation which it analyses. In an ordinary judgment of sense perception, as, e.g., "This is a chair," the subject, the "this," denotes the product of a selection of the relevant *part* of a given whole. The selection is arbitrary, in that it ignores all the rest of the situation "given" along with the "this." If taken in abstraction, as Intellectualism loves to do, it seems *wholly arbitrary*, unintelligible, and indefensible. In the concrete,

244 / Truth and Meaning in Logic and Psychology

however, the judgment *when made* is always purposive, and its selection is justified, or refuted, by the subsequent stages of the ideal experiment. The "objective control" of the subjective freedom to predicate is not effected by some uncomprehended pre-existing fact; it comes *in the consequences of acting out the predication.* So our analyses are arbitrary only if and in so far as we are not willing to *take* their consequences upon us. Similarly the predicate, which includes the "this" in a conceptual system already established, is arbitrary in its selection. Why did we say "chair," and not "sofa" or "stool"? To answer this we must go on to *test* the predication.

For (2) every judgment is essentially an experiment, which, to be tested, must be acted on. If it is really true that "this" is a chair, it can be sat in. If it is a hallucination, it cannot. If it is broken, it is not a chair in the sense my interest demanded. For I made the judgment under the prompting of a desire to sit.

If now I stop at this point, without acting on the suggestion contained in the judgment, the claim to truth involved in the assertion is never tested, and so cannot be validated. Whether or not "this" was a chair cannot be known. If I consent to complete the experiment, the consequences will determine whether my predication was "true" or "false." The "this" may not have been a chair at all, but a false appearance. Or the antique article of ornamental furniture which broke under my weight may have been something too precious to be sat in. In either case, the "consequences" not only decide the validity of my judgment, but also alter my conception of reality. In the one case I shall judge henceforth that reality is such as to present me with illusory chairs; in the other, that it contains also chairs *not* to be sat in. This then is what is meant by the pragmatic testing of a claim to truth.[2]

§ 9. As to the reaction of the consequences of an experimental predication upon its "truth" [§ 3 (6)], the simplest case is that (1) of a successful validation. If, in the example of the last section, I can sit in the "chair," my confidence in my eyesight is confirmed and I shall trouble little whether it ought not rather to have been called a "sofa" or a "stool." Of

[2] Cp. Dewey's *Logical Studies* for the experimental nature of predication, especially ch. VII.

course, however, if my interest was not that of a mere sitter, but of a collector or dealer in ancient furniture, my first judgment may have been woefully inadequate, and may need to be revised. "Success," therefore, in validating a "truth," is a relative term, *relative to the purpose* with which the truth was claimed. The "same" predication may be "true" for me and "false" for you, if our purposes are different. As for a truth in the abstract, and relative to no purpose, it is plainly unmeaning. Until someone asserts it, it cannot become even a claim, and be tested, and cannot, therefore, be validated. Hence the truth of the "proposition" "S is P," when we affirm it on the strength of an actually successful predication, is only potential. In applying it to other cases we always take a risk. The next time "this" may not be a "chair," even though it may look the "same" as the first time. Hence even a fully successful predication cannot be converted into an "eternal truth" without more ado. The empirical nature of reality is such that we can never argue from one case to a *similar* one, which *we take to be* "the same," with absolute assurance a priori; hence no "truth" can ever be so certain that it need not be verified, and may not mislead us when applied. But this only means that no truth should be taken as unimprovable.

(2) Experiments, however, are rarely quite successful. We may have had to purchase the success we attain by the use of artificial abstractions and simplifications, or even downright fictions, and the uncertainty which this imports into the "truth" of our conclusions will have to be acknowledged. We shall, therefore, conceive ourselves to have attained not complete truths without a stain upon their character, which there is no reason to doubt, but only "approximations to truth" and working hypotheses," which are, at most, "good enough for practical purposes." And the principles we used we shall dub *methodological* "truths" or "fictions," according to our bias. And, clearly, the cognitive endeavour will not in this case rest. We shall not have found a "truth" which fully satisfies even our immediate purpose, but shall continue the search for a more complete, precise, and satisfactory result. In the former case, the cognitive interest of the situation could be renewed only by a change or growth of purpose leading to further judgments.

(3) The experiment may fail, and lead to unsatisfactory results. The interpretation then may become extremely complex. Either (a) we may put the blame on our subjective manipulation, on our use of our cognitive instruments. We may have observed wrongly. We may have reasoned badly. We may have selected the wrong conceptions. We may have had nothing but false conceptions to select from, because our previous knowledge was as a whole inadequate. Or we may be led to doubt (b) the basis of fact which we assumed, or (c) the practicability of the enterprise we were engaged in. In either of the first two cases we shall feel entitled to try again, with variations in our methods and assumptions; but repeated failure may finally force even the most stubborn to desist from their purpose, or to reduce it to a mere postulate of rationality which it is as yet impossible to apply to actual experience. And, needless to say, there will be much difference of opinion as to where, in case of failure, the exact flaw lies, and how it may best be remedied. Herein, however, lies one reason (among many) why the discovery of truth is such a personal affair. The discoverer is he who, by greater perseverance or more ingenious manipulation, makes something out of a situation which others had despaired of.

§ 10. We see, then, *how truth is made,* by human operations on the data of human experience. Knowledge grows in extent and in trustworthiness by successful functioning, by the assimilation and incorporation of fresh material by the previously existing bodies of knowledge. These "systems" are continually verifying themselves, proving themselves true by their "consequences," by their power to assimilate, predict, and control fresh "fact." But the fresh fact is not only assimilated; it also transforms. The old truth looks different in the new light, and really changes. It grows more powerful and efficient. Formally, no doubt, it may be described as growing more "coherent" and more highly "organized," but this does not touch the kernel of the situation. For the "coherence" and the "organization" both exist in our eyes, and relatively to our purposes: it is *we* who judge what they shall mean. And what we judge them by is their conduciveness to our ends, their effectiveness in harmonizing our experience. Thus, here again, the intellectualist analysis of knowledge fails to reach the really motive forces.

§ 11. It is important, further, to point out that *looking forward,* the making of truth is clearly a continuous, progressive, and cumulative process. For the satisfaction of one cognitive purpose leads on to the formulation of another; a new truth, when established, naturally becomes the presupposition of further explorations. And to this process there would seem to be no actual end in sight, because in practice we are always conscious of much that we should like to know, if only we possessed the leisure and the power. We can, however, conceive an ideal completion of the making of truth, in the achievement of a situation which would provoke no questions and so would inspire no one with a purpose to remake it, and on this ideal the name absolute truth may be bestowed.

Looking backwards, the situation, as might have been expected, is less plain. In the first place there are puzzles, which arise from the natural practice of *revaluing* superseded "truths" as "errors," and of *antedating* the new truths as having been "true all along." So it may be asked: "What were these truths *before* they were discovered?" This query is essentially analogous to the child's question: "Mother, what becomes of yesterday?" and by anyone who has understood the phraseology of time in the one case and of the making of truth in the other, the difficulty will be seen to be merely verbal. If "true" means (as we have contended) "valued by us," of course the new truth becomes true only when "discovered"; if it means "valuable *if* discovered," it was of course hypothetically "true"; if, lastly, the question inquires whether a past situation would not have been *altered for the better* if it had included a recognition of this truth, the answer is: "Yes, probably; only unfortunately, it was not so altered." In none of these cases, however, are we dealing with a situation which can be even intelligibly stated apart from the human making of truth.[3] Again, it is by no means easy to say how far our present processes of making truth are validly to be applied to the past, how far *all* truth can be conceived as having been made by the processes which we now see in operation.

[3] Cp. Chapter 7, pp. 185–87.

(1) That we must try to conceive it thus is, indeed, obvious. For why should we gratuitously assume that the procedure by which "truth" is now being made differs radically from that whereby truth initially came into being? Are we not bound to conceive, if possible, the whole process as continuous—truth made, truth making, and truth yet to be made—as successive stages in one and the same endeavour? And to a large extent it is clear that this can be done, that the established truths, from which our experiments now start, are of a like nature with the truths we make, and were themselves made in historical times.

(2) Before, however, we can generalize this procedure, we have to remember that on our own showing, we disclaimed the notion of making truth out of nothing. We did not have recourse to the very dubious notion of theology called "creation out of nothing," which no human operations ever exemplify. We avowed that our truths were made out of previous truths, and built upon pre-existing knowledge; also that our procedure involved an initial recognition of "fact."

(3) Here, then, would seem to be two serious, if not fatal, limitations upon the claim of the pragmatic "making of truth" to have solved the mystery of knowledge. They will need, therefore, further examination, though we may at once hasten to state that they cannot affect the validity of what the pragmatic analysis professed to do. It professed to show the reality and importance of the human contribution to the making of truth; and this it has amply done. If it can carry us further, and enable us to humanize our world completely, so much the better. But this is more than it bargained to do, and it remains to be seen how far it will carry us into a comprehension also of the apparently nonhuman conditions under which our manipulations must work.

§ 12. Now as regards the previous knowledge assumed in the making of truth, it may be shown that there is no need to treat it in any but a pragmatic way. For (1) it seems quite arbitrary to deny that the truths which we happen to assume in making new truths are the same in kind as the very similar truths we make by their aid. In many cases, indeed, we can show that these very truths were made by earlier operations. There is, therefore, so far, nothing to hinder us from regarding the volitional factors which actual knowing now exhibits, viz., desire, interest, and purpose, as essential to the process of knowing, and similarly the process by which new truth is now made, viz., postulation, experiment, action, as essential to the process of verification.

Moreover (2), even if we denied this, and tried to find truths that had never been made, it would avail us nothing. We never can get back to truths so fundamental that they cannot possibly be conceived as having been made. There are no a priori truths which are indisputable, as is shown by the mere fact that there is not, and never has been, any agreement as to what they are. All the "a priori truths," moreover, which are commonly alleged, can be conceived as postulates suggested by a previous situation.[4]

(3) Methodologically, therefore, it leads us nowhere to assume that within the truth which is made there exists an uncreate residuum or core of elementary truth, which has not been made. For we can never get at it, or know it. Hence, even if it existed, the theory of our knowing could take no note of it. All truth, therefore, must, methodologically, be treated as if it had been "made." For on this assumption alone can it reveal its full significance. In so far, therefore, as Pragmatism does not profess to be more than a method, it has no occasion to modify or correct an account of truth which is adequate to its purpose, for the sake of an objection which is methodologically null.

(4) It seems a little hard on Pragmatism to expect from it a solution of a difficulty which confronts alike all theories of knowledge. In all of them the beginning of knowledge is wrapped in mystery. It is a mystery, however, which even now presses less severely on Pragmatism than on its competitors. For the reason that it is not a retrospective theory. Its significance does not lie in its explanation of the past so much as in its *present* attitude towards the *future*. The past is dead and done with, practically speaking; its deeds have hardened into "facts," which are accepted, with or without enthusiasm; what it really concerns us to know is *how to act with a view to the future*. And so like life, and as befits a theory of human life, Pragmatism faces towards the future. It can adopt, therefore,

4 Cp. "Axioms as Postulates" in *Personal Idealism*.

the motto *solvitur ambulando,* and be content if it can conceive a situation in which the problem would *de facto* have disappeared. The other theories could not so calmly welcome a "psychological" solution as "logically" satisfactory. But then they still dream of "theoretic" solutions, which are to be wholly "independent" of practice.

§ 13. We must now show (1) that the "making of truth" is necessarily and *ipso facto* also a "making of reality"; and (2) what precisely is the difficulty about accepting the making of truth as a *complete* making also of reality.

(1) (*a*) It is clear, in the first place, that if our beliefs, ideas, desires, wishes, etc., are really essential and integral features in actual knowing, and if knowing really transforms our experience, they must be treated as *real forces,* which cannot be ignored by philosophy.[5] They really alter reality, to an extent which is quite familiar to "the practical man," but which, unfortunately, "philosophers" do not yet seem to have quite adequately grasped, or to have "reflected on" to any purpose. Without, however, going into endless detail about what ought to be quite obvious, let us merely affirm that the "realities" of civilized life are the embodiments of the ideas and desires of civilized man, alike in their material and in their social aspects, and that our present inability wholly to subdue the material, in which we realize our ideas, is a singularly poor reason for denying the difference between the present condition of man's world and that of his miocene ancestors.

(*b*) Human ideals and purposes are real forces, even though they are not yet incorporated in institutions, and made palpable in the rearrangements of bodies. For they affect our actions, and our actions affect our world.

(*c*) Our knowledge of reality, at least, depends largely on the character of our interests, wishes, and acts. If it is true that the cognitive process must be started by subjective interest, which determines the direction of its search, it is clear that unless we seek we shall not find, nor "discover" realities we have not looked for. They will consequently be missing in our picture of the world, and will remain nonexistent for us. To

5 Cp. Prof. Dewey's essay on "Beliefs and Existences" in *The Influence of Darwin on Philosophy,* which makes this point very forcibly.

become real for us they (or cognate realities—for we do not always discover just what we went forth to find, as witness Saul and Columbus) must have become *real objects of interest* hypothetically; and as this making of "objects of interest" is quite within our power, in a very real sense their "discovery" is a "making of reality."[6] Thus, in general, the world as it now appears to us may be regarded as the reflexion of our interests in life; it is what we and our ancestors have, wisely or foolishly, sought and known to make of our life, under the limitations of our knowledge and our powers. And that, of course, is little enough as compared with our ideals, though a very great deal as compared with our starting point. It is enough, at any rate, to justify the phrase "the making of reality" as a consequence of the making of truth. And it is evident also that just in so far as the one is a consequence of the other, our remarks about the presupposition of an already made "truth" will apply also to the presupposition of an already made "reality."

§ 14. The difficulty about conceiving this "making of reality," which accompanies the "making of truth," as more than "subjective," and as affording us a real insight into the nature of the cosmic process, lies in the fact that it is complicated with the difficulty we have already recognized in trying to conceive the making of truth as a completely subjective process, which should yet be self-sufficient and fully explanatory of the nature of knowledge (§ 11). It is because the making of truth seemed to presuppose a certain "acceptance of fact," which was indeed volitional *qua* the "acceptance" and even optional, but left us with a surd *qua* the "fact," that it seems impossible to claim complete objectivity for the making of reality, and that our knowing seems to many merely to select among pre-existing facts those which we are interested to "discover."

It is inevitable, moreover, that the pre-existing facts, which the making, both of truth and of reality, seems to presuppose as its condition, though, properly speaking, it only implies the pre-existence of "primary reality" (§ 5), should be identified with the "real world" of common sense, in which we find our-

6 For the reason why we distinguish between these two cases at all, see Chapter 5, § 5.

selves, and which we do not seem to have made in any human sense. In other words, our theory of knowledge is confronted at this point with something which claims ontological validity, and is requested to turn itself into a metaphysic in order to deal with it.

This, of course, it may well refuse to do. It can insist on remaining what it originally was, and has so far professed to be, viz., a method of understanding the nature of our knowledge. And we shall not be entitled to censure it, however much we may regret its diffidence, and desire it to show its power also in coping with our final difficulties.

We ought, however, to be grateful, if it enables us to perceive from what the difficulty really arises. It arises from a conflict between pragmatic considerations, *both* of which are worthy of respect. For (1) the belief in the world theory of ordinary realism, in a "real world" into which we are born, and which has existed "independently" of us for aeons before that event, and so cannot possibly have been made by us or any man, has very high pragmatic warrant. It is a theory which holds together and explains our experience, and can be acted on with very great success. It is adequate for almost all our purposes. It works so well that it cannot be denied a very high degree of truth.

(2) On the other hand, it is equally plain that we cannot deny the reality of our cognitive procedure and of the human contribution it imports into the making of reality. It, too, is a tried and tested truth. The two, therefore, must somehow be reconciled, even though in so doing we may have to reveal ultimate deficiencies in the common-sense view of the world.

The first question to be raised is which of the two pragmatically valuable truths should be taken as more ultimate.

The decision, evidently, must be in favour of the second. For the "reality of the external world" is not an original datum of experience, and it is a *confusion* to identify it with the "primary reality" we recognized in § 5. It cannot claim the dubious "independence" of the latter, just because it is something better and more valuable which has been "made" out of it. For it is a pragmatic construction *within* primary reality, the product, in fact, of one of those processes of selection by which the chaos is ordered. The real external world is the pragmatically efficient part of our total experience, to which the inefficient parts such as dreams, fancies, illusions, after-images, etc., can, for most purposes, be referred. But though this construction suffices for most practical purposes, it fails to answer the question: "How may 'reality' be distinguished from a consistent dream?" And seeing that experience presents us with transitions from an apparently real (dream) world into one of superior reality, how can we know that this process may not be repeated, to the destruction of what now seems our "real world"?

We must distinguish, therefore, between two questions which have been confused—(1) "Can the making of truth be conceived as a making also of 'primary reality'?" and (2) "Can it be conceived also as a making of the real 'external world' of ordinary life?"—and be prepared to find that while the first formulates an impossible problem,[7] an answer to the second may prove feasible. In any case, however, it cannot be affirmed that our belief in the metaphysical reality of our external world, which it is in some sense, or in no sense, possible to "make," is of higher authority than our belief in the reality of our making of truth. The latter may pervade also forms of experience other than that which gets its pragmatic backbone from the former. Indeed, one cannot imagine desiring, purposing, and acting as ceasing to form part of our cognitive procedure, so long as "finite" minds persist at all. All we can say, therefore, is that so long as, and in so far as, our experience is such as to be most conveniently organized by the conception of a pre-existing real world (in a relative sense), "independent" of us, it will also be convenient to conceive it as having been to a large extent "made" before *we* took a part in the process.[8]

Nevertheless, it is quite possible (1) that this "pragmatic" recognition of the external world may not be final, because it does not serve our ultimate purposes; and (2) that the human process of making reality may be a valuable clue also to the making of the pragmatically real world, because even though

7 Chapter 5, § 7.
8 Cp. *Riddles of the Sphinx*, ch. IX, § 32.

it was not made by us, it was yet developed by processes closely analogous to our own procedure, which this latter enables us to understand. If so, we shall be able to combine the *real* "making of reality" and the human "making of reality" under the same conception.[9]

9 Chapter 5.

PART THREE

Faith, Ethics, and Immortality

Editor's Introduction

IT IS in the realm of religious philosophy that Pragmatism probably scores its greatest success. For here, as in ethics, the postulational approach applies admirably. Thus James spoke of the will to believe, and Schiller of the right to postulate. Religion is for Schiller, like science, "a method of grasping and remoulding our experience." Immortality, like causality, may be taken as a postulate; that is, we behave as if it were true, and our "faith" in a future verification may act to promote that verification. Granted that Schiller greatly overdoes the parallelism between religious and scientific assumptions—can the moral cosmos, for example, ever be "verified" in the same sense that the atomic hypothesis can?—still the pragmatic approach is a fruitful one. It makes no overweening metaphysical leaps, but searches for the "cash value" (O infelicitous phrase!) of religious hypotheses within our experience.

Psychical research was an interest which Schiller shared with such philosophers as Kant, James, and Bergson. No mere vagary, this study was for him at the periphery of science, and therefore illuminating as a possible extension of the method and domain of science. We have noted Dewey's pained dissent, but we must be careful to retain our open-mindedness, in the spirit of a remark of James's[1] on the same subject:

> It is a field in which the sources of deception are extremely numerous. But I believe there is no source of deception in the investigation of nature which can compare with a fixed belief that certain kinds of phenomena are *impossible*.

[1] In a letter to Carl Stumpf, Jan. 1, 1886, in *Selected Letters of William James,* ed. Elizabeth Hardwick (New York, 1960), p. 125.

Chapter 10

Faith, Reason, and Religion[1]

Argument

§ 1. The problem of religious philosophy that of the relations of "faith" and "reason." The rationalistic criticism of religion, and the pragmatic criticism of rationalism. § 2. Faith as a specifically religious principle. Its revival as a philosophic principle, and a presupposition of reason. § 3. The will-to-believe and to disbelieve. Humanism as a recognition of actual mental process. § 4. The analysis of "reason." § 5. Thought dependent on postulation, i.e., "faith." § 6. The definition of "faith." § 7. The pragmatic testing of faith and knowledge. § 8. The incompleteness of this process. § 9. The analogy of scientific and religious faith. § 10. Their differences. § 11. Five spurious conceptions of faith. § 12. The possibility of verifying religious postulates. § 13. Humanist conclusions as to the philosophy of religion. The pragmatic character of Christianity obscured by an intellectualist theology.

§ 1. The NATURE of religion, and the extent to which what is vaguely and ambiguously called "faith" and what is (quite as vaguely and ambiguously) called "reason" enter into it, rank high among the problems of perennial human interest—in part, perhaps, because it seems impossible to arrive at any settlement which will appear equally cogent and satisfactory to all human minds. Of late, however, the old controversies have been rekindled into the liveliest incandescence, in consequence of two purely philosophic developments.

On the one hand, Absolutism, despite its long coquettings with theology, has revealed itself as fundamentally hostile to popular religion (see Chapter 3). In works like Mr. Bradley's

---

[1] This essay appeared in substance in the *Hibbert Journal* for January, 1906. It has been retouched in a few places to fit it more effectively for its place in this volume.

Appearance and Reality, and still more formidably, because more lucidly and simply, in Dr. McTaggart's *Some Dogmas of Religion,* it has reduced Christian theism to what seems a position of grotesque absurdity by an incisive criticism from which there is no escape so long as its victim accepts the rationalistic tests and conceptions of truth and proof with which it operates.

On the other hand, it has simultaneously happened that just these tests and conceptions have been impugned, and to a large extent condemned, by the pragmatic movement in philosophy. It threatens to deprive Rationalism[2] of its favourite weapons just as it is about to drive them home. It promises to lead to a far juster and more sympathetic, because more psychological, appreciation of the postulates of the religious consciousness, and to render possible an unprejudiced consideration of the non-"rational" and non-rationalistic evidence on which religion has all along relied. And so rationalistic philosophers have at once taken alarm.

Hence, though this movement appears to affect immediately nothing but technicalities of the theory of knowledge, it has been extensively taken as an attempt at a revolutionary reversal of the relations of faith and reason. The new philosophy was promptly accused of aiming at the oppression, nay, at the subversion, of reason, of paving the way to the vilest obscurantism and the grossest superstition with the ruins of the edifice of truth which its scepticism had exploded; in short, of attempting to base religion on the quicksands of irrationality. But, it was urged, the dangerous expedients which are used recoil upon their authors; the appeal to the will-to-believe ends by sanctioning the arbitrary adoption of any belief anyone may chance to fancy, and thus destroys all objectivity in religious systems; religious sentiment is freed from the repressive regime of a rigid rationalism only to be ignobly dissipated in excesses of subjective licence.

Now the first thing that strikes one about such denunciations is their premature violence. The opponents of the new Humanism should have met it on the logical, and still more on

---

[2] I am using the term strictly as = "a belief in the all-sufficiency of reason," and not in its popular sense as = "criticism of religion." A rationalist in the strict sense may, of course, be religious, and per contra a voluntarist, or a sensationalist, may be a rationalist in the popular sense.

the psychological, ground whence its challenge proceeded, before they hastened to extract from it religious applications which had certainly not been made, and possibly were not even intended, by its authors, and which there is, as yet, hardly a sign, in this country at least, that the spokesmen of the religious organizations are willing to welcome. And until the leaders of the churches show more distinct symptoms of interest, both in the disputes of philosophers in general and in this dispute in particular, it seems premature to anticipate from this source the revolution which is decried in advance. Theologians, in general, have heard "Wolf!" cried too often by philosophers anxious to invoke against their opponents more forcible arguments than those of mere reason, they have found too often how treacherous were the specious promises of philosophic support, they are too much absorbed in historical and critical researches and perplexities of their own to heed lightly outcries of this sort.

The controversy, then, has not yet descended from the study into the market place, and it seems still time to attempt to estimate philosophically the real bearing of Humanism on the religious problem, and to define the functions which it actually assigns to reason and to faith. It may reasonably be anticipated that the results of the inquiry will be found to justify neither the hopes of those who expect an explicit endorsement of any sectarian form of religion (if such there are), nor the fears of those who dread a systematic demolition of the reason.

§ 2. Perhaps a brief historic retrospect will form the best approach to the points at issue. Thoughtful theologians have always perceived what their rationalistic critics have blindly ignored, viz., that religious truths are not, like mathematical, such as directly and universally to impose themselves on all minds. They have seen, that is, that the religious attitude essentially implies the addition of what was called "faith" for its proper appreciation. This "faith," moreover, was conceived as an intensely *personal* act, as an emotional reaction of a man's whole nature upon a vital issue. It followed that it was unreasonable, on the part of rationalists, to ignore this specific character of religious truth or to treat it as irrational. And it was this perception which prompted a Pascal to array the "reasons of the heart" against the (abstract) reasons of "the head," a Newman to compile his *Grammar of Assent*, and a Ritschl to spurn the pseudo-demonstrations of (a Hegelian) philosophy, and to construct an impregnable citadel for the religious sentiment in the exalted sphere of "judgments of value."

Accordingly, when that great student of the human soul, William James, proclaimed the right of inclining the nicely weighted equipoise of intellectual argumentation by throwing into the scales a will to believe whichever of the alternatives seemed most consonant with our emotional nature, it might well have seemed that he was merely reviving and rewording a familiar theological expedient which philosophy had long ago discredited as the last desperate resource of an expiring religious instinct.

It turned out, however, that there was an important novelty in the doctrine as revived. It reappeared as a *philosophic* doctrine, firmly resting on psychological and epistemological considerations which were, intrinsically, quite independent of its religious applications, and took the field quite prepared to conduct, on purely philosophic grounds, a vigorous campaign against the intellectualist prejudices of the current rationalism. In other words, by conceiving the function of "faith" as an example of a general principle, the religious applications, through which the principle had first been noticed and tested, were rendered derivative illustrations of a far-reaching philosophic view. It ceased, therefore, to be necessary to *oppose* the reasons of the heart to those of the head; it could be maintained that no "reasons" could be excogitated by an anaemic brain to which no heart supplied the life blood; it could be denied that the operations of the "illative sense" and the sphere of value judgments were restricted to religious truths. The new philosophy, moreover, as we have seen,[3] has been taught, by the sceptical results to which the old abstractions led, that knowledge cannot be *depersonalized,* and that the full concreteness of personal interest is indispensable for the attainment of truth. Hence the theologians' insistence on the personal character of "faith," which on the old assumptions had seemed a logical absurdity, was completely vindicated.

3 Cp. Chapters 8, 9.

260 / Faith, Ethics, and Immortality

And so the indications of emotional influence, and the proofs of the ineradicability of personality, multiplied throughout the realm of truth, until the apparently dispassionate procedure of mathematics ceased to seem typical and became a paradox.[4] Thus, throughout the ordinary range of what mankind esteems as "truth," the function of volition and selection, and the influence of values in all recognition of validity and reality, have become too clear to be ignored, and there has resulted the curious consequence that, by the very process of working out the claims of faith fairly to their logical conclusion, "faith" has ceased to be an adversary of and a substitute for "reason," and become an essential ingredient in its constitution. Reason, therefore, is incapacitated from systematically contesting the validity of faith, because faith is proved to be essential to its own validity.

§ 3. The sweeping nature of this change was at first obscured by the accident that the new philosophy was first applied in a paper written for a theological audience, and promulgated as a "will-to-believe," without sufficient emphasis on the corresponding attitudes of a will-to-disbelieve or to play with beliefs, or to suspend belief, or to allow belief to be imposed by what had already been *accepted* as external "fact." Thus it was the special character of the first application that led the less discerning to overlook the general character of the principle and the universal scope of the method. But in itself the new doctrine is perfectly general and impartial in its application to all cognitive states. It proceeds essentially from simple observations that, on the one hand, pure cognition is not an actual process in any human mind, but at best a fiction for theoretic purposes (of the most dubious character); while, on the other, all actual mental procedure is thoroughly personal and permeated through and through with purposes and aims and feelings and emotions and decisions and selections even in such cases where these features are ostensibly abstracted from.

[4] Of course, the discrepant character of mathematical truth as "self-evident" and "independent" of our arbitrament is only apparent. It arises mainly from the ease with which its fundamental postulates are made and rendered familiar, from the general agreement about their sphere of application, from the complete success of their practical working, and from the obvious coherence of truths which are tested in whole systems rather than individually. Cp. *Personal Idealism*, pp. 111–17, and 70 *n*.

Fundamentally, therefore, the new Humanism is nothing but an attempt to dismiss from psychology fictions which have been allowed to engender a brood of logical monsters, which in their turn have tyrannized over human life, and driven back the healthy human instinct to experiment, and thereby to know, from what they perniciously proclaimed forbidden ground. And as this fundamental position has never directly been impugned, does it not become an easy and inevitable inference that the attitude of the denier, the doubter, and the believer cannot be discriminated by the "pureness" of the thought, by the test of the presence or absence of emotion? If no thought is ever "pure," if it is neither "self-evident" nor true in point of fact that the more nearly "pure" it is the better it is for all purposes, if emotion, volition, interest, and bias impartially accompany all cognitive procedures, is it not preposterous to treat the concrete nature of the mind, the personal interests which give an impulse to knowledge and a zest to life, merely as impediments in the search for truth? What emotions, etc., must be repressed, to what extent, for what purposes, depends entirely on the character of the particular inquiry and of the particular inquirer. Thus the anger which leaves one man speechless will add eloquence and effect to the speeches of another; and the desire to prove a conclusion, which impairs the judgment of one, will stimulate another to the most ingenious experiments and the most laborious efforts. It is useless, therefore, to generalize at random about the cognitive effect of these psychological influences. They must be admitted in principle, and evaluated in detail. It *must* surely be futile to protest against the normal functioning of the mind; it must be rational to recognize influences which affect us, whether we approve of them or not. For how can they be estimated and treated rationally, unless we consent to recognize their potency? Has it not then become necessary to examine, patiently and in detail, how precisely these forces act; how, when, and to what extent their influence may be helpful or adverse, how they may be strengthened and guided and guarded or controlled and disciplined? And is it not a strange irony that impels a purblind rationalism to denounce as irrational so reasonable an undertaking?

§ 4. Let us therefore set aside such protests, and proceed

with our inquiry. Like most terms when scrutinized, neither reason nor faith are conceived with sufficient precision for our scientific purpose, and it would be hard to say which of them had been misused in a more flagrant or question-begging way. Reason to the rationalist has become a sort of verbal fetish, hedged round with emotional taboos, which exempt it from all rational criticism. It is credited with supramundane powers of cognition a priori; it is sacrosanct itself; and when its protecting aegis is cast over any errors or absurdities, it becomes blasphemy and "scepticism" to ask for their credentials. Hence it is only with the utmost trepidation that we can dare to ask: What, after all, does reason mean in actual life? When, however, we ask this question, and ponder on the answer, we shall not be slow to discover that, in the first place, *reason is not reasoning*. Reasoning may, of course, enter into the "rational" act, but it is by no means indispensable, and even when it does occur, it only forms a small part of the total process. Ordinarily instinct, impulse, and habit account for by far the greater number of our "rational" acts. On the other hand, it is *not* rational to "reason" three hours a day about the clothes one is going to put on; the reasoning of the victims of such "abulia," so far from being taken as a mark of superior rationality, is taken as a symptom of a *loss of reason*.

In the next place, "reason" is *not a faculty*. It stands for a group of habits which men (and to some extent some animals) have acquired, and which we find extremely useful, nay necessary, for the successful carrying on of life. Among these habits may be mentioned that of inhibiting reaction upon stimulation, i.e., of checking our natural and instinctive tendencies to act, until we have reflected what precisely it is we are dealing with. To determine this latter point, we have developed the habit of *analysis,* i.e., of breaking up the confused complex of presentations into "things" and their "attributes," which are referred to and "identified" with former similar experiences, and expressed in judgments as to what the situation "really is." This enables us to rearrange the presented connexions of attributions, and the whole reasoning process finds its natural issue and test in an action which modifies and beneficially innovates upon the original habit of reaction.

§ 5. In other words, thinking or judging is one of the

habits that make up man's "reason," and thinking or judging is a highly artificial and arbitrary manipulation of experience. The "rational" connexion of events and the "rational" interpretation of experiences are very far removed from our immediate data, and arrived at only by complicated processes of thought. Now, thinking involves essentially the use of concepts, and depends ultimately upon a number of principles (identity, contradiction, etc.), which have long been regarded as fundamental "axioms," but which reveal themselves as *postulates* to a voluntarist theory of knowledge which tries to understand them.

Now a postulate is not a self-evident "necessary" truth— it ceases to be necessary so soon as the purpose which called it into being is renounced. Neither is it a passively received imprint of experience. It is an assumption, which no doubt experience has suggested to an *actively inquiring* mind, but which is not, and cannot be, proved until after it has been assumed, and is often assumed because we desire it, in the teeth of nearly all the apparent "facts." It is therefore a product of our volitional activity, and initially its validity is uncertain. It is established *ex post facto* by the experience of its practical success. In other words, it is validated in just the same way as are the other habits that make up our "reason." In so far as, therefore, reasoning rests on postulates, and postulates are unproved and open to doubt at the outset, our attitude in adhering to them implies "faith," i.e., a belief in a "verification" yet to come. Must we not say, then, that at the very roots of "reason" we must recognize an element of "faith"? And similarly it would seem that as the fundamental truths of the sciences are attained in the same way, they all must presuppose faith, in a twofold manner—(1) as making use of reasoning, and (2) as resting upon the specific postulates of each science.

§ 6. That the principle of faith is commonly conceived very variably and with great vagueness has already been admitted, though its critics seem unfairly to incline towards the schoolboy's definition that it is "believing a thing when you know it's not true." Even this definition would not be wholly indefensible, if it were only written "believing when you know it's not *true*," and if thereby proper attention were drawn to the fact that a belief sustained by faith still stands in need of verification to become fully "true." On the whole, however, it would seem preferable to define it as the mental attitude which, for purposes of action, is willing to take upon trust valuable and desirable beliefs, *before* they have been proved "true," but in the hope that this attitude may promote their *verification*. About this definition it is to be noted (1) that it renders faith pre-eminently an attitude of will, an affair of the whole personality and not of the (abstract) intellect; (2) that it is expressly concerned with values, and that the worthless and unimportant is not fitted to evoke our faith; (3) that it involves risk, real stakes, and serious dangers, and is emphatically not a game that can be played in a casual and halfhearted way; (4) that a reference to verification is essential to it, and that therefore it is as little to be identified with, as to be divorced from, knowledge. Now verification must come about by the results of its practical working, by presuming the "truth" of our faith and by acting on its postulates; whence it would appear that those theologians were right who contended that real faith must justify itself by works. On the other hand, we might anticipate that spurious forms of faith would fall short in one or more of these respects, and so account for the confusion into which the subject has drifted.

§ 7. Such, then, being the nature of the faith which is said to envelop and sustain reason, and to engender knowledge, can it be fairly charged with forming a principle of unbridled individualism which abrogates all distinctions between subjective fancy and objective reality? Nothing surely could be further from the truth. At first, no doubt, it looks as though to recognize the psychological necessity and logical value of the will to believe opened the door to a limitless host of individual postulates. But the freedom to believe what we will is so checked by the consciousness of the responsibility and risk attaching to our choice that this part of the doctrine becomes little more than a device for securing an open field and a fair trial to every relevant possibility. Furthermore, all such subjective preferences have to submit to a severe sifting in consequence of the requirement that our postulates must stand the test of practical working, before their claim to truth can be admitted. Whatever our faith, it must be confirmed by works, and so prove itself to be objectively valid.

Alike, therefore, whether it is applied to knowledge or to faith, the pragmatic test is a severe one. It allows, indeed, the widest liberty to experiment; but it inexorably judges such experiments by the value of their actual achievements, and sternly withholds its sanction from insincere phrasemongering, from ineffectual aspiration, from unworkable conceptions, from verbal quibblings and dead formulas. Throughout the intellectual world the pedantry of the past has heaped up so much rubbish which the application of this pragmatic test would clear away that it is not always easy to repress a suspicion that much of the philosophic alarm at the consequences of applying our test may have been inspired, more or less unconsciously, by an unavowed dread lest it should insist on pensioning off some of the more effete veterans among philosophic traditions.

For really the pragmatic value of much that passes for philosophy is by no means easy to discern. Metaphysical systems, for instance, hardly ever seem to possess more than individual value. They satisfy their inventors, and afford congenial occupations to their critics. But they have hitherto shown no capacity to achieve a more general validity or to intervene effectively in the conduct of life. Again, it is inevitable that the pragmatic inquiry as to what difference their truth or falsehood can be supposed to make should be raised concerning many metaphysical propositions, such as that the universe is "one" or "perfect," or that truth is "eternal," or that "substance" is immutable, which, in so far as they are not taken as merely verbal (and this is all they usually profess to be when criticized), seem only very distantly and doubtfully connected with life. Their *prestige,* therefore, is seriously imperilled.

Now similar dogmas abound in religion, and are not wholly absent even from the sciences. But their occurrence is outbalanced by that of assertions which carry practical consequences in the most direct and vital way. Hence the pragmatic importance and value of science and religion can hardly be contested. And as tested by their material results in the

266 / Faith, Ethics, and Immortality

one case and by their spiritual results in the other, they both indisputably "work." It is inevitable, therefore, that we should regard them as resting on conceptions which are broadly "true," or "true" at all events until superseded by something truer. They have nothing, consequently, to fear from our method of criticism; if anything, its application may be expected to invigorate their pursuit, and to relieve them of the burden of nonfunctional superfluities with which an officious formalism has encumbered them.

Selection, then, of the valuable among a plurality of alternatives is essential to the life and progress of religious, as of secular, truth. Truth is not *merely* "what each man troweth," but (in its fullness) also what has stood its tests and justified our trust.

§ 8. But experience would seem to show that (at least while the winnowing process is still going on) the results of this testing are not so decisive as to eliminate all the competitors but one. Over an extensive range of subjects the most various opinions appear tenable, and are successfully maintained. But why should this astonish us? For (1) what right have we to expect final results from an incomplete process? (2) What right have we to assume that even ultimate "truth" must be one and the same for all? The assumption is no doubt convenient, and in a rough and ready way it works; but does it do full justice to the variety of men and things? Is the "sameness" we assume ever really more than agreement for practical purposes, and do we ever really crave for more than this? And provided we achieve this, why should not the "truth" too prove more subtly flexible, and adjust itself to the differences of individual experience, and result in an agreement to differ and to respect our various idiosyncrasies? (3) It is difficult to see why a phenomenon which is common in the sciences and normal in philosophy, without exciting indignation, should be regarded as inadmissible in the religious sphere. It is a normal feature in the progress of a science that its "facts" should be established by engendering a multitude of interpretations, none of which are capable, usually, of covering them completely, and none so clearly "false" as to be dismissible without a qualm. Why, then, should we be alarmed to find that the growth of religious truth proceeds with an analogous exuberance? (4) Anyhow, whether we like or dislike the human habit of entertaining divergent beliefs, the plurality of the opinions which are held to be "true" is an important fact, and forms one of the data which no adequate theory of knowledge can afford to overlook.

§ 9. It is useless, therefore, to close our eyes to the fact that faith is essentially a personal affair, an adventure, if you please, which originates in individual options, in choices on which men set their hearts and stake their lives. If these assumptions prosper, and if so, by faith we live, then it may come about that by faith we may also know. For it is the essential basis of the cognitive procedure in science no less than in religion that we must start from assumptions which we have not proved, which we cannot prove, and which can only be "verified" after we have trusted them and pledged ourselves to look upon the facts with eyes which our beliefs have fortunately biased. Of this procedure the belief in a causal connexion of events, the belief which all natural science presupposes and works on, is perhaps the simplest example. For no evidence will go to prove it in the least degree until the belief has boldly been assumed. Moreover, as we have argued (in Chapter 8), to abstract from the personal side of knowing is really impossible. Science also, properly understood, does not depersonalize herself. She too takes risks and ventures herself on postulates, hypotheses, and analogies, which seem wild, until they are tamed to our service and confirmed in their allegiance. She too must end by saying *Credo ut intelligam.* And she does this because she must. For, as Professor Dewey has admirably shown,[5] *all values and meanings rest upon beliefs,* and "we cannot preserve significance and decline the personal attitude in which it is inscribed and operative." And the failure of intellectualist philosophy to justify science and to understand "how knowledge is possible," we have seen to be merely the involuntary consequence of its mistaken refusal to admit the reality and necessity of faith.

I find it hard, therefore, to understand why a religious assumption, such as, e.g., the existence of a "God," should

5 In his important paper on "Beliefs and Existences" in *The Influence of Darwin on Philosophy.*

require a different and austerer mode of proof, or why the theologian should be debarred from a procedure which is always reputable, and sometimes heroic, in a man of science.

We start, then, always from the postulates of faith, and transmute them, slowly, into the axioms of reason. The presuppositions of scientific knowledge and religious faith are the same. So, too, is the mode of verification by experience. The assumptions which work, i.e., which approve themselves by ministering to human interests, purposes, and objects of desire, are "verified" and accepted as "true." So far there is no difference. But we now come to the most difficult part of our inquiry, viz., that of applying our general doctrine to the religious sphere, and of accounting for the different complexion of science and religion. For that there exists a marked difference here will hardly be denied, nor that it (if anything) will account for the current antithesis of faith and reason. It must be, in other words, a difference in the treatment of the same principles which produces the difference in the results.

§ 10. Now it is fairly easy to see that certain differences in treatment are necessarily conditioned by differences in the subjects in which the verification of our postulates takes place. In ordinary life we deal directly with an "external world" perceived through the senses; in science with the same a little less directly: in either case our hypotheses appeal to some overt, visible, and palpable fact, by the observation of which they are adequately verified. But the data of the religious consciousness are mainly experiences of a more inward, spiritual, personal sort, and it is obvious that they can hardly receive the same sort of verification. The religious postulates can hardly be verified by a direct appeal to sense, we think; and even if theophanies occurred, they would not nowadays be regarded as adequate proofs of the existence of God.

But this difference at once gives rise to a difficulty. The opinion of the great majority of mankind is still so instinctively averse from introspection that it is not yet willing to treat the psychical facts of inward experience as facts just as rightfully and in as real a way as the observations of the senses. It does not recognize the reality and power of *beliefs*. It does not see that "beliefs are themselves real without discount," "as metaphysically real as anything else can ever be," and that "belief, sheer, direct, unmitigated, personal belief," can act on reality "by modifying and shaping the reality of other real things."[6] And because it has not understood the reality of beliefs as integral constituents of the world of human experience, and their potency as the motive forces which transform it, it has disabled itself from really understanding our world.

But it has disabled itself more seriously from understanding the dynamics of the religious consciousness. It rules out as irrelevant a large and essential part of the evidence on which the religious consciousness has everywhere instinctively relied. It hesitates to admit the historic testimony to the "truth" of a religious synthesis which comes from the experience of its working through the ages, even though it may not, like the old rationalism, dismiss it outright as unworthy of consideration. It suspects or disallows many of the verifications to which the religious consciousness appeals. And this is manifestly quite unfair. The psychological evidence is relevant, because in the end there is a psychological side to all evidence, which has been overlooked. The historical appeal is relevant, because in the end all evidence is historical, and the truth of science also rests on the record of its services. The controversy, therefore, about the logical value of religious experience will have henceforth to be conducted with considerably expanded notions of what evidence is relevant. Nor must we be more severe on religion than on science. But it is plain that we are. We ought not to be more suspicious of the religious than of the many scientific theories which are not capable of direct verification by sense perception. But even though the ether, e.g., is an assumption which no perception can ever verify, it is yet, in scientific theory, rendered so continuous with what is capable of perceptual verification that the discrepancy is hardly noticed. The system of religious truths is much less closely knit; the connexion of the postulates with our spiritual needs and their fulfilling experiences is much less obvious; the methods and possibilities of spiritual experiment are much less clearly ascertained.

The reason, no doubt, partly is that in the religious sphere the conceptions for which the support of faith is invoked are much more vaguely outlined. It would be a matter of no

6 *Ibid.*, pp. 192, 188, 187.

slight difficulty to define the conception of religion itself so as to include everything that was essential, and to exclude everything that was not. And it would not be hard to show that at the very core of the religious sentiment there linger survivals of the fears and terrors with which primitive man was inspired by the spectacle of an uncomprehended universe.

Again, consider so central a conception of religion as, e.g., "God." It is so vaguely and ambiguously conceived that within the same religion, nay, within the same Church, the word may stand for anything, from the cosmic principle of the most vaporous pantheism to a near neighbour of the most anthropomorphic polytheism. And it is obvious that while this is so, no completely coherent or "rational" account can be given of a term whose meanings extend over almost the whole gamut of philosophic possibilities. But it is also obvious that there is no intrinsic reason for this state of things, and that theologians could, if they wished, assign one sufficiently definite meaning to the word, and then devise other terms as vehicles for the other meanings. It may be noted, as a happy foretaste of such a more reasonable procedure, that already philosophers of various schools are beginning to distinguish between the conceptions of "God" and of "the Absolute," though it is clear to me that the latter "conception" is still too vague and will in its turn have to be either abolished or relegated to a merely honorary position.

§ 11. It must be admitted, thirdly, that a widespread distrust of faith has been, not unnaturally, provoked by the extensive misuse of the principle in its religious signification. Faith has become the generic term for whatever religious phenomena coexisted with an absence of knowledge. Under this heading we may notice the following spurious forms of faith: (1) Faith may become a euphemism for unwillingness to think, or, at any rate, for absence of thought. In this sense faith is the favourite offspring of intellectual indolence. It is chiefly cherished as the source of a comfortable feeling that everything is all right, and that we need not trouble our heads about it further. If we "have faith" of this kind, no further exertion is needed to sustain our spiritual life; it is the easiest and cheapest way of limiting and shutting off the spiritual perspective. (2) It is not uncommon to prefer faith to knowledge because of its uncertainty. The certainty about matters of knowledge is cold and cramping; the possibilities of faith are gloriously elastic. (3) Our fears for the future, our cowardly shrinkings from the responsibilities and labours of too great a destiny, nay, our very despair of knowledge itself, may all assume the garb of faith, and masquerade as such. (4) Faith may mean merely a disingenuous disavowal of a failure to know, enabling us to retain dishonestly what we have not known (or sought) to gain by valid means. To all these spurious forms of faith, of course, our Humanism can furnish no support, though it is alert to note the important part they play (and especially the first) throughout our mental life.

The fifth form of faith is not so much fraudulent as incomplete; its fallacy consists in allowing itself to be stopped short of works, and to renounce the search for verification. This is the special temptation of the robuster forms of faith; if our faith is very strong it produces an assurance to which, psychologically, no more could be added. Why, then, demand knowledge as well? Does not this evince an unworthy distrust of faith at the very time when faith has shown its power? To which it may be replied that we also can and must distinguish psychological assurance from logical proof, even though the latter must induce the former, and the former must lay claim to logical value as it grows more nearly universal. The difference lies in the greater psychological communicability of the "logical" assurances and their wider range of influence. At first sight emotional exhortations (sermons, etc.) may seem to produce far intenser and more assured beliefs than calmer reasonings. But they do not appeal so widely nor last so well, and even though it is hazardous to assume that "logical" cogency is universal,[7] it is certainly, on the whole, of greater pragmatic value.

Moreover, the motives of an unreasoning faith are easily misread; the faith which is strong enough to feel no need of further proof is interpreted as too weak to dare to aspire to it. And so a properly enlightened faith should yield the strongest impetus to knowledge; the stronger it feels itself to be, the more boldly and eagerly should it seek, the more confidently

[7] Cp. Chapter 3, § 8.

should it anticipate, the more probably should it attain, the verificatory experiences that recompense its efforts.

§ 12. It must be admitted for these reasons that the mistaken uses of the principle of faith have retarded the intellectual development of the religious view of life. It has lagged so far behind the scientific in its formal development that theologians might often with advantage take lessons from the scientists in the proper use of faith. But intrinsically the religious postulates are not insusceptible of verification, nor are religious "evidences" incapable of standing the pragmatic test of truth. And some verification in some respects many of these postulates and much of this evidence may, of course, be fairly said to have received. The question how far such verification has gone is, in strict logic, the question as to the sphere of religious "truth." The question as to how much further verification should be carried, and with what prospects, is strictly the question of the sphere of the claims to truth which rest as yet only upon faith.

§ 13. To attempt to determine with scientific precision what amount of established truth must be conceded to religion as it stands, and what claims to truth should be regarded as reasonable and valuable, and what not, is a task which probably exceeds the powers, as it certainly transcends the functions, of the mere philosopher. It would in any case be fantastic, and probably illusory, to expect any philosophy to deduce a priori and in so many words the special doctrines of any religion which bases its claims on historic revelation, and *may*, by its working, be able to establish them. For what would be the need and the use of revelation if it added nothing to what we might have discovered for ourselves? Moreover, in the present condition of the religious evidence, any attempt to evaluate it could only claim subjective and personal interest. No two philosophers probably would evaluate it just in the same way and with the same results.

It seems better, therefore, to make only very general observations, and to draw only general conclusions. As regards the general psychology of religion, it is clear (1) that all our human methods of grasping and remoulding our experience are fundamentally one. (2) It is clear that the religious attitude towards the facts, or seeming facts, of life is in general valid.

(3) It is clear that this attitude has imperishable foundations in the psychological nature of the human soul. (4) It is clear that the pragmatic method is able to discriminate rigorously between valid and invalid uses of faith, and offers sufficient guarantees, on the one hand, against the wanderings of individual caprice, and, on the other, against the narrowness of a doctrinairism which would confine our postulates to a single type—those of the order falsely called "mechanical."[8] It can show that it is not "faith" to despise the work of "reason," nor "reason" to decline the aid of "faith"; and that the field of experience is so wide and rough that we need never be ashamed to import religion into its cultivation in order to perfect the fruits of human life.

As regards the concrete religions themselves, it is clear (1) that all religions may profit by the more sympathetic attitude of Humanism towards the religious endowment of human nature, and so towards their evidences and methods. And this for them is a gain not to be despised. For it invalidates the current rationalistic attacks, and secures religions against the ordinary "dialectical" refutations. It gives them, moreover, a chance of proving their truth in their own appropriate way. It is clear (2) that all religions work pragmatically to a greater or less extent. And this in spite of what seem, theoretically, the greatest difficulties. The obvious explanation is that these "theoretical" difficulties are really unimportant, because they are either *nonfunctional* or *pragmatically equivalents,* and that the really functional parts of all religions will be found to be practically identical. It follows (3) that all religions will be greatly benefited and strengthened by getting rid of their nonfunctional accretions and appendages. These constitute what may, perhaps, without grave injustice be called the *theological* side of religion; and it nearly always does more harm than good. For even where "theological" systems are not merely products of professional pedantry, and their "rationality" is not illusory, they absorb too much energy better devoted to the more truly religious functions. The most striking and

[8] Strictly interpreted, the word *confirms* the Humanist position which it is so often used to exclude. For a "mechanism" is, properly, a *device*—a means to effect a purpose. And, in point of fact, it is as a means to ordering our experience that "mechanical" conceptions are in use. To abstract from this teleological function of all "mechanism" therefore, is to falsify the metaphor: a device of nobody's, for no purpose, is a means that has no meaning.

familiar illustration of this is afforded by our own Christianity, an essentially human and thoroughly pragmatic religion, hampered throughout its history, and at times almost strangled, by an alien theology, based on the intellectualistic speculations of Greek philosophers. Fortunately the Greek metaphysic embodied (mainly) in the "Athanasian" creed is too obscure to have ever been really functional; its chief mischief has always been to give theological support to "philosophic" criticisms, which, by identifying God with "the One," have aimed at eliminating the human element from the Christian religion.[9] As against all such attempts, however, we must hold fast to the principle that the truest religion is that which issues in and fosters the best life.

[9] Cp. Prof. Dewey, *op. cit.*, pp. 178–80.

Chapter 11

The Ethical Significance of Immortality[1]

Argument

I. *Is immortality an ethical postulate?* Yes, if it can be shown to be implied in the validity of our ethical valuation of the world. Objections: (1) *a pure morality needs no reference to another world*. But there is moral waste if goodness of character perishes, and ultimate moral failure when physical life becomes impossible on earth; (2) *it is immoral to relegate the sanctions of morality to another world*. Not if future happiness and misery are conceived as the intrinsic consequences of moral goodness and badness; (3) *we cannot live for two worlds at once*. Depends on how they are conceived. The thought of a future life morally bracing, and, like all forethought about the future, a mark of superior mental development.

II. *What is the value of an ethical postulate?* The postulate is not emotional but rational, and affirms the validity of our moral judgments. It is part of a system of postulates which all proceed similarly. Moreover, the ideals we postulate are coincident and bound up together. Ultimately truth, goodness, happiness and beauty must all be postulated or rejected together. The alleged superior validity of the ideal of truth explained.

An ethical postulate, however, does not prescribe any special mode of its realization, for which we must look to scientific experience. There are also other questions which may modify, though they cannot subvert, our ethical demand.

WE ARE so accustomed in these days to hear the world-old traditions of the human race denied or ignored simply because

1 First published in the *New World* for September, 1897.

they are old that the antique flavour inevitably attaching to any argument about immortality almost suffices to secure its condemnation unheard. Yet such scornful treatment of authority is not justified by the present state of our knowledge. On the contrary, the antiquity and wide prevalence of an idea in themselves constitute a prima-facie claim upon the attention of the unprejudiced. Even on our most modern principles of evolutionist explanation, it means that the idea is somehow a response to a widely felt and persistent element in our experience. Its very antiquity, therefore, gives it an authority which may not be lightly set aside.

Still I do not wish to argue this question of immortality on the basis of authority. There is another side also to the influence of authority, when that authority is old. It is probable in such cases that the idea supported by authority will be disfigured by the dust of ages, overgrown by all sorts of parasitic fungi of fancy, and rendered ridiculous by the incrustations of fossil formulas, until its best friends hardly know it and it becomes intellectually contemptible, morally outrageous, and aesthetically repulsive to its foes. As something of this sort has probably happened to the idea of immortality, it will be the plan of this paper to argue the question on the sole ground of reason; its only stipulation being that the appeal be really made to the light of reason, shining without let or hindrance, and so far as possible, freed from all coloured spectacles of religious or scientific orthodoxy that might check its transmission.

The subject of immortality is, however, too extensive for me to attempt to discuss it as a whole, and my efforts will be confined to a single aspect of it—the ethical. That is, I shall *not* try to determine whether there is immortality as a fact, but only whether the science of ethics needs this conception for its own perfection. Putting the question more technically, I propose to consider two things. First: Is immortality an ethical postulate? Must a moral being, i.e., a being that can be judged good or evil, as such be deemed immortal? Secondly: If so, what does an ethical postulate prove? What is its general significance or logical status in the world of thought? The first of these questions is exclusively ethical. The second enters upon the realm of metaphysics, and may be expected to involve so much subtler and more difficult considerations that I would gladly evade it altogether if possible. But, unfortunately, to enforce the due respect for an ethical postulate, the case must be carried to the supreme court of metaphysics. Moreover, it is only the discussion of its metaphysical value that gives the ethical argument any direct bearing on the question, not here to be discussed as such, whether there is immortality as a matter of fact.

I

Let us take up, then, the first question, whether immortality is an ethical postulate. What can be urged in favour of this view? The argument for it is exceedingly simple: it consists in showing that without immortality it is not possible to think the world as a harmonious whole, as a moral cosmos. To show this, one has not to appeal to anything more recondite than the fact that in our present phase of existence the moral life cannot be lived out to its completion, that it is not permitted to display its full fruitage of consequences for good and for evil. Whenever might triumphs over right; whenever the evil-doers succeed and the righteous perish; whenever goodness is trampled under foot and wickedness is exalted to high places —nay, whenever the moral development of character is cut short and rendered vain by death—we are brought face to face with facts which constitute an indictment of cosmic justice, which are inconsistent with the conception of the world as a moral order. Unless, therefore, we can vindicate this order by explaining away the facts that would otherwise destroy it, we have to abandon the ethical judgment of the world of our experience as good or bad; we have to admit that the ideal of goodness is an illusion of which the scheme of things recks not at all.

But if we refuse to do this (and whether we are not bound to refuse to abandon our ideals at the first show of opposition will presently be considered), how shall the ethical harmony be restored if not by the supposition of a prolongation and perfection of the moral life in the future? Only so can character be made of real significance in the scheme of things; only so is it something worth possessing, an investment more permanent and more decisive of our weal and woe than all the outward goods men set their hearts upon, rather than a transitory bubble to whose splendour it matters not one whit whether it be pure translucence refracting the radiance of the sunlight, or the iridescent film that coats decay.

The ethical argument for immortality, then, is simply this: that if death ends all, the moral life cannot be lived out, moral perfection is impossible, and the universe cannot be regarded as at heart ethical. But in spite of its simplicity, this argument has been misunderstood in a variety of ways. Let us briefly consider the chief of these.

It is objected by well-meaning people, who rather pride themselves on their advocacy of a purer and higher morality, that the ethical sphere does not need supplementing by a future life. They grow indignant at the thought that "the good men do is buried in their graves," and does not survive to inspire and direct succeeding generations. They bid us therefore fight the good fight disinterestedly and without selfish reward, in order that our grandchildren, if we have any, may enjoy the fruits of our self-denial, and that the world may be the better for our efforts.

To this the reply is twofold. It is idle to say that goodness is not wasted because the results of actions reverberate throughout the ages. The good men *do* may persist and work well or ill, but the good men *are* surely perishes. The human character itself passes away, and its effects are transmitted only through the characters of others. The character itself is an indefeasible and inalienable possession of the owner, and by no flight of the imagination can it be transferred to others. Whatever worth, therefore, we assign to character, that worth is lost to the world if immortality be denied. And, moreover, it is only in their effect upon his own character that a man's actions can be surely classified as good or bad. What the effect of actions will be on others, now or subsequently no one can foretell; the real objection to doing too much for posterity is not that "posterity has done nothing for us," but the uncertainty as to what the effect on posterity will be. For that depends largely on the character of others, and *quisque suos patimur Manes.* Each can assume full responsibility for his own actions and his own character alone; the rest lies largely on the lap of the gods. If, then, you deny the persistence of character, you have denied the real basis of the moral order.

But, secondly, supposing even that humanity profited by our efforts, how far would this go towards re-establishing the moral order of the world? If the immortality of the individual be an illusion, surely that of the race is a transparent absurdity. If there is certainty about any prediction of science, it is surely, as I have elsewhere put it, this: that our racial destiny is "to shiver and to starve to death in ever-deepening gloom."[2] The prospective fortunes of the race, then, do not redeem the moral character of the universe. If the view of mechanical science be the whole truth about the universe, the race is of just as little account as the individual; suns and stars and the hosts of heaven will roll on in their orbits just as steadily and unfeelingly whether we prosper or perish, struggle on or resign ourselves to despair. Cosmically, the earth and all it bears on its surface is of infinitesimal importance; what does it matter then whether any one brood of mites that crawls upon it is better or worse than its successors, any more than whether it laboriously grubs up a few atoms of a shining yellow or of a shining white metal and fights about the ratio? No; the worthy people who think that George Eliot's "choir invisible" can make a noise to compete with the whirl of worlds decidedly delude themselves, and "an immortality of influence" is no adequate ethical substitute for personal immortality.

A second objection does not pretend to improve on the ethic of immortality, but criticizes it by descanting on the turpitude of basing morality on "fears of hell and hopes of Paradise." This objection also is urged by many worthy persons; and I have known some who have been sustained through life by the pride they took in showing that they could be just as moral without knowing why, as they were when they thought their eternal salvation depended on their conduct. But theoretically this objection surely rests on a misconception. The rewards and punishments for conduct are not to be looked upon as *motives* to conduct, but as the natural *results* of conduct, inevitable in a morally ordered universe. In an ethical universe, goodness cannot be associated with persistent misery, because that would be an outrage upon the moral order; badness must ultimately involve unhappiness, because only such retribution

2 *Riddles of the Sphinx,* p. 105; new ed., p. 104.

will reaffirm the outraged supremacy of the moral order. Rewards and punishments, then, are but incidents in that completion of the moral life for the sake of which immortality was postulated; they are not in themselves the sole motives for leading such a life. The very suggestion that they may be supposed to be, on whatever side it is urged, shows an imperfect appreciation of the nature of the moral life, indicative of a coarser moral fiber and of a lower stage of ethical development.

But we need not on this account entirely condemn this mode of regarding immortality. Fears and hopes of what may happen hereafter may not be the highest motives to morality; they may enforce as an external sanction what should be an intrinsic conviction; but they are not therefore valueless. For, if they are effective, they at least *accustom* men to right conduct, and thus form the basis of sound habit, which is the actual foundation of all conduct in any case, and the necessary prerequisite for sound reflection upon conduct and the attainment of any higher view of morality. Our moral enthusiasm, therefore, need no more frown upon these lower motives than it need disband the police on the ground that a truly moral community should not need policing.

Still more radical than the objections we have considered is a third objection, which denounces the essential immorality of looking to a future life at all in connexion with our conduct here. The habit of contemplating a future life, it is urged, engenders a pernicious "other-worldliness" most detrimental to proper behaviour in this world. We cannot live for two worlds at once. The future life dwarfs the present; the supposed significance of the eternal life hereafter destroys the real significance of our life here and now.

Again, I think the objection labours under a misconception. It holds good only against a conception of immortality which, like the Buddhist Nirvana, for example, conflicts and competes with the ethical view of this world. We cannot "live for two worlds at once," only if the principles of conduct required in them are fundamentally different. If extinction is the end to which we should aspire hereafter, then certainly it would be folly to prepare for it by a strenuous life on earth. The objection is irrelevant to an immortality which is postulated as the *completion* of mundane morality, which is not so much *other-worldliness* as *better-worldliness*, suggested by the ethical defects of our actual experience. In reality such a view indefinitely deepens the significance of the present life. Think what is involved in the assertion that character is permanent and indestructible, and passes not from us however the fashion of our outward life may change! Think of it, that we can never escape from ourselves, from the effect of our deeds on our character, and that every deed leaves its mark upon the soul, a mark which may be modified and counterbalanced, but can never be undone to all eternity! Will not the effect of such a belief be to make us realize the solemnity of life as we never did before, to nerve us to that unremitting self-improvement without which there is no approximating to the moral ideal? Instead of losing its significance, does not every act of life become fraught with infinite significance? Instead of becoming careless about ourselves, will it not, then, become worth our while to bestow upon our own character-building a care that would otherwise have been disproportionate? For, as most of them are thoroughly aware, ordinary people are quite good enough for ordinary purposes. Why then, should they strive laboriously to change and remould themselves, and fall, perchance, into the exaggerated virtue of Jane Austen Beecher Stowe de Rouse, who was "good beyond all earthly need"? Is it not much more convenient to stay as one is, and to reply to the ambitions of an unquiet conscience as the General of the Jesuits replied to the Pope who wished to reform them: *Sint ut sunt aut non sint*—"Let them be as they are or not be at all"? Is it not always inconvenient to think of the future, and is not the future life altogether too big a thing to think of? And is not this, and not any logical or scientific difficulties which the thought involves, the real reason why men seek to banish it from their consciousness—why it is hardly ever more than a half belief in most men's minds? Human inertia, all that keeps us commonplace and sordid, unheroic and unaspiring, is, and always has been, dead against it. And that is why moral reformers have always insisted on it. For their function is to overcome moral inertia.

It is, however, some consolation to think that the past course of evolution seemingly sanctions the belief of those who would have us take account of a future which extends into another life. Certainly the expansion of the future, of which our action takes account, is one of the most marked characteristics of a progressive civilization. The animal looks into the future not at all, and the savage but little; but, as civilization grows, the future consequences of action become more and more important, and are prepared for more and more. When we have dared to forecast the future of the race when our coal supply shall be exhausted; when we have looked unflinchingly upon that unimaginably distant period when the sun's light shall fail, shall we shrink from rising to the contemplation of a future that extends immeasurably further?

II

By thus replying to these three objections I hope to have sufficiently established the first part of my thesis—that immortality is in truth an ethical postulate. But the second part still remains to be answered, namely, the question: What is an ethical postulate really worth? What is its value metaphysically? Is it more than an impulse of ethical emotion which shrinks into nothingness under the calm gaze of scientific truth? Does it amount to demonstration?

One often hears it said that immortality is an emotional postulate, unreasoning if not unreasonable; and that hackneyed phrase "the hope of immortality" bears involuntary witness to the fact that the argument is not supposed to amount to demonstration. Now this is just the mental attitude towards the subject which I deprecate and wish to controvert. The people who cherish the *hope* of immortality I regard as people who, for the reasons given above, *sometimes hope there is no immortality,* or at least have not much faith in their own argument. It is more especially for the benefit of such weak-kneed brethren that I would maintain the following doctrine:

The ethical postulate of immortality is not an emotional postulate, but as rational as any postulate, and has as good a claim for recognition in our ultimate metaphysic. Or, if they still prefer to regard it as emotional, and quote von Hartmann's remark on the subject that metaphysical truths cannot be based on emotional postulates, I shall reply that, ultimately, truths will nowhere be found to rest on any other grounds.

(1) Hence immortality, as an ethical postulate, is of the same nature as certain other postulates without which we cannot harmonize our experience.

(2) It is bound up with those other postulates.

(3) Its assumption is justified in precisely the same way as that of the other postulates.

(4) If they cannot accept this as demonstration, they will get no better anywhere in the world.

(1) Taking these points in order, let us ask what is the nature of an ethical postulate. It is nothing but the affirmation of the cosmic significance of the ideal of *goodness,* of our *ethical valuation* of things. It claims that the universe is not merely a fact, but has a certain value which we call ethical. It is at bottom a moral universe, and potentially resolves itself into an ethical harmony. Now the logical method by which this argument proceeds is this: given a part, to find the whole; given a few fragmentary data, to construct therefrom an ideal which may validly be used to interpret the data. It is the same method which is used by the palaeontologist when, from a tooth or a bone, he reconstructs some long-extinct form of life. The question, then, resolves itself into this: Have we the right to assume that our ethical data cohere and may be fitted together into an ethical ideal?

And (2) in sustaining this procedure, the ethical consciousness does not stand alone. Its claim is supported by our procedure elsewhere. *All* the ideals of ultimate value are constituted in the same manner. How do we make good the claim that anything in the universe is beautiful? We assume that our judgments concerning beauty are not devoid of significance, but may be harmonized in an ideal of beauty to which the nature of things is somehow akin. How do we make good the claim that happiness is possible? We believe in the prophetic significance of the pleasurable states of consciousness in our experience, and out of them frame the ideal of happiness which we assume reality may realize.

Lastly, how do we make good the claim that the world is knowable? We assume that its facts somehow cohere, and may be arranged in an orderly system of truth or knowledge. In other words, we try to look upon reality as realizing our ideals of knowledge, beauty, goodness, and happiness, and thereby constitute it a cosmos, knowable, beautiful, ethical, and delightful. But in each case we are checked by the same obstacles. The ideals certainly do not float on the surface of life. They are not congruous with the raw facts of experience. They have to be sought with infinite pains and ere we have dragged them forth and proved them valid, lo, death comes and, ruthlessly impartial, cuts short the careers of the man of science and of the man of pleasure. Life is imperfect and fragmentary all round—not only in the eyes of ethics. Emotionally, intellectually, and aesthetically, life as it stands is no less inadequate than ethically. The ideals of happiness, knowledge, and beauty postulate realization no less and in no other way than goodness; the murky atmosphere of earth, poisoned by the breath of death, no less derides their possibility. What we ask, then, for one we ask for all, and we ask it in obedience to the same law of our being—that life *must* show itself congruous with the ideals from which it draws its value.

And (3) these ideals are not only cognate, but coincident; we cannot in the last resort affirm one while denying the rest; nothing short of a complete harmony can wholly satisfy us. Truth, goodness, happiness, and beauty are all indispensable factors in perfection, the varying facets which the one ideal reveals to our various modes of striving.[3]

This is generally denied only by the votaries of the ideal of truth, and so it will perhaps suffice if I content myself with pointing out to them how untenable is their position. We have all heard some postulate of human feeling met with the cold sneer of a shortsighted science and the query: Why should the universe take account of goodness and its completion? Well, I contend that if this sneer is worth anything, it must be extended so as to include all human activity, that we might with equal cogency go on to ask: Why, then, should the universe take acount of knowledge and its establishment, or of happiness and its attainment? We have, I claim, no logical ground for supposing the world to be knowable, and yet utterly disregardful of happiness and goodness. For a world supposed to be wholly knowable, i.e., wholly harmonious with our intellectual demands, while remaining wholly discordant with our emotional nature, would *ipso facto* include an intellectually

3 See *Riddles of the Sphinx*, ch. XII, § 9.

insoluble puzzle which would render it fundamentally *unknowable*. Nay, more, is not the supposition directly self-contradictory? Does not a knowable world satisfy at least one of our emotional demands—the desire for knowledge? It cannot be then, as alleged, *utterly* out of relation to our emotional nature. But if it can satisfy one such postulate, why not the rest?

The ideals, then, stand and fall together. They are rooted in the unity of the human soul, in the final solidarity of life's endeavours. And when the supreme need arises, the outcry of the soul can summon to its aid all the powers that minister unto its being; it wields a spell that reaches from the iciest altitudes of scientific abstraction to the warmest pulsations of concrete emotion, and from the most ethereal fancy of the purest intellect to the blindest impulse of agonizing passion; it can extort from every element of our nature the confession of its solidarity with the rest of life, and set it in array on that dread battlefield whereon the Gods contend against the Giants —of Doubt, Disorder, and Despair.

For it is because of this solidarity of the ideals that the denial of them confronts us with the gravest issues. They all assert, in varying form but with unvarying intent, the same great principle—the conformity of the world with the capacity of our nature. And unfamiliar as some of the applications of this principle may be to our ordinary habits of thinking, we have to remember that the principle itself can hardly be impugned. For inasmuch as in the end our "world" is human experience, and a world which we neither did nor could experience would not be one we need argue or trouble about, this principle really amounts to an assertion of the intrinsic coherence and potential harmony of the whole of experience. Without it where should we be? What would our attitude have to be towards a world in which the ultimate significance of our ideals was denied, that is, a world which was no world, a world in which nothing really meant anything, nothing was really good or beautiful or true, and in which the hope of happiness was nothing but illusion? To say that the prospect of such a world would reduce us to the most despairing depths of the most abject pessimism hardly depicts the full horror of the situation: it would be a world of which the hopelessness would disarm even the suicide's hand. For, in a world which had really renounced its allegiance to the ideal, all action would be paralysed by the conviction that nothing we desired could ever be attained, because the existent was irreconcilably alienated from the desirable. The foundations of the cosmos would be shattered, and we should have to realize that nothing is worth doing because nothing has any worth, because human valuations have no significance in establishing the nature of things. We should be plunged, in other words, in that unfathomable abyss where Scepticism fraternizes with Pessimism, and they hug their miseries in chaos undisguised.

(4) We can reject, then, the principle on which the ethical postulate of immortality rests only at the cost of entire scepticism and utter pessimism. By those not prepared to pay that price the principle must be accepted, like the other assumptions that render the world a fit sphere for the satisfaction of other human activities. Take, for instance, the assumption that the world is a knowable cosmos. Is this proved? Certainly not; nor can it be until everything is known; until then it always remains possible that the world may not turn out really knowable at the last. Can we avoid assuming it? Certainly not; without it we could not take a single step towards any science or practice. We simply *must* assume that the world is an intelligible world, if we are to live in it. As a matter of fact we do assume it, all except a few who bury their dissent in the seclusion of the madhouse. Is the assumption confirmed? Yes, in the only way in which such fundamental assumptions ever are confirmed: the further we trust it the more we know, the more confident in it we grow.

The assumption of a moral cosmos is made and confirmed in the same way. We cannot prove it to be correct so long as the world is not morally perfect; we cannot wholly exorcize the recurrent dread that, after all, the moral order may of a sudden lapse into chaos before our eyes; but we cannot organize our moral experience without this assumption, and in the course of moral development our confidence in it grows.

But, it may be said, if there is no essential difference between the assumption of a moral and that of an intellectual order in our experience, how is it that the former appears so much less certain than the latter? Why are we so much more confident that the world is subject to natural than to moral law? Why are *moral* so much more common and more successful than *intellectual* sceptics? These facts are not to be disputed, but perhaps they can be explained. Undoubtedly the moral order is not so strong as the scientific, and its principles have not such a hold on human nature. The rebels against the moral order are not all in prison; our rascals largely run about unhanged. "Moral insanity" is pleaded in mitigation of the punishment which it should render inexorable. But the difference is due simply to the different amounts of experience behind the two assumptions. Historically man was a knowing being long before he was an ethical being. He had lived long, as Aristotle said, before he had lived well; both in time and in urgency, perceptual adaptation to the physical order took precedence over ethical adaptation to the social order. Man had to assume, therefore, the principles that constituted the world a knowable cosmos long before he needed to assume a moral order. Hence the beliefs in the uniformity and calculability of Nature and the like have a much greater and more unequivocal mass of racial experience and hereditary instinct behind them than any moral instinct we have yet acquired. But this does not show that the nature of the several assumptions is not essentially the same.

If the argument of this paper has commended itself so far, there will probably be little difficulty in granting the last point, that the demonstration of immortality proffered by the ethical argument is as complete as any that can be devised. But, to enforce the point, allusion may be made to the fact that demonstration is in its very nature what the logicians call *hypothetical*. It proceeds in the form: If A is, then B must be. But how are we to know that A is? The premiss has to be assumed or conceded in every demonstration. The utmost we can do is to rest our demonstration on an assumption so fundamental that none will dare to question it; and this we here seem to have accomplished. For what could be more fundamental than the assumption on which the ethical argument rests—that the elements of our experience admit of being harmonized, that the world is truly a *cosmos?* If this be not absolute certainty, it is at least certainty such that, while no assertion of any special science is *less* hypothetical, none rests upon an *equally* indispensable assumption.

On the whole, then, the ethical argument for immortality seems logically as sound and metaphysically as legitimate as any argument can well be; but it will not be amiss to allude in closing to two points about which nothing has so far been said. The first is the fact that, when immortality has been shown to be an ethical postulate, nothing has been decided as to the *content* of that idea. All we know is that immortality must be of such a sort as to be capable of being an ethical postulate. And it is quite possible that the science of ethics would on this ground find much to protest against in many of the traditional forms of the belief in immortality, while it would find little to object to in others which are less familiar. It is difficult, for instance, to see how eternal damnation could be regarded as an ethical postulate, while some appropriate modification of the Hindu notion of *karma* might seem ethically welcome. But though ethics could thus *prohibit* certain ethically outrageous beliefs in immortality, it cannot aspire *positively to determine* the way in which its postulate is to be realized. That problem lies beyond its scope, and has to be determined, if at all, by considerations of a scientific and metaphysical character. Hence the moral argument for immortality is in a manner incomplete: first, because a moral postulate cannot as such inform us as to the method of its realization; and secondly, because, disguise it as we may, our faith in a cosmic order which includes the moral remains still capable of further confirmation. For, however firm our trust in the rationality of life, few would contend that the discovery of scientific facts consonant with our ethical demands would add nothing to the assurance of their faith.

And so, lastly, a word must be said on the subject of these scientific and metaphysical arguments about immortality which were excluded as irrelevant to the ethical aspect of the question, in order to bring out the important fact that, however they may be supposed to result, the ethical argument maintains its independent validity. So far as I can see, these further arguments may result in three different ways. They may confirm the ethical argument—in which case our confidence in immortality will be strengthened. They may balance each other—in which case they will leave the field open for the ethical argument. Or, in the worst event, they may preponderatingly conflict with it. But, even so, it would not follow that they were right and the ethical argument was wrong, at least until the plea for the essential solidarity of the ultimate postulates had been invalidated. A world in which the ethical ideal is abrogated and annulled cannot be a harmonious world; and if it be not harmonious throughout, we can feel no confidence that it is harmonious in any part. In other words, so long as we trust in the ultimate presupposition of all knowledge and all action, we could never quite trust the nonethical arguments that are supposed to plunge us in perplexity.

Chapter 12

Philosophy and the Scientific Investigation of a Future Life[1]

Argument

I. The use of philosophy in scientific inquiry—the general logical criticism of fundamental postulates and working methods. This is most necessary and helpful in a new science, and safest in one which, like psychical research, has not yet obtained professional endowment. Special interest of a discussion of the assumptions made in a scientific inquiry into the possibility of a future life. The general scientific assumption of "law," i.e., knowableness. The axiom of proceeding from the known to the unknown. This life must give the clue to our interpretation of an "other" life, which could not be wholly "other" without paralysing thought. Misconceptions on this score explain (1) the practical weakness of the "belief" in a future life; (2) the prejudice against an anthropomorphic future life; and (3) against the spiritist hypothesis. Assuming, therefore, that as a working theory personal survival is conceivable, how can it be verified? The future life must be conceived (1) as natural; (2) as psychically continuous with the present, in spite of the difficulty of obtaining proofs of identity; (3) as only dissociated from our world by secondary processes traceable in our normal psychology. Result that a future life scientifically provable would necessarily *seem* humdrum and unsensational.

II. The philosophic basis of the conception of a future life. Philosophies which reject it a priori are gratuitous. For an idealistic experientialism the conception has no difficulty. How we pass into another world.

1 An expanded form of a paper originally read before the Society for Psychical Research, and published in its *Proceedings*, Part 36, February, 1900.

How, why, and to what extent are dream worlds
"unreal"? "Death" as "awakening" to a more real
world. Philosophers on death. Four paradoxes about
death. Their explanation by idealism. The construction and dissolution of the common world of waking
life. The ambiguity of death. Does it leave the
chances equal? Impossibility of disproving a future
life wholly severed from the present. Possibility of
empirical evidence that the severance is *not* complete.
Philosophy clears away prejudices that obstruct investigation, but leaves discovery to science.

I

THE philosopher, as the genius of Plato long ago perceived,[2]
is a very strange being. He is in the world, but not of it, resid-
ing mainly in a "Cloud-cuckoodom" of his own invention,
which seems to have no relation to the actual facts of life, and
makes no difference to anything or anybody but the philosopher himself. Its sole function seems to be to make the philosopher himself feel happy and superior to everybody who
does not understand his philosophy enough to enter into it,
that is, to everybody else in the world.

But even so the philosopher is not happy in his paradise—
of sages. He is terribly worried by all the other philosophers,
each of whom is quite as cantankerous and cranky as himself,
and wants to carry him off into his own private Nephelococcygia. And as he will not, and indeed cannot, enter into it,
they all get very angry. They get so angry that they cannot
even laugh at each other. But when they get a little calmer
(not that there is really such a thing as calm among philosophers any more than among cirrus clouds—only they live so
far aloof and aloft that people cannot see how they behave)
they fall to criticizing. And so when one of them has built
himself a nice new Nephelococcygia high up in the clouds, the
rest all try to pull to pieces the abode of his soul, and bombard
him with buzzing chimeras bottled in vacuum tubes and riddle
him with sesquipedalian technicalities. In this they are usually
successful, for, though so perverse, they are immensely clever,
and their critical acumen is as wonderful as their unconscious-

2 *Republic,* 490.

ness of their own absurdity. And so, one after the other, each loses his scalp, and is buried in the ruins of his system.

Or rather he is *not;* for the burial customs of philosophers are as strange as the rest of their behaviour, and unlike those of any other tribe of men. Among the scientists, for instance, there are also savage wars, and they practise vivisection. But the scientists are not head-hunters. They forget the errors of their vanquished warriors and bury their remains, preserving only the memory of the work they did for Science. And thus do they keep clean the face of Science, and every morning wash away every blood stain and every speck of error in the waters of Lethe, so that the many may believe that Science is infallible and its history is one unbroken progress; which is both more Christian and more worldly-wise.

But not so the philosophers. They still believe in the discipline of dirt, and keep the face of the fair goddess they profess to worship like unto the face of Glaucus the sea god,[3] and the thicker grow the incrustations of historic error the better they are pleased. For they are simply devoted to the memory of ancient errors. They venerate them and collect them and dry them (in their histories of philosophy), and label them and exhibit them in glass cases with the scalps of their authors. They compile whole museums of such antiquities, and get themselves appointed the curators thereof. One of our universities is popularly believed to have appointed about two dozen such curators of the relics of the great fight between Aristocles, the son of Ariston, and Aristoteles, the son of Nicomachus. And the cause thereof was not Argive Helen, if you please, but the transcendence of the universal! Verily philosophic immortality is as terrible a thing and as hard to bear as that of Tithonus!

Such, I cannot help suspecting, are the real sentiments of intelligent men of the world concerning philosophers, though only a philosopher could be rude enough to set them down in black and white. But calumny, like murder, will out, and only so can it be met. And so those who, like Plato, have had the deepest faith in the value of philosophy have ever also been the readiest to admit and to confront the allegations of detractors.

[3] Cp. Plato, *Republic,* 611 D.

And yet, at bottom, this was never quite an easy thing to do. The weaknesses of philosophy are manifest; its obscurity, its flimsiness, its intense individuality,[4] its remoteness and uselessness for the ordinary purposes of life, cannot but catch the public eye. Its virtues (if any) are hidden out of sight. It seems safer, therefore, on the whole, for the sage to flaunt his shame and to assume its burden; boldly to disavow all purpose to better or instruct the world, cynically to confess that whether or not his astounding feats of conceptual prestidigitation can entertain the gaping crowd, they do at least amuse himself, honestly to disclaim the search for some more subtle service springing from his exercises. It may have happened here and there that the prescience of some wild and philosophic guess outstripped the plodding march of science. It may have happened now and then that in some reflective soul the conduct of life has been improved by study of its theory. But over most men habit bears such sway that this would be a marvel, and such precarious incidents are not enough to prove the useful nature of philosophy.

And yet if it were permitted to appeal to the philosophic heresy which just now is stirring up in all the bottled chimeras a buzzing fit to burst their vacuum tubes, if we might argue as pragmatists, it would seem obvious that even philosophy must have some use. For if it had not, society would scarce continue the endowment of philosophy, whose professors might thereupon find themselves reduced to breaking stones instead of systems. It is quite true that there is always a flavour of impertinence about the intervention of a philosopher in a subject of scientific research. For he cannot, as such, be trusted to make original contributions to the facts, and when he makes an attempt to criticize the contributions of others, it is quite true that he is terribly prone to do so from the a priori basis of some farfetched cosmic theory which nobody else in the world besides himself believes in or even understands, and so achieves a comic rather than a cosmic interest. If, again, he contends himself with ponderously pondering on the accepted facts of a science, he becomes a bore, consuming time and getting in the way of more practical workers.

It must be admitted, therefore, that the usefulness of a phi-

4 For the explanation of which see *Personal Idealism*, pp. 50–1.

losopher is very limited. It is undeniable only in cases where he is needed to clear out of the way other philosophers who have become obstreperous and obstructive; but such occasions do not occur frequently, and no really vigorous movement pays much heed to what philosophers are saying.

Nevertheless, philosophy seems to me to have also a more important function, which may enable it to be scientifically suggestive and serviceable, at all events at a certain stage in the development of a science.

The function in question is that of discussing the working methods of a science, of exhibiting their full scope and logical implications and connexions, and considering the merits of the alternative ways of treating the subject. Such a critical *methodology* of a science is necessarily dull, but, perhaps, on that account, all the better adapted for philosophic discourse. And in view of the intellectual myopia which scientific specialism engenders, there are, perhaps, few things more salutary, as an unpleasant medicine is salutary, than for a science to become conscious of the working assumptions, or methodological postulates, on which it proceeds.

In the case of psychical research, in particular, the discussion of such methodological assumptions seems to be more novel, easier and more useful than in disciplines which have already reached a more assured position among the sciences. It is likely to be more novel, because of the novelty of the whole subject. It is likely to be easier to dissect out and contemplate in abstraction the methodological assumptions of an inchoate and infant science, because its organism is not so strongly knit and the flesh of fact does not so closely shroud the bone of method by which it is supported; it is still in a low stage of organization in which the whole may be taken to pieces and put together without much injury to the vitality of its parts. An advanced science, on the other hand, is far more difficult to handle. It imposes on the philosophic critic by its very mass of coherent and consistent interpretation; it appeals to him by its noble record of service to the human race; it crushes him by the sheer weight of immemorial authority. In it facts and theories have long been welded together into so indissoluble a union that the former can no longer be questioned, while the latter have for the most part risen to the dignity of indispensable "necessary truths" implied in the very nature of the human mind and underlying the whole structure of human knowledge.[5] We gain little help, therefore, from the assumptions of sciences like mathematics and mechanics in considering what assumptions should be made in a new subject like psychical research; we learn little about the making of a science from sciences which can neither be unmade nor remade, and in whose case it requires a considerable effort of philosophic thought to realize the methodological character of their fundamental postulates. More might perhaps be learnt from the assumptions of parvenu sciences which have but recently obtained full recognition, but for the fact that a critical dissection of their methods is decidedly dangerous. For the *arbor scientiae* seems in their case to have developed a symbiotic arrangement greatly resembling that whereby certain trees protect themselves; just as any attack on the latter is ferociously resented by a host of ants which the tree provides with food and shelter, so any interference with such a science is sure to draw down upon the mildest critic the onslaught of an infuriated professor who lives upon the science. In psychical research, on the other hand, no such danger is to be apprehended; we have not yet developed any professionals whose mission it is, as William James has wittily remarked,[6] to kill out the layman's general interest in the subject, and hence the philosopher may proceed at his leisure to observe how the science is made and to try instructive experiments with its working methods, without fear of offending vested interests.

Again, a philosophic discussion of possible methods is likely to be more useful in psychical research because such methods are still plastic cartilage, as it were, which has not yet grown into rigid bone, and may be moulded into a variety of forms. Hence by reflecting betimes upon the advantages of alternative methods, the philosopher may flatter himself that he can be of real service in guiding the course of investigation, or at least in helping it to avoid certain pitfalls. Not, of course, that even here he would be wise to presume to lay down the law a priori as to the actual working and merits of the various methods; he should content himself with expounding the logical charac-

[5] See *Axioms as Postulates*.
[6] *Human Immortality*, init.

teristics which sound methods in psychical research must possess, and explaining why exactly they must possess them.

I do not propose, however, on this occasion to discuss the methodological value of the assumptions made in psychical research generally, but only in so far as they affect the question of a future life. The reasons for this are obvious. The possibility of a future life provides much of the motive force in such inquiries. Most of the active members of the Society are probably interested in this question, and whether they desire or fear a future life, they agree in wanting to know what chance or danger there is of it. It is true that the S.P.R. is unique in aiming to solve this problem in a scientific way, but though we are scientific, we may yet be honest—in avowing the existence of a practical motive. If attacked on this score, let us meet our critics with the doctrine that in this respect at least we are *not* unique, inasmuch as in the end all true science is inspired by practical motives, and that it is the fear, no less than the hope, of a future life that renders its possibility so urgent a subject for scientific consideration. Moreover, just now the evidence in connexion with Mrs. Piper's trances seems to have brought this possibility well above the horizon of the S.P.R., while at the same time much confusion and prejudice still seem to prevail about it which philosophic criticism may help to dissipate. For a comprehensive statement of the new evidence and new interpretations of old evidence which render it the bounden duty of the philosopher to readjust himself and his formulas to the growth of knowledge, I can now (1903) point to Frederic Myers' valuable work on *Human Personality and Its Survival of Bodily Death*.

I may begin by passing over with a merely formal mention the assumptions which are required for every scientific investigation. As a matter of course we must assume that the phenomena under investigation are knowable and rational in the sense of being amenable to determinable laws. The need for this assumption is so plain that a priori attacks on psychical research on the score of undermining the fundamental principle of all scientific research can hardly be put down to anything but voluntary or involuntary ignorance of the grossest kind.

Next we must enunciate a methodological axiom with

which at first sight few will be disposed to quarrel, viz., that we must proceed to the unknown from what is known to us. The remark is Aristotle's,[7] and I may be suspected of quoting it merely because Oxonians can but rarely resist a temptation of quoting Aristotle. But in reality it is not such a truism as it appears, at least in the meaning I propose to put upon it. It means in this connexion that, both psychologically and logically, we must interpret any supposed future life by the knowledge we have acquired of our present life. It is a methodological necessity, in other words, that we must project this world into the next, if ever we purpose scientifically to know it. Our assumption may be wrong in the sense that it may be wrecked on barrier reefs of impenetrable fact—possibly it will be—but, right or wrong, we can work with no other at the outset. As we go on we shall no doubt detect the initial crudities of our assumptions, and correct them as our knowledge grows. But whatever differences we may discover between the two worlds must rest upon the postulate of a fundamental identity, in default of which our reason would be merely paralysed. From a complete otherness of the other world nothing would follow; a future life in which everything was utterly different would mean nothing to us, and in proportion as the difference grows the practical efficacy and theoretical knowableness of the conception diminish.

Now this, I venture to think, is a philosophic result of no small practical importance.

(1) It goes a long way towards explaining the anomaly of the feebleness of most people's religious beliefs about the future life. For the heavens and hells of the various religions, in spite of their pretensions to evoke forces which should utterly dwarf their threescore years and ten of our mortal life, are found in practice to constitute motives so weak that they are continually routed and set aside by the trivial temptations of the moment. The reason is that they have ordinarily been conceived as differing too radically from the known conditions of life to excite the same serious belief, to require the same matter-of-fact forethought as, e.g., next year's crops or tomorrow's money market. And so the belief in a future life, even where it has not been degraded into a merely verbal assent to

7 *Eth. Nic.,* I. 3. 5.

a traditional formula, has commonly lacked that intimacy of association with the ordinary concerns of life which is needed to render it psychologically efficacious as a stimulus to action.

(2) Again, it turns out that the spiritists were by no means wrong in principle when they proceeded to construe the future life, of which they believed themselves to possess cogent evidence, very much on the lines of our earthly life. Their constructions may in detail be as crude and absurd as their adversaries allege—I am neither familiar enough with the literature to discuss this point nor convinced that they are—but it is a mistaken prejudice to reject such accounts a priori as too trivial or undignified to be ascribed to the inhabitants of another world. Owing, no doubt, to the unduly tragic view we have come to take of death, the prejudice that the decease of Brown, Jones, and Robinson must instantly transmute them into beings of superhuman powers and tastes, and transport them into regions where they are initiated into the uttermost ecstasies and agonies of the scheme of things, has become inveterate. Indeed, I have often been amused to see how strongly this notion influences people who are really entire disbelievers in the possibility of any future life; while scorning everything "supernatural," they reject the spiritist's version thereof as *not supernatural enough,* because they are quite sure that if there were a future life at all, it would have to be as full of angels and demons as what they would call "the traditional mythologies." In a more respectable form the same feeling shows itself in the large number of persons who refuse to accept the evidence, e.g., in the Piper case, because they think they would not like the sort of life to which it seems to point. This may seem a somewhat naïve *ignoratio elenchi,* but the psychical researcher can hardly afford to smile at it, for he is continually having it impressed upon him how very serious are the obstacles which prejudices of this sort form to the discovery and recognition of the facts, and how manifestly the "will-to-believe" is the *ratio cognoscendi* of truth. Hence a systematic challenge of the whole assumption that another world must be as different as is conceivable (or rather inconceivable) from this is needed to clear the atmosphere.

And inasmuch as the groundlessness of a false assumption

is never revealed more clearly than by a request for the reasons on which it rests, I should like, for my own part, to add to the general challenge a particular request, asking philosophers to show cause why a hypothetical "other" world must necessarily be conceived as out of time and out of space. The conviction that this must be so underlies, I am sure, much of the high philosophic scorn of empirical spiritism and popular theology, but I do not think it would be easy to support it by a valid and cogent philosophic argument. For so long as temporality and spatiality form indispensable characteristics of the only real world we experience, the presumption surely is that they will pervade also any other, until at least a definite method has been suggested whereby they may be transcended.

(3) Thirdly, it must be recognized that the methodological principle of interpreting the unknown by the known tells strongly in favour of the simpler, and prima facie easier, theory of the agency of personal spirits as against the more complex and unfamiliar notions of an impersonal clairvoyance, or subliminal consciousness, or nonhuman modes of cognition by gods, devils, or cosmic principles of a more or less unknowable kind. I am very far from thinking that we should in such matters hastily commit ourselves to the interpretation which prima facie seems the most plausible, or, indeed, to any definitive theory whatsoever, and I should be sorry to see the ingenious attempts to provide a nonspiritistic explanation of the phenomena in question prematurely abandoned—if only on account of their excellence as mental gymnastics—but I cannot admit that such attempts are one whit less anthropomorphic in principle than the "spiritist" hypothesis (they only stray further from their human model), while I cannot help admitting that methodologically they are more cumbrous and so considerably inferior. The spirit hypothesis has the same kind of initial advantage over its rivals as the "solid" atom has in physics over the "vortex ring" or the "ether stress." And while our knowledge remains in its rudiments, this advantage is considerable, though, as the parallel shows, it may easily become problematical.

Admitting, therefore, that as a working theory the hypothesis of the persistence after death of what we call the human personality possesses considerable advantages over rival theories, let us inquire further by what methods, resting on what postulates, that theory may be verified.

(1) We may rule out once more the notion that such a future life is essentially supernatural in character. This notion has been a favourite with believers, but it is easily turned into a terrible weapon in the hands of their adversaries. For the supernatural is, as such, conceived to be insusceptible of investigation, and belief in it must be mere faith, exposed to every doubt and jeer, if indeed it can be even that, seeing that a real faith must be nourished by at least partial and prospective verification in fact. Hence the answer to this notion is simply this: that if the future life be really "supernatural" in the sense of having no connexion of any sort with nature, there could not possibly be any evidence of it, and it would have to be for us nonexistent; while if there be evidence of it, this would *ipso facto* include it in the widest conception of nature, and render the nature of the connexion between this world and the next a legitimate subject for scientific research. If, therefore, the connexion be rare and precarious, the reason cannot possibly be that from time to time some audacious spirit has impiously achieved the impossible by breaking through the natural order; it must lie in the peculiarities of the natural order itself. Or, to sum up in a single phrase a discussion which would long have become needless but for the persistence of attempts to dispose of an inconvenient investigation into facts by logical quibbles about words, if "supernature" is to be retained, it must not be in the sense of something alien and hostile to "nature," but strictly as meaning a higher department or aspect of nature itself.

(2) We must suppose a certain continuity of psychological constitution in the human spirit throughout every phase of its existence. Without this we should not know ourselves again after death. This does not imply that death may not be a great event, involving a great gain (or loss) in the intensity and extent of consciousness and memory; it asserts only that if we are to have knowledge of a future life at all, we must assume that the general characteristics of mental life will persist. Without this, too, there could be no proof of "spirit identity" to others; without "spirit identity" there could be no proof of

a future life. Unfortunately, however, this assumption of ours would lead us to expect that the proof of "spirit identity" would be difficult. For it is psychologically far more probable that the moral character and the feelings would traverse the shock and change of death unshaken, than that little bits of knowledge about terrestrial affairs would persist in equal measure. Yet it is these latter that afford the best tests of "spirit identity," and it is suggestive that whereas at first Mrs. Piper's "G.P." communications abounded in such tests, they have gradually grown rare.

(3) As we must try to explain all the facts by principles already known to be valid, we must account for the remarkable dissociation between this world and the next by the principle of psychological continuity. That such dissociation must exist will hardly be denied by anyone who has realized how very rare an experience a "ghost" is, even with the most expert of ghost seers and in its most favoured haunts. But it would seem that if the departed still retained their personality and psychical continuity, "ghosts" ought to be more plentiful than blackberries, and unhedged by that divinity which makes people so reluctant to make a clean breast of their ghost stories. Prima facie, therefore, it requires explanation that in spite of psychic continuity so much dissociation should prevail.

Nevertheless, it may, I think, be shown that the assumption of psychical continuity would be quite compatible with the prevalence of an almost complete dissociation between this world and the next. For any great event tends to dissociate us from our past, and this would apply a fortiori to an event like death, which *ex hypothesi* launches us into a new world. A new world, moreover, would engross us not only by its novelty, but also by the practical need of accommodating ourselves to new conditions of existence. Hence the psychological conditions for great concern about the world we had left behind us would hardly be present. This argument, moreover, could be considerably strengthened by psychological observations with regard to the interest which is taken in the affairs of our world by the aged. For it would be unlikely that an interest which had already grown faint should effectively maintain itself amid the distractions of a new life.

And even if the desire to communicate were felt, it could

hardly be assumed that the knowledge and power to do so would at once be at the disposal of the newcomer, who, for aught we know, might find that, as upon his entry upon this scene, a period of helplessness and dependence analogous to infancy had to be passed through.

It would seem probable, therefore, that to render communication effective, quite as systematic and sustained an effort would be needed on the other side as is being made by the S.P.R. on this, while the self-regarding motives for making it would be indefinitely less potent. For while each of us *ought to have*[8] the strongest personal interest in determining what his prospects may be after death, no such case could be made out for a retrospective interest of the departed in our world. And in their world the prevalent social sentiment might esteem it better to leave us in our present doubt and discourage attempts to pry into the possibilities of communication with another world. That would only be to suppose that their social sentiment is the same as ours. Only it would in their case be more reasonable. For why should they incommode themselves to impart to us a knowledge which each one of us is bound to gather for himself within a few years more? And this suggestion will appear the more probable when we remember that, according to the principle of psychic continuity, the *same* people will be making the same sentiment in both cases. Nevertheless, it is conceivable that someday a fortunate coincidence of the efforts of an infinitesimal minority on both sides should succeed in establishing spirit identity and forcing upon the reluctant masses of men the scientific fact of a future life which they did not in the least desire to have so established. Even then, however, we should still be very far from any definite and detailed knowledge of the nature of the future life in itself, the difficulties of transmitting which would increase enormously in proportion as the dissociation between the two spheres of existence became greater.

Thus the general upshot of our discussion so far would be that a future life which was accessible to scientific methods of proof would necessarily appear to be of a somewhat homely

---

[8] I emphasize the "ought," for, as a matter of empirical fact, the present number of those who are *scientifically* interested in the question to the extent of a guinea per annum appears to be about 1,400!

and humdrum character, displeasing to spiritual sensationalists. Broadly speaking, our conceptions of it would rest on the assumption of social and psychic continuity, and they would tend to suppose that the reward and punishment of the soul consisted mainly in its continuing to be itself, with the intrinsic consequences of its true nature revealed more and more clearly to itself and others. Hence there would be but little scope for epic flights of a lurid imagination, and those who hanker after the ecstasies of the blessed and the torments of the damned would have to go, as before, to the preachers and the poets. We may, however, trust these latter to work up a more copious material into pictures quite as edifying and thrilling as those of Homer, Dante, and Milton.

II

I have assumed hitherto, without a hint of doubt, the general possibility of the conception of a future life. But, after all, this also is an assumption, of a very vital character, and one which has been strongly impugned on a priori grounds. I shall devote, therefore, my concluding remarks to disposing of such philosophic attempts at an a priori suppression of the question and to stating some of the philosophic considerations which lead me to think the conception of a future life a valid and non-contradictory one, whether or not we are able or anxious to find empirical evidence of its actual existence. On the first point I may be brief: I should not deny that it is possible to devise metaphysical systems which will render the persistence of the individual consciousness improbable and even impossible, and which consequently close the question to all who conscientiously adopt them. Personally, I believe those systems to be demonstrably wrong, but it is enough for our purpose that they should be gratuitous, and that we may, at least equally well, adopt metaphysical views which leave the question open, or even lead us to regard a future life as a priori probable enough, and needing only verification a posteriori.

Hence, speaking for myself—and in so personal a matter it is best to speak for oneself if one wants to speak to the point —I cannot at all appreciate the enormous antecedent difficulty which so many philosophers profess to feel about the conception of a future life. Even its most difficult implications, like, e.g., the transition from one world to another, seem to become quite easy, if we start from the proper philosophic basis. Let us, for instance, assume—as I think we must do in any case— the philosophic position of an idealistic experientialism. I use this clumsy phrase to designate the view that "the world" is primarily "my experience," *plus* (secondarily) the supplementings of that experience which its nature renders it necessary to assume, such as, e.g., other persons and a "real" material world. In that case, the world, in which we suppose ourselves to be, is, and always remains, relative to the experience which we seek to interpret by it, and if that experience were to change, so necessarily would our "real" world. Its reality was guaranteed to it, so long as it did its work and explained our experience; it is abrogated so soon as it ceases to do so. Hence we may conceive ourselves as passing through any number of worlds, separated from each other by (partial) discontinuities in our experience, each of which would be perfectly real while it lasted, and yet would have to be declared unreal from a higher and clearer point of view.

Nor would this conception remain an empty form, which we could not find anything in our experience to illustrate. I venture to affirm that we are all of us perfectly familiar with what it feels like to pass from one world into another. When we fall asleep and dream, we pass into a new world, with space, time, persons, and laws (uniformities) like our own. But though these fundamental features *persist in principle,* they are *not the same* space, etc., and have no very obvious connexion with the corresponding characteristics of our waking life. It is true that the reality of each dream world is very precarious: it is dissolved by every clumsy interruption from a more "real" world, in the *ex post facto* judgment of which the dream world is fleeting, chaotic, and unmanageable. But the philosophic critic cannot thus presume the theoretical correctness of our ordinary judgment. To him all modes of experience are, in the first instance, real. He can find no standing ground outside experience whence to judge it.

All our distinctions, then, between the "real" and "unreal" are *intrinsic:* it is the dream world's character itself that leads us to condemn it. And if in our dreams we found ourselves transported into worlds more coherent, more intelligible, more beautiful, and more delightful than that of daily life, should we not gladly attribute to them a superior reality, and, like Mohammed, hold that in our sleep our souls had been snatched up to heaven and privileged to commune with the gods? The fact, indeed, that such experiences have played a signal part in the lives of nearly all the world's greatest heroes, and thereby left an indelible mark upon its history, should make us chary of dogmatic denials of the value of such dream worlds. But as a rule we do deny without a scruple, and, reasoning as pragmatists, do ruthlessly reject them for yielding nothing that sense can use and sanity can tolerate. Hence the consensus of common sense declares dream experiences to be unreal—though, it may be noted, it has taken men a long time to arrive at this conclusion and to disabuse themselves of the notion that after all there must be a literally veridical and inspired meaning in all their experiences. What has not been realized with equal clearness—probably because the observation seemed to have no direct practical bearing—is that the existence of unreal worlds of dream experience casts an indelible slur on the claim of our present waking life to absolute reality. What has happened once may happen again, and when we wake to another world our terrestrial life may appear as grotesque a parody, as misleading a distortion, of true reality as the most preposterous of dreams.

Nay, more; even in this life we cannot call it an illicit and unthinkable ambition to discover modes of rising from our waking world to one of a higher order, whose superior reality would demand acknowledgment from all so soon as either its experience had become communicable to an appreciable fraction of society, or it had proved to be of use for the purposes of "waking" life. Philosophy could not indeed provide the Columbus of such idealist discovery. But it might sanction his assumption of such risks. Just as an enlightened physics might have contended, long before Magellan, that the earth was circumnavigable if it could find the daring soul to sail right round it, so philosophy may declare that if the whole world be experience, *new worlds* may be found by psychical transformation as probably and validly as by physical transportation. And it must decline to treat the fact that the other worlds we know are apparently less real than that of waking life[9] as being a conclusive proof that more real worlds are nowhere to be found.

Thus the passage from world to world is familiar enough to our experience. But, as experienced by us in sleep, it is not *irrevocable*. We *return*, that is, to the same waking world. And that makes a difference between sleep and its twin brother death. For from death we are bidden to believe that there is no return. Still we must not exaggerate the difference; for *to* our dream worlds also we do not (usually) return.

Hence this return, which is regarded as an *awakening* of the soul from the point of view of the subject of the experience, is at the same time the *dissolution* of his dream world and life. The severance of his relations with the world of his former experience, therefore, has a double aspect. On the one hand, his "dream" passes away as he passes into a region of higher reality; on the other, *he passes away* out of the dream world that imposed itself upon him into his "waking" life. For we have seen that even dreams are not entirely unreal. Even at their lowest, the features they present refer to the truth, and foreshadow the reality, of a superior world: they are to some extent *veridical*. Hence we must contemplate the situation also from the point of view of the beings who interacted with the "dreamer" in the "dream" life and world. For them, his awakening means his *withdrawal* from their world. When Alice awakes, she of course declares Looking-Glass Land to have been a dream, and its inhabitants to have been the creatures of her fancy. But while she was with them they were vividly real. And Alice, after all, herself was not *quite* satisfied with this vulgar explanation. It will be remembered that she suspected the black kitten of having transformed herself into the Red Queen of Looking-Glass Land. And this would raise an interesting question: if we should chance to survive death, should we merely declare earth life to have been unreal, or should we not rather trace in its happenings some subtle presage of a fuller truth?

9 A remark subject always to certain reservations on the score of the subjective worlds of the mystics and founders of religions. Common sense hardly realizes how its principles here cut away the foundations of all the religions which, nevertheless, it imagines itself to value and believe.

It seems quite worth while, therefore, to look at the situation from the point of view of Looking-Glass Land, to whose denizens it would appear quite different. Tweedledee, no very cogent reasoner, perhaps, but a thoroughgoing idealistic monist in his argument, asseverated that the dream was not Alice's at all, but the Red King's, and that if and when he left off dreaming her, the phenomenon called Alice would simply disappear. His notion as to the manner of her disappearance was that she would "go out bang!—just like a candle," but herein he may have been mistaken. Still he has at least suggested to us that when one of us withdraws from a world, the world may misinterpret his action as his *death*.

Now death is a topic on which philosophers have been astonishingly commonplace. The reason of this cannot have been that it was not a splendid topic for reflection, nor yet that their doctrines were not capable of throwing light upon its nature. Perhaps they have lived in as great terror of it as more ordinary mortals, and so lacked the courage to think about it at all. At all events, I can readily believe, from a study of their doctrines, that Spinoza was quite right in maintaining that there is no subject concerning which the sage *thinks less* than about death.[10] Which, nevertheless, is a great pity. For the sage is surely wrong. There is no subject concerning which he, *if he is an idealist and has the courage of his opinions,* OUGHT to think more, and OUGHT to have more interesting things to say.

In partial proof of which let me attempt to arouse him to reflection by propounding some old[11] *paradoxes about death* which will, I think, be germane to our subject.

(1) No man ever yet perished without annihilating also the world in which he lived.

(2) No man ever yet saw another die; but if he had, he would have witnessed his own annihilation.

(3) The world is the greatest of all conventions; but all are unconventional enough to leave it.

(4) To die is to cut off our connexion with our friends; but do they cut us, or we them, or both, or neither?

Now these paradoxes contain nothing but necessary infer-

---

10 *Eth.,* IV, Prop. 67.
11 Cp. S.P.R. *Journal* for March, 1898, VIII, 204.

ences from the idealistic view of the world, if it is applied practically to the phenomenon of "death," and no philosopher who really and seriously accepts that view should have the slightest difficulty with them. But for the sake of the others I feel that it may be better to add a short commentary. "No man ever yet perished without annihilating also the world in which he lived," i.e., the world of *his* experience, or as we may perhaps say with still more accuracy, the objective world, in so far as it was assumed to explain *his* experience. Moreover, "no man ever yet saw another die, but if he had he would have witnessed his own annihilation": inasmuch as he could never see the other's self and so a fortiori could not observe its destruction; what he saw was the "death" of a "body" which was merely a phenomenon in his own world of experience. But if, *per impossibile*, he could have witnessed the destruction of the subject of a world of experience, his own destruction, as a phenomenon in such a world, would have been included in the catastrophe. Thus both these paradoxes are designed to bring out the essential and incurable philosophic ambiguity of "death."[12] Death is not the same thing for him who experiences and for him who witnesses it. It forms the limiting case which involves the breakdown of the great social convention, whereby we postulate (for practical purposes) a common world which is experienced by us all (No. 3). Even during life that convention is maintained only at the cost of excluding from "reality" all such experiences as are personal, or divergent, or incapable of forming a basis for common action. At death it breaks down altogether, and the long-suppressed divergence between the world of "my" experience and the "objective" world, which is nobody's experience but is supposed to account for everybody's, dominates the situation.[13]

[12] Cp. also *Riddles of the Sphinx*, ch. XI, § 8.
[13] This is the simplest description of the actual situation and begs the fewest questions. The monistic metaphysicians who arrogate to themselves exclusive rights to an idealism which they cannot use, and which dies away in their hands either into Naturalism or into platitude, prefer to distort it by postulating as its explanation a "divine" consciousness which somehow embraces or contains all the subject-consciousnesses of our fellows, and thereby (*sic*) guarantees the absolute commonness of the "common" world which is really the "object" of the divine consciousness. But the expedient proves utterly futile. For (1) the conception of one consciousness (divine or diabolical) including another has never yet been shown to be capable of anything like intelligible statement (cp. Dr. Rashdall in *Personal Idealism*, pp. 382–84). The only clue in experience to anything of the sort is to be found in the highly suggestive, but quite in-

When a man dies, his relation to the common world apparently ceases, and so "to die is to cut off our connexion with our friends; but do they cut us, or we them, or both, or neither?" But for what reason we cannot say. It may be that the deceased has ceased to be; it may also be that he has ceased to interact with us—until we also have followed his example. Similarly, when we witness a death, all that we can safely and scientifically say is that a peculiar feature in our experience which impelled us to assume a self-conscious spirit, analogous to our own, in order to account for the behaviour of the complex of phenomena we called the body of our fellow-man, has undergone a change such that the behaviour of his "body" no longer warrants the inference of the presence of his "spirit." Again, the reason may be either that the spirit is

---

adequately studied, facts of "multiplex personality," and it seems extremely doubtful whether even these would lead to the desired conclusion. The metaphysicians in question, moreover, are about the last people in the world to concern themselves with empirical phenomena of this sort. (2) The divine world image, so far from explaining the plurality of our individual world images, only adds one to their number. It remains involved in the old Platonic difficulty of the transcendent universal. Or, if it is taken as really immanent, it becomes merely a hypocritical description of the "harmony" of the individual images, and lapses into atheism. And (3) in many cases the "harmony" is very imperfect, and there is not, strictly, a "common" world at all. That is, the communion is neither pre-existent nor absolute. It is an *achievement*, reached by infinite labours and unending struggles, to a limited degree, for a limited period. We do not, as a matter of fact, experience our common "objects" alike. Hence the infinite diversity of individual judgments and valuations. But if this were all, there would be no possibility of what Prof. Ward has well called "intersubjective intercourse." So we have managed to some extent to act concordantly with regard to the "objects" of our most pressing practical concerns. You and I, e.g., are said to perceive a "common" red, when we classify colours alike. But whether your experience in perceiving "red" is the same as mine, it is meaningless to ask. For the "common red" means merely such practical agreement. And when we go on to ask what is "beautiful," and "good," and "right," and "pleasant," we soon discover how narrow are the limits of such practical agreement, and are forced to realize that to a large extent we still literally live in different worlds. And, as noted above, "death" seems to terminate the common world in time as completely as individuality limits its extent. (4) The Absolute or "universal consciousness" on scrutiny turns out to be neither divine nor conscious. Or rather the connotation both of "God" and of "consciousness" has to be radically changed to accommodate it. An all-containing consciousness cannot be a moral being. It is the Devil just as much as God, and indeed the "Absolute" must be defined in Hegelian terms as the synthesis of God and the Devil. And however much it may "contain" consciousness, it is hard to see how it can be itself conscious. Indeed in the end it seems describable in negatives alone, and by contrast with the contents of our experience; it "has" all things, but *is* not any of the things it "has." For the whole cannot *be* anything that we predicate of its parts.

In short, it seems impossible really to think out the conception of a single subject of all experience except upon solipsistic lines. If one consents to solipsism, it is easy enough, but not a bit more satisfactory. For solipsism is just the view we are driven out of by the considerations which induce us to construct a common world.

destroyed, or that it has ceased to animate the "body." Thus it would seem as though all that could be affirmed for certain about death was that it was a disruption of the common world in which spirits acted together; what else or what more it was would remain in doubt—the spirit may have perished or it may just have "passed away."

Thus, so far as philosophy can determine, it would seem as if the chances of destruction and survival were exactly equal, and that we were doomed to doubt forever. Nevertheless, considerations may be adduced which must add decisively to the weight of the latter alternative. For it should be noted that the two alternatives are not equally well situated with respect to empirical evidence. No conceivable empirical evidence can suffice to establish the destruction of the soul at death, because none can even be relevant to the real issue as it presents itself from our philosophic point of view. For it can only concern appearances in the common world of the *survivors,* it can only prove that the rupture of connexion with it at death is utter and entire. But that is not enough. Even if a ghost returned to announce to us the complete extinction of the soul at death, we could not credit so Hibernian an assertion. A scientific proof, therefore, of the annihilation of the soul is rigorously impossible. On the other hand, there is no such intrinsic impossibility about a scientific proof of the persistence of consciousness through death; there is, in fact, no particular difficulty about conceiving empirical evidence sufficient to establish this doctrine with as high a degree of certainty as we have for any of our beliefs as to matters of fact. The whole difficulty consists in getting the evidence. If we had succeeded, the theoretic readjustment of our opinions would be easy; all we should need to do would be to modify our original assumption that death meant an *absolute* rupture of relations, an utter dissolution of the common world. We should have to say instead that death altered the mode of communication of spirit with spirit, rendering it different and difficult, without interrupting it altogether. But properly interpreted and manipulated, the common world would persist through death. What exactly would be the nature of the common world, thus extended to include a life after death, philosophy could not, of course, forecast; that would remain a question for positive research to determine.

Here then we reach the limits of philosophic speculation. When the philosopher has shown that no a priori impossibilities block the pathway of discovery, and no authentic fact can be too anomalous for explanation, when he has cleared men's eyes of the prejudices which obstruct a clear prevision of the goal and has aroused a sufficient will to know, a sufficient conviction that it is well to look before we plunge, and to try to see whither we go before we go, he must modestly stand aside, and leave the empirical explorer into the puzzling mazes of psychical science to cut down the barbed-wire entanglements of hostile human prejudice, and step by step to fight his way through the thickets of complex and perplexing fact. And so the glory of discovery will not be his, but will reward the scientist who has borne the labour and danger of the day of battle. And yet the discoverer will owe perhaps the faith which sustained his courage and endurance in no small measure to the apparently unmoved spectator who watched the struggle from afar, and this faith may justify the thinker also when he is called upon to render an account of the use to which he has put his powers.

Appendix

Selections From *Mind!*

IN 1901, there was published in London a periodical entitled *Mind!* It was an elaborate parody of that esteemed philosophical journal *Mind*. Though unsigned, there is little doubt that most if not all of its contents were written by Schiller. We would regard it today as somewhat topical, but philosophic humor is so rare a commodity that we are happy to reprint parts of it.

— Editor

A Triad of the Absolute

By H. Dele

I

"Ω" ON

A contribution to the forthcoming *Hegelian Hymnal*
(Republished by permission)[1]

O BEING for Self,
    O End of all Ends,
O Something, O Nothing
    Where everything blends!
Identical Absolute,
    Thee we acclaim,
Though empty of Content
    Thy vacuous Name.

True Sun of the Realm,
    Where the Bodiless move,
Insensible Object
    Of Sensuous Love,
Sole Pattern supernal,
    First Form without Stuff,
Why wasn't pure Being
    Existence enough?

Ah! why did you suffer
    The "slim" Demiurge
In endless Becoming
    Your Being to merge.
Oh! Where was your *Noûs*?
    Oh! What was the Good?
You resemble the Babes
    Who were lost in the Wood.[2]

[1] From the *Oxford Magazine*.
[2] ὕλη·

Oh! why did you take
   All the trouble and bother
Involved in becoming
   A Manifold Other?
Ah! now you are Many,
   You find it such Fun,
You'll never go back
   To the Form of the One.

II

A BALLADE OF YE ABSOLUTE[3]

For the usage of a Hegelian Nursery

The Absolute was very High—
   More high than seasoned game;
"I have been *kept* too long," It said,
   "Identically Same."

The Absolute was very Broad—
   It filled all Time and Space;
It couldn't see Its Aspects—for
   It hadn't got a face.

The Absolute lay very Low,
   Veiled in a misty phrase;
It was the only way, C——d said,
   To elongate Its days.

The Absolute lay very Deep
   In protoplastic Sludge,
With metaphysic fumes replete
   And philosophic Fudge.

In Self-identity Alone,
   Sans Father, Wife, or Mother,
It sobbed, "It would console me to
   Be Something or An Other."

[3] Republished from the *Oxford Magazine*.

By Hegel's help It Was, and yet,
  Its sad plight scarcely mended,
The fickle Elf returned to Self
  Before Its hour was ended.

The Absolute for once to be
  Intelligible sighed;
It read Itself in B——y's book,
  And then, poor soul, It died.

III

THE COMPLAINT OF THE ABSOLUTE[4]

Remote, unfriended, melancholy, slow,
  More slow than words can say,
I *Was,* unmixed, unfeeling, without go,
  A Hamlet minus play.

Incarnate Boredom, absolute Ennui,
  Oyster shut tight in shell,
Devil-less, defecated deity,
  Heaven unenhanced by Hell.

And then—it almost makes me disbelieve
  My own Totality—
Through my "unlimited inwards" passed a Heave
  Of Spontaneity.

I felt a kind of Fidgets in my frame,
  A twinge of Cosmic Schism;
I felt a little Other than the Same,
  A nascent Dualism.

Was it a humid Vortex-ring that stirred,
  Or dim primordial Cell?
The mirror of my consciousness was blurred,
  I—wasn't very well.

4 Cp. *Pelican Record,* V, No. 6.

Then—I forget the manner of the birth
   Distraught by this world's worries:
But there proceeded from me with fell mirth
   A scheme of Categories.

They took and bound me in a causal Chain,
   To cure my trend chaotic:
On Mother Hegel's Syrup fed, my brain
   Feels still quite idiotic.

Then as an *Aspect* from me there exhaled
   My own efficient Double,
Him Cause, Creator, Demiurge I hailed;
   He saves me all the trouble.

And They and He between them this world made
   Of semblances and shows;
And what the Deuce it means I am afraid
   That no sane person knows.

I'm Everything and Nothing, here's my pain!
   Supreme, yet on the shelf!
When shall I be my own true I again,
   Sweetly regarding Self?

Specimens of the *Critique of Pure Rot*

By I. Cant

From the Remains of a Philosopher[5]

[*Note:* I must make time to translate the whole of this eye-opening work, being deeply sensible that to publish such bare outlines as these would do no justice to the author, especially in the matter of style, which I have translated as mere English, sacrificing the profundity of the original sentences that "have been measured by a carpenter," and whose dragon-tailed involutions of many a winding bout both de- and im-press the reader: he rightly judging that the effort of exegesis measures the value of the meaning when discovered, and compensates its absence when undiscoverable—labour being its own exceeding great reward: and which style I do not despair of imitating with the help of a certain brownish drench that I wot of: *verb. sap.*—S.T.C.]

CRITIQUE OF PURE ROT

Preface

EVERY new world-moving Philosophy is generated by a new method. Now my method of seeing things as they really are is to stand upon my head; for the images of all things being inverted on the retina, a man may by this means, in a manner, correct the perversity of nature without trusting to psycho-physiological processes that have the double fault of being mechanical and empirical. If anyone think this an obvious device, I remind him of Copernicus and the egg.

The method was, to be sure, suggested to me by a Scotch philosopher's account of how the English open the eyes of their children by making them "see London." For one brief moment, flashing over in a whirligig, they beheld the world in its true posture. This hint broke my dogmatic slumber. It explained why London merchants over-reach the rest of the

---

5 It is known that Samuel Taylor Coleridge left much MS. (chiefly in the margins of his friends' books) that is still unpublished. We take it that this fragment was written in 1801, although (like Aristotle's works) it contains "anticipations" that might suggest a later date; and we congratulate the readers of MIND! upon obtaining in 1901 a synopsis of doctrines so well calculated to initiate and direct the New Philosophy of a New Age.—ED.

world; for in ȳouth, under the name of City-Arabs, they turn cart wheels on the pavement, and thus learn to see things in their true relations; no one can be Lord Mayor till he has turned 5,000 cart wheels. Also English aristocrats, browbeating a demagogue, accuse him of "turning everything upside down"; such is their antipathy to popular education. But all this is English empiricism; whereas we begin with a *petitio principii* and proceed upon universal and necessary assertions *a priori.*

Book I, Part I, Chapter I, Article I

§ 1, etc. Now, to cut matters short, let us begin by inquiring into the possibility of Rot in general. That Rot exists you may take my word. And there are two kinds of it: Damp Rot and Dry Rot, besides certain Fungoid Growths; but how are such things possible in the best of possible worlds?

Damp Rot being nothing else than the corruption of woody fibre, the possibility of it manifestly depends upon the presence of C and H_2O, into which the Manifold is received and judiciously distributed.

H_2O, popularly called "water," is an intuition and not a concept; for all water is *in* water and not *under* water. Moreover, water is *a priori,* since without it there could be no Damp Rot; but painting in water colours absolutely presupposes water.

Similarly C is an intuition; for to intuit a thing is to *see* it. And the *a priori* necessity of C is given, in a manner, in the bare possibility of Music in general.

Thus the only possible genesis of Damp Rot is demonstrated as a synthetic construction in a pure heterogeneity. Only splash in the Manifold and the thing is done.

Observe, finally, that whilst C and H_2O are real as a matter of fact, yet on reflexion they are unreal. You will see this by standing on your head, and there is no other way of seeing it.

Book II. Transcendental Dodges of Blunderstanding, Part I, Chapter II, Article II

§ 3. Well then, the possibility of Dry Rot depends on the system of the pure Caterwaulings, which are functions of Papperception, or Milk-for-babes.

To find the pure Caterwaulings need give us no trouble, as we may conveniently take them from the newspapers, and list them as follows:

Quantity	Quality	Relation	Modality
Bottle	Imperialism	Paedagogue and Pupil	Ignorance
Half-bottles	Pro-Boerism	Praise and Profits	Prejudice
Bottle-and-a-half	The Closure	Log-rolling	Superstition

§ 4. Now there is a certain difficulty in applying these Caterwaulings to phenomena, which is not felt in distributing the Manifold within the province of Damp Rot. For if, as a matter of Damp Rot, I perceive that *a publisher is a fraud,* "publisher" and "fraud" are homogeneous intuitions in the synthesis of H_2O. For H_2O, being a synthetic function of Reason, is amenable to reasonable analysis, and (as the future will know) whatever is convenient is reasonable. Hence, a publisher being no doubt H (or *homo*), $_2O$ is the symbol of his fraud, meaning that he owes *too* much; and such an apprehension of the facts is both easy and elegant.

But if, in the sphere of Dry Rot, I judge that *a criticism in* MIND! *is praise,* how can such heterogeneous elements be brought together? For the "criticism" is a given fact, whereas "Praise" is pure Caterwauling. Now all such difficulties are overcome by scheming and skirmishing with C, which is the natural intermediary between pure Caterwaulings and all phenomena.

§ 5. To apply the pure Caterwaulings to matter-of-fact needs Imagination. This can surprise nobody; for all Philosophies are works of Imagination, or sportive essays in the fine art of Reason. In this case we want Imagination badly, and we will call it no mere imitative but "productive Imagination," because that sounds better. The labourer sings at his work; and in the severe work of labelling matters of fact with suitable Caterwaulings it is the function of Imagination to represent the pure Caterwaulings by generalised tunes in the form of C —that is, by the rhythms of tunes, abstracting from their particular notes and all heterogeneous sensuosity—such as a professor may hum without being able to sing them. They are called Sing-songs, and their correspondence with the Cater-waulings is exhibited in the following table:

Caterwauling	Sing-song
Bottle	The Leather Bottel
Half-bottles	Drink to Me Only with Thine Eyes
Bottle-and-a-half	We Won't Go Home till Morning
Imperialism	Rule Britannia
Pro-Boerism	Down among the Dead Men
The Closure	Donnybrook Fair
Paedagogue and Pupil	Said the Old Obadiah to the Young Obadiah
Praise and Profits	See the Conquering Hero
Log-rolling	The same, hummed alternately forwards and backwards
Ignorance	Nobody Knows What I Know
Prejudice	Sally in Our Alley
Superstition	Home, Sweet Home!

If with such incentives you can't stick the labels, I can't; and without standing on your head you will hardly be convinced that they stick fast.

§ 6. However, the humming of these Sing-songs by way of illustration may always be relied upon to enliven a lecture and to fill the class-room of the dullest pedant. The Sing-song of Log-rolling will be most effective if the professor, instead of humming it forwards and backwards alternately, shall hum it forwards and get his *famulus* to hum it backwards at the same time. This will illustrate the struggle for existence and demonstrate the special applicability of the third Caterwauling of Relation to Biology and social affairs.

§ 7. But further difficulties in applying the Caterwaulings to the Manifold may arise from not knowing which should be applied to what; so that whilst universally necessary they are particularly contingent: but here again the Sing-songs ought to help us. As to the Caterwaulings of Quality for example—if hastily and erroneously you call a man as big as yourself a Pro-Boer to the tune of *Down Among the Dead Men,* and he closes with you to the tune of *Rule Britannia,* there is a dead-lock whilst both sing *Donnybrook Fair.* Or again, in the Caterwaulings of Quantity—if you think you have drunk only Half-a-bottle, when in fact you have finished a Bottle-and-a-half, there is an irresistible impulse to sing *We Won't go Home till Morning;* and the chances are that you will even be late for breakfast, passing most of the interval in strict seclusion, and arriving fresh from an interview with the functionary at Bow Street. I shall show hereafter that the blame for all such slips lies ultimately at the door of the *Unding-an-sich;* but it will not be of much use, as the *Unding's* oak is always sported.

If after these illustrations any one fails to see how the Sing-songs help us in inflicting the Caterwaulings upon matters of fact, I can only say that it is a mystery hidden in the depths of the soul.

Book II, Part I. Walpurgisnacht, Chapter I, Article II

§ 1. The worst thing you can do, my young friend, is to try to apply your blunderstanding to Ideas: it was never designed for such use and is quite incompetent. For the new dialectic shows that *noumena,* far from being the only objects of real knowledge, are just the things that the mind can't know. I cant.

Nevertheless, you can't help experimenting with Ideas; and thereby are generated three Fungoid Growths.

Chapter II. First Fungus: the Common Mushroom

§ 2. Träume eines Geistersehers. . . .

.   .   .   .

§ 3. Now all this fine confused thinking results from mistaking the Bottle of Papperception for Spirit *per se.*

Chapter III. Second Fungus: the Antilogistic Toadstool

§ 3. Donnybrook Fair *in vacuo,* by our special Reporter. . . .

.   .   .   .

Therefore, A is both B and not-B.   Q.E.D.

But if A is B, it is impossible to know anything; and if it is not-B, it is impossible to believe anything; so since it is both, *tant pis.*

§ 4. The ground, however, of these conclusions (equally odd and inevitable) is, that we take A for granted; whereas *per se* it is not granted, but only Hay; and to make hay of A, or A of hay, is a solecism.

Chapter IV. Third Fungus

§ 1. Die scholastische Götterdämmerung fängt an. . . . .

. . . .

[*Note:* Angels and ministers of grace! least said, soonest mended. Indeed, there may be some things in this book which my friend Leighton would hardly sanction: it deserves to be not only translated but edited. Judicious commentators, however, will not be wanting:—

Wenn die Könige baun, haben die Kärrner zu thun.[6]

—S.T.C.]

6 A translation that has been proposed for this verse—One fool makes many— is more spirited than literal, and sacrifices urbanity to emphasis.—ED.

Pre-Socratic Philosophy

BY LORD PILKINGTON (OF MILKINGTON)

THERE was a time before the teaching of philosophy had taken the form of a dictation lesson, when students ventured beyond the covers of their note-book and even attempted a little dialectic on their own account. Small blame to them if their Dialogue sometimes assumed a playful air, or if, in those walks up Shotover or round the Hinkseys and the "Happy Valley," which have lost their charm for cycling Oxford of the present generation, they capped each other in amoebean verse like Vergil's shepherds. As a remembrance of these happier methods of study, which the publication of MIND! may do something to revive, we print, before they are forgotten, a few fragments upon the Pre-Socratics which originated under the conditions described.

Damon.

> The Ionic philosophers trace
> The World to a physical base—
>> Thus while Thales sought a
>> First 'Αρχή in Water
> Anaximenes put Air in its place.

Pythias.

> From the Concrete Xenophanes fleeing
> Found the world to consist in pure Being;
>> Said, "Πᾶν = ῾Εν,"
>> And "Gods ain't like men,
> But all-thinking and hearing and seeing."[7]

Damon.

> Heracleitus said everything came
> From a Strife which he sometimes calls Flame.
>> The illustrious Hegel
>> Thought this quite *"en règle,"*
> Meaning *"Seyn* and *Nicht-seyn* are the same."

7 See *Ritter und Preller*, p. 79, § 85.

Pythias.

> It's all very well when you're tight
> To say that white's black, and black white;
> > But this will never do,
> > As Parmenides knew,
> For the Footpath which leads to the Right.[8]

Damon.

> There was an old man of Abdera
> Whose language grew queerer and queerer;
> > With his Δὲν and his Κρᾶσις
> > And other odd phrases
> He perplexed the good folk of Abdera.

Pythias.

> Pythagoras thought that Creation
> Was a mere Arithmetic Relation,
> > Said "you must not eat beans
> > By no manner of means,"
> And believed in the Soul's Transmigration.

[8] See *Ritter und Preller*, p. 88, § 94.

New Platonic Dialogues

I. An Aporia[9]

JONES was a congenital genius, and we always expected he would come to a bad end, poor fellow. Hence I was not surprised to find that after an early marriage and a brief but brilliant matrimonial career (including two pairs of twins and a triplet), he should have taken up his residence in an asylum which shall be nameless, but where I occasionally visit him. The doctors consider him a hopeless case, but the chief thing I can find the matter with him is an excessive conscientiousness which unfits him for practical work and leads him to raise scruples about what everybody else takes for granted. For instance, the last time I saw him he startled me with a fallacy which seemed to me not unworthy of mention by the side of the *Liar* and the *Crocodile*.

Jones had been greatly depressed; he declared himself a murderer, and would not be comforted. Suddenly he asked me a question. "Are not the parents the cause of the birth of their children?" said he. "I suppose so," said I. "Are not all men mortal?" "That also may be admitted." "Then are not the parents the cause of the death of their children, since they know that they are mortal? And am I not a murderer?" I was, I own, puzzled. At last I thought of something soothing. I pointed out to Jones that to cause the death of another was not necessarily murder. It might be manslaughter or justifiable homicide. "Of which of these then am I guilty?" he queried. I could not say because I had never seen the Jones family, but I hear Jones has become a great bore in the asylum by his unceasing appeals to every one to tell him whether he has committed murder, manslaughter, or justifiable homicide!

Curiously enough, when I told the tale to a learned friend of mine, he showed me what appears to be a new fragment of Plato's *Lysis,* on an Egyptian papyrus recently discovered. It distinctly anticipates Jones in its statement of the problem,

9 Cp. *Pelican Record,* IV, No. 4.

and testifies aloud to the saying that there is nothing new under the sun, and that truth is eternal.

ΣΚΩΠΤΑΔΗΣ,[10] ΛΥΣΙΣ

S. Whom then, Lysis, do you consider your best friends, and love most? *L.* My father and my mother, as is most fitting. *S.* Why do you so love them? *L.* Both for other reasons and because they are the cause of my living. *S.* And does that seem to you a great benefit? *L.* Surely the greatest of all. *S.* What then do you esteem the greatest evil? *L.* Of all evils death seems to me the greatest and most hateful. *S.* Then you would not love those who are the cause of your coming death (τοῦ μέλλοντος θανάτου), if you knew them? *L.* That is impossible. *S.* And what would you call those who knowingly cause the death of others? *L.* Evil-doers and murderers. *S.* You would not call them your friends? *L.* Certainly not; for did you not convince me that a friend does good only to his friend, and not evil. *S.* And yet perhaps, Lysis, you escape your own notice loving your own murderers, and thinking them your greatest friends. *L.* I do not understand you, Skoptades. *S.* Tell me, Lysis, are not all men mortal? *L.* Assuredly. *S.* Then all who are born must also die? *L.* Of course. *S.* And if anyone knowingly put you in a place where you must die, such as a desert island or a den of lions, would you not consider him the cause of your death? *L.* Most certainly I should. *S.* But have not your parents done this very thing to you? *L.* How so? *S.* Did you not say that they were the authors of your being in a world where you must die? *L.* So it would appear. *S.* And does it not follow that they are the authors of the greatest evil, namely death, and not friends, but murderers? *L.* By Zeus, Skoptades, the argument has turned out a most unholy one. *S.* And the worst of it is that we do not yet know what is a friend and whom we ought to love most. . . .

This then is the ἀπορία of the *Lysis*; but what is the λύσις of the ἀπορία?

[10] This is the MS. reading, but ΣΩΚΡΑΤΗΣ surely must be intended.

II. A Sequel to the *Republic*[11]

The following interesting fragment of a Platonic dialogue has been found on a papyrus recently discovered in the belly of an ancient crocodile of literary tastes, which Messrs. Grenfell and Hunt have imported from Egypt. With their leave we publish a translation, which will doubtless be recognised as the most important addition to our knowledge of Plato's lost writings since the recovery of the fragment of the *Lysis* printed above.

ΣΩΚΡΑΤΗΣ, ΚΕΦΑΛΟΣ, ΠΛΑΤΩΝ

Soc. Methinks, Plato, I see Kephalos hastening round the corner into yonder side-street. Will you not quickly run after him and tell him that it is not good for a man at his age to be in such haste, and that moreover we have seen him, and that he cannot escape us, since there is no thoroughfare at the other end?

Plato. Assuredly, Socrates, I will put on my running foot.

Soc. I hail thee, Kephalos, breathless though I am. It seems to me a long time since I met you. Indeed I do not think I have seen you since we visited you at your house on the festival of Bendis and had a famous argument on the nature of Justice.

Keph. I think you are right.

S. It was a great pity you did not stay and listen to the whole argument.

K. I had to go out and attend to some domestic matters.

S. You *said* it was a sacrifice.

K. You are right again, Socrates, as I now remember.

S. It must have been a very long sacrifice.

K. The argument, too, was very long, I have heard.

S. Nevertheless, you would have enjoyed it. But it does not matter; Plato here has written it all out beautifully and he shall send you a copy. You deserve it in return for the drinks wherewith we kept up our spirits in the long search for justice.[12]

---

[11] Cp. *Pelican Record*, V, No. 5.
[12] There is no mention of them in the existirg MSS. of the *Republic*.

K. I thank you both.

S. And now, Kephalos, while we accompany you home to the Piræus, I want to ask you concerning a point which I was eager to inquire into when last we met, but which escaped my notice owing to your[13] having raised the question of justice. It is this. You are rich, are you not?

K. Moderately so.

S. To whom then do you intend to leave your riches when you die?

K. To my children, of course.

S. I thought you would say this. But tell me why you propose to do this?

K. Because they stand first in my love, I suppose.

S. Ah! I am afraid, Kephalos, that is impossible.

K. Are you not escaping your own notice talking nonsense?

S. I wish I were. But it really is impossible and contrary to nature for you to love your own children first.

K. How so?

S. You must first love other people's children and then your own.

K. I do not understand you.

S. How can you, being a man, have children of your own to love until you have first loved the children of others?[14]

K. By Zeus, Socrates, you are right. For he alone of the gods could do what you say, if indeed he was the only parent of Athena.

S. You agree then that it is absurd to love your own children first, and on this account to leave the money to them rather than to those of others?

K. I suppose so.

S. Consider this also. Do you not wish good to your children?

K. Of course.

S. Then you do not wish that they should get that which would harm them?

---

[13] Our traditional account hardly bears this out.

[14] An indignant scholiast—probably an Alexandrine—has here written in the margin, "Look at the Greek, Socrates; look at the Greek." But Socrates was no doubt quite capable of using φιλεῖν in the sense of ἐρᾶν·

K. Certainly not.

S. But are not good things for the bad?

K. Very likely.

S. Then wealth being a good thing in itself will be bad for the bad?

K. This we see in many cases.

S. In proportion then as your children are bad it will harm them to have wealth?

K. So at least the argument shows.

S. You ought not therefore to leave your wealth to them.

K. Would you have me leave it to my enemies?

S. Not at all.

K. To whom then?

S. To those to whom the intrinsically good is really good.

K. Are you thinking of yourself, Socrates?

S. Have you never heard of my Little Demon (δαιμόνιον)? And would not the wealth which benefited me do harm to Xanthippe?

K. I doubt whether she would get much of it.

S. Even if I took care to prevent this, would it not make her temper worse to think of me spending my wealth in the pursuit of the beautiful?

K. Your pursuit would always be in vain.

S. That is why I am a philosopher. Still, as you know, we Athenians φιλοκαλοῦμεν μετ᾿ εὐτελείας.[15]

K. So I have observed. But will you not finish telling me to whom I ought to leave my wealth?

S. Most willingly. Do you know Plato here?

K. Yes, and I have long desired to ask him whether he be truly the son of Apollon as well as the descendant of Poseidon. He certainly looks it.

S. Hush! you see how he blushes. Plato, let me tell you, is about to found an Academy, the first there has been, and the most famous there ever will be. How better could you bestow your wealth than by giving it to Plato's Academy?

K. I would rather leave it to Xanthippe!

S. Even if we promise you immortality of fame?

K. You are far more likely to confer an eternity of infamy.

15 Love the beautiful on the cheap.

However, I will do what you ask on one condition, and that is that you, Plato, should write down this conversation exactly as it occurred, in order that men may know whether Socrates always got the better in words of those he conversed with.

P. I agree, Kephalos.

S. And I no less; I will this time content myself with getting the better in deeds, if only they be good.

The Absolute at Home

By A Troglodyte

A Tragedy

IN

One Act (*Actus Purus*)

Dramatis Personæ

The Absolute, absolutely at home
Her Fossilliness the Universal, housekeeper to the Absolute
The Father of Lies, *alter ego* to the Absolute
Truth, a lovely maiden who has just come out
Experience, a wise old teacher
Inexperience, her sister
Philosophers, fools, fogies, pedants, categories, schemata, etc.

Scene I

The Father of Lies. Hallo, who is this sitting by the well? A lovely girl, by Brahma, attractively disarrayed! I must accost her. (*Goes up to her.*) Who art thou, pretty one? What is thy name and of what parents wert thou born?

Truth. It is borne in on me that my name is Truth, but what I am I hardly know as yet. You see I have only just come out.

F. of L. Out of what?

T. Out of this well.

F. of L. You are well out of it! Ha ha! And of your parents?

T. I know nothing, save that I read on the notice-board that "Truth is evolved out of Error by the immanent self-criticism of Experience." But I know neither Error nor Experience.

F. of L. Then you must be as wholly *a priori* as you are charming. I am delighted too to find that we must be nearly related.

T. How?

F. of L. Why, I am not only well acquainted with Experience, but Error is indissolubly wedded to Falsehood, who is the offspring of Lies, of whom I boast myself to be the father!

T. I cannot follow the relation which, you say, results. It ought to be worked out on the notice-board. And in any case it seems to me that to be "nearly related" is not to be really related. A miss is as good as a mile!

F. of L. (*Aside.*) How easily innocence is sophisticated in these days! (*Aloud.*) At all events you are not a miss, but a most egregious—

T. Sir, do you doubt my honour?

F. of L. (*Aside.*) Pulled up again! (*Aloud.*) You mistake me! I know you are a Miss in one sense, but in that I meant you are Nature's most stupendous hit, and do not come amiss to me!

T. You puzzle me, but if you mean well, you might tell me what I ought to do. You see, I do not know my way about the world as yet.

F. of L. (*Aside.*) Already she is trying to be practical! Really the Absolute and I must take steps to stop this pestilent growth of Pragmatism. (*Aloud.*) I will see that you are properly launched upon the world. Come with me now and be introduced.

T. To whom?

F. of L. To everybody.

T. Where are you going?

F. of L. To the Absolute's, which is At Home to-day. So the whole world will be there and the half as well. It will be a great lark, for as Hesiod says "the half is more than the whole."

T. What half?

F. of L. The better half of course! (I must not yet shock her!) The Universal too will be charmed to meet you.

T. What are the Absolute and the Universal?

F. of L. Sancta simplicitas! What is the Absolute! Why everything! I can't possibly explain It. You must take It on trust. But the philosophers all say that It is absolutely real. However I dare say, though It is at home to-day, you will soon find It out for yourself. (*Aside.*) I did long ago, but I always find it pays to praise It to others. (*Aloud.*) As for the Universal, there is a great deal I might tell you about her.

T. Pray tell me.

F. of L. In the first place she's the Absolute's housekeeper, and people do say a good deal more. But why should I corrupt your innocent mind with the vile slanders of those who cannot see that to the profound all things are profound, and that a mystery and a deity can be made out of the most unpromising materials, if only you keep them dark enough? Let it suffice you that without her the Absolute can or will do nothing, and that she receives all Its guests.

T. I am surprised that people go.

F. of L. Oh, one must not be too particular. Especially about the Universal. Besides, everybody has to go.

T. I cannot.

F. of L. Nonsense! Why not?

T. You see how little of a dress I have for such a function.

F. of L. Oh, that doesn't matter. The Absolute will like you, will address you and, I dare say, still think you overdressed.

T. I don't like your account of the Absolute at all. And how about the Universal?

F. of L. Oh, Her Fossilliness will mind still less. You see she isn't particular and indeed can't afford to be so.

T. But why do you call her 'Her Fossilliness'? What does it mean?

F. of L. It's a little pet name I gave her, because the philosophers haven't yet found out how stupid she really is. But come you *must,* it's your chance and you ought to think yourself lucky.

T. I suppose I must, but I never dreamt of becoming a "necessary truth" so soon.   *Exeunt.*

Scene II

A crowded reception at the Absolute's Home, commanding a fine view out of Space and Time.

Experience and Inexperience

Inexperience. Do you know, sister, who the lovely girl was that old Father of Lies was taking into the Reception Room to be presented? She seemed to me to be the realisation of all one's ideals of Beauty, Truth and Goodness in one.

Experience. I feel sure that was Truth, though I can never quite make out whether she is three or one. I have never seen her here before.

In. It seems a pity that she should be sacrificed to the Absolute.

Exp. A burning shame. But I see no way to stop it, so long as the philosophers approve of whatever happens to be traditional, and will not listen to me.

In. Ah, there she comes again, running, and flushed and excited.

(*Truth runs up and throws herself at the feet of Experience.*)

Truth. Oh, protect me, you who look so wise and good. It was too horrible! How could they offer me to such a hideous ogre!

Exp. Don't be frightened, dear, you are safe here and can trust me. Calm yourself and tell us what has happened. That is right.

T. Well you saw how that horrid, wicked old Father of Lies took me in. When we got there it was quite dark, and I could make out neither the Absolute nor the Universal. But he stopped and cried out: "Oh, Thou that art the Being of all beings, the Incomprehensible, the All-embracing, that wantest Nothing and hast Everything, lo, I present to Thee Truth, the fair, the virgin, to have and to hold through all Eternity!" What right had he, I should like to know, to present me, seeing that I wasn't his to present?

Exp. You see you are so very presentable. And the Absolute, being utterly unpresentable, loves those like you, to absorb them.

T. The horror! But I must tell you what followed. Very soon after a hideous, shapeless, incomprehensible, intangible Something gathered round me. I could feel that It was trying to embrace me and nearly lost my senses. Still I struggled violently, but the cold, clammy, filthy Thing slobbered all over me. It was too disgusting for words. At last, in my despair, I drew out the sword with which I do up my hair, and stabbed at It furiously. Whether I killed It or not I do not know, but It relented. I got free, and managed to rush out as you saw.

Exp. My darling Truth, how brave, what a heroine you are! I see it all.

T. But can you understand it?

Exp. In a way, yes. It is when the Absolute is *absent-minded* that It behaves like that, or even worse. You see ordinarily It is both the Same and the Other, Self and Not-Self, Identity in Difference, through Difference, by, with and from Difference. It is Itself through not being Itself, and thereby returning to Itself reconciled with Itself. When It is like that It generally behaves Itself; at least the philosophers say they can manage It. But when It is *absent-minded,* It is as it were *beside* Itself, and wholly Its Other (what the vulgar would call material), and then It thinks of nothing. Unfortunately this happens very often of late, indeed, almost constantly, and produces "the absolute identity of absolute Idealism and absolute Materialism." Nevertheless the philosophers defend Its "going on the loose," on the wretched plea that this is what It is etymologically bound to do, and that being thereby "set loose," It is more Absolute, more Itself: *i.e.,* such is Its intrinsic form of "Self-realisation." But even so, it seems very sad and bad. Especially as, even at the best of times, It is firmly convinced (by Bradley) that Morality is Appearance, and so not binding upon It. And when It thinks, It thinks so much of Itself that It always thinks that everybody is only too glad to be part of Itself. [*Truth,* indignantly, "The idea!"] and that It ought to embrace them. [*Truth,* "Not me, thank you!"] The Father of Lies of course knew all this and wanted you to be sacrificed, and absorbed by the Absolute, so as to become a mere *aspect* of It. But I am unspeakably glad that you have not only escaped from Its clutches, but helped others. For though you can hardly have killed It, you have certainly scotched it, and I fancy It will not readily recover. For the least resistance irritates It so much that it sets up a process of Self-diremption and disintegrates the lies which compose Its tissue. And the philosophers also it will make so mad that they will become inarticulate, as well as unintelligible. And then, you know, it will be quite clear that they are no longer men, but either gods or beasts.

T. I am delighted to hear all this.

Exp. Come home then with me. We'll wash and have tea!

The Welby Prize

LADY WELBY, whose interest in clearing up intellectual fogs and purifying the philosophical atmosphere is well known, has offered a prize of £1,000 to any philosopher who can produce adequate documentary evidence to show that he

    (1) Knows what   he   means.
    (2)   "   "   anyone else   "
    (3)   "   "   everyone   "
    (4)   "   "   anything   "
    (5)   "   "   everything else   "
    (6) Means what   he   says.
    (7)   "   "   "   means.
    (8)   "   "   everyone else   "
    (9)   "   "   "   "   says that he means.
    (10) Can express what he means.
    (11) Knows what it signifies what he means.
    (12)   "   "   it matters   "   "   signifies.

At first sight it might seem as though the Twelve Labours of Hercules would be in comparison with this a slighter achievement. But in view of the extensive and peculiar knowledge of the Absolute's Mind which is now possessed by so many philosophers, a large number of solutions may confidently be expected. These should be sent in to the Editors of MIND! Corpus Christi College, Oxford, *before the issue of the next number.*

The M.A.P. History of Philosophy

RHYMES BEYOND REASON

THIS important *History of Philosophy* is the fruit of long and anxious cogitation upon the proper method of teaching the subject. Its merits are novelty and conciseness. The Editors, however, neither guarantee the historical accuracy of the facts alluded to in these rhymes, nor hold themselves responsible for any of the opinions or sentiments expressed. Any one who has ever seriously tried to be a poet *knows* that all such matters are principally determined by the exigencies of rhyme. For the same reason we have had to omit many distinguished names which we should gladly have inserted, if it had been possible to obtain rhymes for them for love or money. The names of the persons concerned have been suppressed—for obvious reasons. They will be found however in the index.[16] Contributors to MIND! have enjoyed the singular privilege of writing their own "Limericks," without being charged the usual advertisement rates.

The order is both chronological and logical.

I. ANCIENT PHILOSOPHY

1

Though T—— held all things were water,
He married a wine merchant's daughter:
    From a corner in oil
    He gathered great spoil,
And routed the "City" with slaughter.

2

"At one time," said A——,
"We sprang from a great Salamander,
    Grew smoother and drier,
    Democratic and higher,
Evolving a vast Gerrymander."

16 If not before.

* * *

4

"I, sternly monistic, P——,
The Many consign to the Eumenides,
All Being is One!"
"Yet, pardon the pun,
'Tis true you yourself are ¶ *many* D's!"

* * *

6

Young Z—— had only one notion—
To prove that there couldn't be Motion.
But his father said, "D——!
Why *solvitur am—
bulando:* go fetch me a potion!"

* * *

8

"All's woeful and vain," said Heraclitus,[17]
"All's Atoms and Void," said D——.
" 'Tis Matter for laughter,
'Gay Science' I'm after,
Or even a tale of Theocritus!"

* * *

10

An idle old lounger was S——
(Though Plato a martyr the bloke rates);
When they asked "Is it sooth

[17] "Isn't the 'I' long?"—ED., MIND! "No—shortened by poetic license."—
AUTHOR. "Won't do: must draw the line somewhere. I shall draw it over the
eye. You must try again"—ED., MIND! "All right—How's this?
    "With fooling one must meet men's folly—
      D——found it quite jolly;
        In Atoms and Void
        He really enjoyed
      Specifics against melancholy"—AUTHOR.
"That will do much better, thank you." ED., MIND!

You're corrupting the youth?"
"You clearly don't know 'em!" said S——[18]

11

The divinest philosopher, P——,
Proved comforting very to Cato;
    But our wiseacres laugh,
    Immortality chaff,
And think him the smallest potato.

12

An Asklepiad, great A——,
Felt terribly tempted to throttle
    Alexander, his pup;
    But they asked him to sup,
So he buried his wrath in a bottle.

13

We hedonists, said A——,
Discomforts detest when they grip us,
    So wealth we adore,
    The moment live for,
And take what the rich *'Arries tip us.*

        *   *   *

16

A Stoic and slave, E——,
With courtesy ventured to greet us:
    But his master, enraged,
    In prison him caged
And told us to go, or he'd beat us!

17

Said the paragon Emperor, M——,
"On ponderings let us embark us,
    All virtues we'll borrow,

[18] "Is this a fact?"—ED., MIND! "Yes, on the authority of a recent examination paper, in which I found it almost verbatim!"—AUTHOR.

Take thought for the morrow,
The world cannot fail to remark us."

*   *   *

20

Of Egypt's weird wisdom Great T——
The mysteries showed me on oath,
    Neith's Image unveiled,
    Ra's Boat with me sailed:
Such secrets to tell you I'm loth!

21

Life's Struggle than thou, Z——,
Who pictures us finer or vaster?
    Poetic and true,
    I marvel thy view
The world has not managed to master!

*   *   *

25

Of India's *Trimurti* dark S——
I fear was the gayest deceiver;
    He carried off *Maya,*
    And made her his *ayah;*
So people refused to receive her.

26

A famous Scholastic, named A——,
Quite morbidly every tabby barred;
    Cried the Canon, "What's that?
    I'll give him the cat!"
And terribly hurt him, the blaggyard!

27

Said Tom, the great Saint of A——,
"*Theology's sum* is what we know,
    My creed is scholastic,
    God's very elastic,
Don't dare to expect that of *me!* No!"

28

The *Doctor Subtilis,* old D——,
A Scotsman addicted to puns,
    Maintained the Haecceity
    Of Man and the Deity;
On fast days he lived upon buns.

29

"To multiply beings," said O——,
"Is needless, 'tis better to dock 'em!"
    So he seized on his razor,
    This pestilent phraser,
And ran out to bloodily block 'em.[19]

30

A Frenchman, whose name was D——,
Enlarged Geometrical Art,
    His X, Y, and Z,
    Although he's long dead,
Still play a most prominent part.

*   *   *

32

Thought the wily Lord Chancellor B——,
Whose faith in old methods was shaken,
    "I'll simply set to
    And start things anew
On the path that Posterity's taken!"

33

With his mythical monsters old H——
Gave his readers some terrible jobs;
    Now they've put on Hobbs Locke,
    At Behemoths they mock,
And jeer at Leviathan's sobs.

---

[19] "Don't understand. O——'s razor—yes: to 'block' razors, also; but why 'bloodily'?"—ED., MIND! "To cut off their *blockheads,* of course! You also need it."—AUTHOR.

Now this is the legend of L——,
Of Christ Church a Student and *hock;*
    On primary Matter
    He did not grow fatter;
But dealt at innateness a knock.

Sir Isaac, our chroniclers say,
Slept under an apple all day;
    When it fell on his nose,
    And disturbed his repose,
"Gravitation!" he shouted, "Hooray!"

High-minded was good Bishop B——,
Through Matter he saw his God darkly:
    His notions of Vision
    Excited derision,
And multitudes stared at him starkly.

A canny old Scotchman was H——,
Of dogmas he sounded the doom;
    They call him a sceptic,
    His thought's antiseptic,
In "answers" there isn't a boom.

'Twixt Monads, Herr L——, you see,
Communion can't possibly be:
    You are one; so am I,
    So it's useless to try
To fathom your *"Philosophie."*

*   *   *

40

A Prussian professor named K——,
Proposed to his own maiden aunt;
    Cried she in a huff:
    "I've heard quite enough!
What, marry you? Nonsense! I shan't!"[20]

41

Das Ich mit dem Nicht-Ich sich F——
Besah einst bei unsicherm Lichte;
    Er rief: "Das Ich setzt sich!
    Unding! Es entsetzt mich!
Das Ich macht das Nicht-Ich zu Nichte!"

42

A German professor named S——
His doctrines proved simply *by yelling;*
    He shouted aloud,
    And attracted a crowd,
When questioned, he'd say: "That is telling!"

*   *   *

45

A pessimist, great S——,
Found living exceedingly sour,
    At Hegel he cursed,
    His grievances nursed,
And poured forth his wrath by the hour.

*   *   *

53

A staid Merton Fellow, named B——,
Fell in love with the Absolute madly;

---

[20] "Surely this is not historical?"—ED., MIND! "Not altogether. She really uttered only two words—the rest is poetical licence."—AUTHOR. "What were they?"—ED. "*Anti-Kant!* See? Can *you* see what *Aunty can't?*"—AUTHOR.

A big book he wrote
Its perfections to note:
The Absolute looked at him, sadly.

* * *

73

An astute Asst. Tutor named S——,
Of MIND!'s Essence the subtle distiller,
    Above Corpus gate
    Jokes early and late,
While the Pelican grins on her pillar.

* * *

76

At Manchester Sam A——
Conducted a new propaganda;
    Cried he, when a goose
    Approached with abuse,
"Away with you, improper gander!"

77

Though hardly a moralist, T——
O'er perilous seas is a sailor,
    He imitates B——,
    And does it not badly,
Some think him at ethics a nailer.

78

The greatest American J——
The Kantians call *other* names;
    Let them say what they will,
    We adhere to it still,
The Will to believe is Will J——.

79

A Cambridge idealist, W——,
Relentlessly put to the sword

The naturalist crew,
Till they cried: "That will do!
Professor, you've certainly scored!"

80

I'm Herbert the Sage, the De S——
Of truths that grow daily immenser,
My thought is synthetic,
Please take (with emetic!)—
In Collins' patent condenser.

* * *

91

A portly professor inclined
To think Matter a function of Mind:
Each day after dinner
He *thought* himself thinner,
No matter how well he had dined!

92

Another, who daily grew fatter,
Held Mind was a product of Matter,
Said he: "Mental growth
And bodily, both
Proceed from a well supplied platter."[21]

21 "Who are these? Can't guess. Give more data."—ED., MIND! "Leave it to
you. The verses are universal—their application only is particular. Only be
particular about the application!"—AUTHOR.